AI Marketing

How AI is Transforming Marketing and Business Growth

Edited by
Hamed Taherdoost
Mitra Madanchian

CRC Press
Taylor & Francis Group
Boca Raton London New York

CRC Press is an imprint of the
Taylor & Francis Group, an **informa** business
A CHAPMAN & HALL BOOK

Cover image adapted from artwork by Ultrashock, sourced via Shutterstock
(Image ID: 17154961)

First edition published 2026
by CRC Press
2385 NW Executive Center Drive, Suite 320, Boca Raton FL 33431

and by CRC Press
4 Park Square, Milton Park, Abingdon, Oxon, OX14 4RN

CRC Press is an imprint of Taylor & Francis Group, LLC

ISBN: 978-1-041-03806-1 (hbk)
ISBN: 978-1-041-03804-7 (pbk)
ISBN: 978-1-003-62545-2 (ebk)

DOI: 10.1201/9781003625452

Typeset in Minion
by SPi Technologies India Pvt Ltd (Straive)

To Parents,

the generation that taught us the value of authenticity before algorithms.

Your wisdom continues to shape how we navigate a world driven by data, but grounded in trust.

Contents

About the Editors

Dr. Hamed Taherdoost is a globally recognized technology leader and academic, with an extensive career that bridges four continents. He has held C-level executive roles, including Chief Technology Officer (CTO), in companies across Europe, the Middle East, Asia, and North America, spearheading innovation in industries such as IT, healthcare, transportation, and energy. As the founder of Hamta Business Corporation and Director of R&D at Q Minded | Quark Minded Technology Inc., he has led numerous cross-sectoral projects and served as a strategic advisor and consultant to international firms.In academia, Dr. Taherdoost is a Full Professor and serves as Chair of the Research Standards and Advancement Committee at University Canada West, Vancouver. With over 15 years of academic experience, he has held faculty positions and supervised research in Southeast Asia, the Middle East, Europe, and North America. His teaching and mentoring roles have included appointments at Westcliff University (USA), and Gisma University of Applied Sciences (Germany), among others.A prolific and widely cited scholar, Dr. Taherdoost has published more than 350 scientific works, including journal articles, book chapters, and authored and edited volumes. He is a well-known figure in the fields of technology management and research methodology, with several of his books, particularly in digital transformation and e-business, adopted as core texts in universities such as the University of Malta, Yarmouk University, University of Macau, University of Kerala, USIM (Malaysia), and University Canada West. His academic distinction is further underscored by his inclusion in the Stanford-Elsevier list of the world's top 2% of scientists (2021–2024) and as one of the top 10 SSRN Business Authors globally (2021–2024). Dr. Taherdoost also plays a vital role in scholarly publishing. He is the editor of two prominent book series: Mastering Academic Excellence: Research,

Teaching, Learning, and Publishing (Routledge, Taylor & Francis Group) and Quantum Computing. Additionally, he holds editorial board positions and serves as a reviewer and advisor for several esteemed journals published by Taylor & Francis and other leading publishers. He has organized and chaired numerous conferences and workshops, and he actively contributes to over 400 international events as a scientific or technical committee member.His achievements have earned him numerous accolades, including THE BIZZ Business Excellence Award, PeerJ Award, Asia Corporate Excellence & Sustainability Award, and multiple Best Paper and Outstanding Reviewer awards. He is also a certified cybersecurity professional and a senior member of IEEE, as well as a working group member of IFIP TC 11. His ongoing research explores cutting-edge domains including blockchain, cybersecurity, innovation in information systems, and digital technology acceptance.

Dr. Mitra Madanchian is a distinguished scholar, strategic leader, and industry expert with deep expertise in business management, leadership, human resources, and technology-driven innovation. She currently serves as an Associate Professor at University Canada West (UCW), where she is also the vice chair of the Department of Arts, Communications, and Social Sciences in the School of Arts, Science, and Technology. In addition, she holds an adjunct professorship at Fairleigh Dickinson University.

Dr. Madanchian is also an accomplished entrepreneur and R&D strategist, serving as the director of Quark Minded Technology Inc. and Hamta Business Corporation, where she leads initiatives focused on applied research and strategic innovation.

She holds a Ph.D. in business management and a Master of Administrative Science in Human Resources, with over 15 years of industry experience, including leadership roles in small and medium enterprises (SMEs) and one of the Big Four firms, Klynveld Peat Marwick Goerdele (KPMG). Her work bridges theory and practice in areas such as business strategy, HR development, marketing, and organizational innovation.

As a prolific academic, Dr. Madanchian has authored over 80 high-impact, peer-reviewed publications across top-tier journals published by Elsevier, Springer, IGI Global, and Multidisciplinary Digital Publishing Institute (MDPI). She has also contributed to multiple book chapters and authored five books in the areas of leadership and human resource management. Her interdisciplinary research spans business management, human resources, marketing, IT management, and emerging leadership models, earning her a strong citation record and h-index that reflect her influence within the global academic community.

Her recent research focuses on the integration of artificial intelligence (AI) in HR and marketing, exploring how digital tools are reshaping the future of workforce engagement and customer experience. She is a regular speaker and the session chair at international conferences, an active member of the Chartered Professionals in Human Resources (CPHR), and a mentor to emerging scholars.

Contributors

Mostafa Ahmadi
Department of Marketing, Strategy and Entrepreneurship
University Canada West (UCW)
Vancouver, Canada

Barzi Ghizlane
Research Laboratory in Finance, Audit and Governance of Organisations
National School of Business and Management
Hassan the First University Settat
Settat, Morocco

Badrane Hasnaa
Research Laboratory in Finance, Audit and Governance of Organisations
National School of Business and Management
Hassan the First University Settat
Settat, Morocco

Badrane Nohayla
Research Laboratory in Finance, Audit and Governance of Organisations
National School of Business and Management
Hassan the First University Settat
Settat, Morocco

T. Shirley Devakirubai
Department of Commerce
Madras Christian College
Chennai, India

A. Ghayathri
Department of Commerce
Madras Christian College
Chennai, India

Jash Khatri
Department of Arts, Communications and Social Sciences
School of Arts, Science and Technology
University Canada West
Vancouver, Canada

Mitra Madanchian
Department of Arts, Communications, and Social Sciences, School of Arts, Science, and Technology
University Canada West
Vancouver, Canada

Nirmala Mohan
Department of Commerce
Madras Christian College
Chennai, India

Alireza Rafiee
Department of Arts, Communications and Social Sciences
School of Arts, Science and Technology
University Canada West
Vancouver, Canada

Hamed Taherdoost
Department of Arts, Communications, and Social Sciences
School of Arts, Science, and Technology
University Canada West
Vancouver, Canada
and
GUS Institute, Global University Systems
London, United Kingdom

Preface

In the 21st-century digital landscape, marketing has evolved from an art guided by intuition to a science empowered by data, algorithms, and real-time analytics. At the core of this evolution lies artificial intelligence (AI), a technology that is not only enhancing the capabilities of marketers but fundamentally transforming the way businesses connect with consumers, understand their needs, and deliver value. This book, *AI Marketing: How AI is Transforming Marketing and Business Growth*, offers a comprehensive exploration of this transformation, combining theoretical insight with practical application to illuminate the path forward for marketers, business leaders, data scientists, and students alike.

AI has moved from being a buzzword to becoming a critical component of business strategy. In marketing, its applications are vast and continually expanding. From machine learning algorithms that power targeted advertising to personalized recommendations that tailor customer experiences in real time, AI is enabling organizations to engage customers in more meaningful, relevant, and timely ways. By leveraging vast amounts of structured and unstructured data, companies are now capable of predicting customer behavior, optimizing marketing spend, and crafting hyper-personalized content tasks that were once considered aspirational or resource-intensive.

To set the stage, the book opens with *Chapter 1 – The Role of Machine Learning in Targeted Advertising* – where we explore how AI models are revolutionizing the way marketers reach specific audiences. Through real-time bidding, segmentation, and predictive analysis, machine learning enables advertisers to deliver highly personalized ads that convert more effectively.

Following this, *Chapter 2 – AI-Enhanced Personalization: Crafting Tailored Experiences for Every Customer* – delves into how brands are creating unique journeys for individual users. With advanced algorithms analyzing customer behavior and preferences, marketers are now able to offer dynamic, one-to-one experiences at scale, enhancing both satisfaction and loyalty.

The book then shifts focus to the cross-functional collaboration between departments in *Chapter 3 – Marketing-Finance Collaboration in the Age of AI: Toward a Reinvented Era Where Predictive Analysis in Cash Management Drives Marketing Performance.* Here, we explore how AI facilitates synergy between marketing and finance, allowing better alignment in budgeting, forecasting, and performance tracking, ultimately making marketing more accountable and measurable.

In *Chapter 4 – Data-Driven Decision-Making and Predictive Analytics* – we examine how AI tools are empowering marketers to make more strategic decisions. Predictive analytics is transforming how organizations identify market trends, customer needs, and potential risks, enabling timely, data-informed actions rather than relying solely on intuition or retrospective reporting.

Continuing this theme, *Chapter 5 – AI-Driven Finance Function and Marketing: A Close Partnership for Performance* – expands on how AI is redefining the finance function in relation to marketing. We discuss how real-time analytics, budget optimization, and return on investment (ROI) modeling are now essential components of marketing strategy, making financial acumen a necessary skill for modern marketers.

Content remains a vital part of marketing, and in *Chapter 6 – AI-Driven Content Creation and Curation* – we explore how AI tools are enabling marketers to generate, edit, and distribute content efficiently without sacrificing creativity. From natural language generation and sentiment analysis to automated video editing and visual recognition, AI is helping content teams manage increasing demands across diverse platforms.

Chapter 7 – Optimizing Marketing Campaigns with AI Automation – focuses on how automation is transforming campaign execution. AI not only streamlines processes such as A/B testing, email marketing, and real-time targeting, but it also provides insights that help marketers continuously improve their tactics for maximum impact.

The customer journey does not end with acquisition, and *Chapter 8 – Enhancing Customer Loyalty with AI Solutions* – highlights how AI is reshaping loyalty strategies. We discuss AI-powered segmentation, retention modeling, and personalized engagement that help companies build deeper, more sustainable relationships with their customers.

Implementation is key, and *Chapter 9 – Strategic Selection and Integration of AI Tools in Data-Driven Marketing* – provides practical guidance on how organizations can select, evaluate, and integrate the right AI technologies to suit their specific goals. This chapter outlines a framework for aligning technological capabilities with marketing needs, organizational readiness, and ethical considerations.

Finally, *Chapter 10 – AI-Driven Marketing Strategies in the Digital Era* – brings together the key insights of the book and presents a forward-looking vision. It explores how organizations can build adaptive, AI-driven marketing ecosystems that support agility, innovation, and sustained growth in an increasingly complex digital marketplace.

This book does not merely examine the technological facets of AI; it reflects on the broader strategic, operational, and cultural implications of its adoption in marketing. Readers will encounter case-based insights, actionable frameworks, and future-facing perspectives that together form a holistic understanding of AI's role in marketing transformation. The aim is not just to educate but also to inspire innovation and encourage strategic thinking in the face of change.

Whether you are a seasoned marketing executive aiming to integrate AI into your strategy, a finance professional seeking to understand marketing performance through a predictive lens, a data analyst exploring marketing applications, or a student preparing to enter a digitally driven workforce, this book has something to offer.

As AI continues to advance, it presents both immense opportunities and complex challenges. Embracing AI in marketing is not about replacing human creativity or decision-making; it is about augmenting them with tools that enhance our ability to deliver value. The future of marketing will be defined by those who can combine the power of data with the depth of human insight, and this book is your guide to that future.

Acknowledgments

The completion of this book, *AI Marketing: How AI is Transforming Marketing and Business Growth*, would not have been possible without the collaboration, expertise, and dedication of numerous individuals and organizations. We take this opportunity to express our heartfelt appreciation to everyone who played a role in bringing this project to life.

First and foremost, we extend our sincere gratitude to the contributing authors. Their knowledge, research, and thought leadership have formed the backbone of this volume. Each chapter reflects countless hours of rigorous analysis, creative insight, and a shared passion for exploring the evolving landscape of artificial intelligence (AI) in marketing and business. Thank you for your commitment to excellence and for contributing such high-caliber work to this collective endeavor.

We are also deeply grateful to the peer reviewers and editorial advisors who provided invaluable feedback throughout the development of this book. Their critical insights, constructive comments, and academic rigor have helped ensure the quality, clarity, and relevance of the content. Your dedication to upholding the highest standards of scholarly work is truly appreciated.

A special thank you goes to GUS Institute | Global University Systems, Hamta Business Corporation, Q Minded | Quark Minded Technology Inc., and University Canada West, whose support and encouragement have been instrumental throughout this process. Their commitment to fostering innovation, research, and technological advancement has provided a strong foundation for this publication. We are proud to be associated with organizations that value interdisciplinary knowledge and the practical applications of emerging technologies.

Finally, to our readers – thank you.

Whether you are an academic, practitioner, student, or curious mind exploring the frontier of AI in marketing, we hope this book offers valuable insights and sparks new ideas. It is your engagement that gives this work its true purpose.

This book is the result of collective intelligence, global collaboration, and a shared belief in the transformative power of AI. We are honored to contribute to this important and ever-evolving conversation.

CHAPTER 1

The Role of Machine Learning in Targeted Advertising

Mitra Madanchian and Hamed Taherdoost

1.1 INTRODUCTION

Targeted advertising has become a cornerstone of modern marketing, allowing businesses to reach specific audiences with tailored messages that resonate deeply. Unlike traditional advertising methods that cast a wide net, targeted advertising focuses on delivering personalized content to individuals based on their demographics, behavior, preferences, and interests. This approach is increasingly vital in an era where consumers are inundated with digital advertisements. By leveraging data and advanced technologies, businesses can ensure that their marketing efforts are not only relevant but also impactful, minimizing wasted resources and maximizing engagement. The effectiveness of targeted advertising lies in its ability to connect brands with the right audience at the right time, fostering meaningful interactions and driving conversions [1, 2].

The rise of machine learning has revolutionized targeted advertising by enhancing its precision and scalability. Machine learning algorithms analyze vast amounts of consumer data, such as browsing history, purchase patterns, and social media activity, to identify trends and predict future behaviors. This predictive capability allows advertisers to anticipate consumer needs and deliver ads that align with their interests even before they actively seek products or services. For example, machine learning can segment audiences into micro-groups based on nuanced behavioral patterns,

DOI: 10.1201/9781003625452-1

enabling hyper-personalized campaigns that address individual preferences. This level of personalization not only improves the user experience but also increases the likelihood of engagement and conversion [3, 4].

Moreover, machine learning has transformed the feedback loop in advertising. Traditionally, advertisers relied on manual analysis of campaign performance metrics to refine their strategies. With machine learning, this process is automated and continuous. Algorithms evaluate user interactions with ads, such as clicks, views, and purchases, and use this data to optimize future campaigns in real time. This dynamic approach ensures that advertisements remain relevant as consumer preferences evolve. For instance, if a particular ad format or message garners higher engagement among a specific demographic, machine learning systems can adjust targeting parameters to replicate this success across similar audience segments [5, 6].

The integration of machine learning into targeted advertising has also addressed long-standing challenges such as ad fatigue and inefficiency. By analyzing user behavior patterns, machine learning can determine the optimal frequency and timing for ad delivery, reducing the risk of oversaturation while maintaining consumer interest. Additionally, it enables advertisers to allocate budgets more effectively by identifying high-performing channels and strategies. This data-driven approach not only enhances campaign efficiency but also provides valuable insights into consumer preferences that can inform broader business decisions [7].

1.2 UNDERSTANDING MACHINE LEARNING IN ADVERTISING

Machine learning has emerged as a transformative force in advertising, redefining how marketers approach data analysis and campaign optimization. At its core, machine learning refers to a subset of artificial intelligence (AI) that enables systems to learn and improve their performance by analyzing data and identifying patterns without explicit programming for every task. In advertising, this technology processes vast datasets to uncover insights about consumer behavior, preferences, and trends. By leveraging algorithms capable of self-improvement, machine learning systems can predict outcomes, segment audiences, and refine strategies with remarkable precision. This ability to "learn" from data and adapt over time makes machine learning a powerful tool for advertisers seeking to maximize their impact in an increasingly competitive digital landscape [8, 9].

One of the defining characteristics of machine learning in advertising is its ability to automate complex tasks that traditionally required human intervention. Unlike traditional methods that rely on manual analysis or predefined rules, machine learning systems dynamically process incoming data and adjust their operations accordingly. For example, traditional advertising methods might involve segmenting audiences based on static demographic data, whereas machine learning can analyze real-time behavioral patterns to create dynamic audience profiles. This shift from static to adaptive targeting allows advertisers to respond to changing consumer preferences instantly, ensuring campaigns remain relevant and effective [10].

Another key distinction between machine learning and traditional advertising techniques lies in the depth of insights generated. Traditional methods often focus on surface-level metrics, such as click-through rates or impressions, which provide limited information about consumer intent. Machine learning, however, delves deeper by analyzing correlations and trends within datasets that may not be immediately apparent to human analysts. For instance, algorithms can identify subtle connections between browsing habits and purchase behaviors, enabling advertisers to predict future actions with greater accuracy. This predictive capability empowers marketers to craft personalized messages that resonate on a deeper level with their target audience [11, 12].

Machine learning also excels in optimizing the efficiency of advertising campaigns. Traditional approaches often involve trial-and-error processes where marketers test various strategies and gradually refine them based on performance metrics. In contrast, machine learning systems continuously evaluate campaign data in real time and make adjustments automatically. These systems can optimize ad delivery by determining the best times to display ads, selecting the most effective platforms, and even tailoring content for specific audience segments. This level of automation not only saves time but also reduces costs by minimizing wasted ad spend on ineffective strategies [13].

1.3 EVOLUTION OF AD TARGETING

The evolution of ad targeting has been shaped by technological advancements and the growing availability of consumer data, transitioning from broad demographic-based strategies to highly sophisticated behavior-driven approaches (Figure 1.1). In its early stages, targeted advertising relied on general demographic information such as age, gender, and

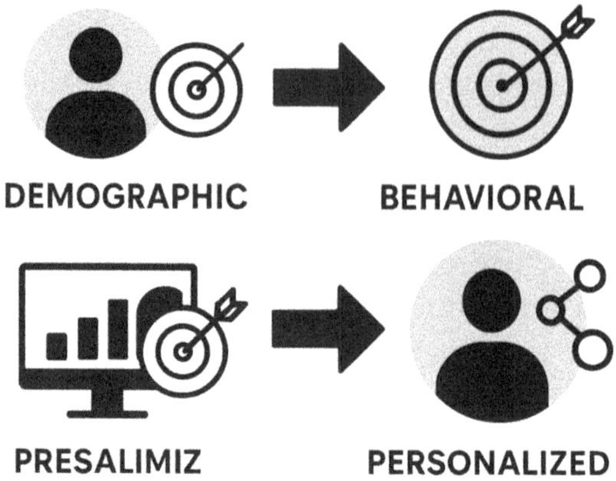

FIGURE 1.1 Evolution of AD targeting.

income to craft marketing campaigns. For instance, advertisers placed ads in magazines or TV programs that catered to specific groups, assuming that the audience shared common interests. While this method was effective to some extent, it lacked precision and often resulted in irrelevant messaging for many consumers within the target group. This approach dominated advertising for decades until the advent of the internet introduced new possibilities for data collection and analysis [14, 15].

The rise of digital platforms marked a significant turning point in ad targeting. By utilizing cookies and tracking user activity online, advertisers gained access to detailed insights about individual browsing habits and preferences. This allowed for more personalized advertising strategies, such as retargeting users who had previously visited a website or interacted with a product. Programmatic advertising further revolutionized the field by automating the buying and placement of ads based on real-time data, optimizing campaigns for relevance and efficiency. Search engines like Google also played a pivotal role by introducing keyword-based targeting through paid search models, enabling advertisers to reach users actively searching for related products or services. These developments laid the foundation for behavior-driven strategies that prioritize individual user experiences over generalized assumptions [16].

Social media platforms amplified the precision of ad targeting by providing granular data about user interests, activities, and connections. Platforms like Facebook pioneered interest-based targeting, allowing advertisers to deliver content tailored to specific hobbies, preferences, or life events. This level of personalization was unprecedented and significantly improved engagement rates compared to traditional methods. Machine learning algorithms enhanced these capabilities by analyzing vast datasets to identify patterns and predict future behaviors. For example, algorithms can segment audiences into micro-groups based on nuanced behavioral trends, enabling hyper-personalized campaigns that resonate deeply with individual users. This shift from demographic-based targeting to behavior-driven strategies has transformed advertising into a more dynamic and responsive field [17].

Machine learning has had a profound impact on the precision and personalization of ad targeting. Unlike traditional methods that rely on static rules or manual analysis, machine learning systems continuously adapt to new data inputs in real time. These systems can predict consumer preferences with remarkable accuracy by analyzing complex correlations within datasets that may not be immediately apparent to human analysts. For instance, machine learning can identify subtle connections between browsing habits and purchase decisions, allowing advertisers to anticipate needs before they are explicitly expressed by consumers. This predictive capability ensures that advertisements are not only relevant but also timely, increasing the likelihood of engagement and conversion [18].

Another key advantage of machine learning in ad targeting is its ability to optimize campaigns dynamically. Traditional approaches often involve trial-and-error processes where marketers test various strategies and refine them based on performance metrics after campaigns conclude. In contrast, machine learning systems evaluate user interactions, such as clicks, views, and purchases, in real time and adjust targeting parameters automatically. This continuous feedback loop enables advertisers to maximize their return on investment by focusing resources on high-performing channels and strategies while minimizing wasted efforts on ineffective ones [19].

The integration of machine learning into ad targeting has also addressed challenges such as ad fatigue and inefficiency. By analyzing user behavior patterns, algorithms can determine the optimal frequency and timing for ad delivery, reducing the risk of oversaturation while maintaining consumer interest. Additionally, machine learning facilitates budget optimization by identifying cost-effective opportunities for engagement across different platforms and audience segments. These capabilities not only enhance campaign efficiency but also contribute to a more positive user experience by ensuring that ads are relevant rather than intrusive [7, 20].

1.4 KEY APPLICATIONS OF MACHINE LEARNING IN TARGETED ADVERTISING

Machine learning has become a cornerstone in the realm of targeted advertising, enabling marketers to refine their strategies and deliver highly personalized content to the right audiences. One of its most impactful applications is audience segmentation, where machine learning algorithms analyze vast datasets to divide users into distinct groups based on shared characteristics, behaviors, or preferences. Traditional segmentation methods relied on broad demographic categories, but machine learning allows for deeper insights by identifying nuanced patterns within the data. For instance, algorithms can segment audiences into micro-groups that reflect specific interests or purchase behaviors, such as frequent travelers or eco-conscious consumers. This granularity not only enhances the relevance of advertising campaigns but also improves engagement rates, as users are more likely to respond positively to ads tailored to their unique profiles [21].

Predictive analytics is another transformative application of machine learning in targeted advertising. By analyzing historical data on consumer behavior and purchasing patterns, machine learning models can forecast future actions with remarkable accuracy. These predictions help advertisers anticipate which users are most likely to engage with specific products or services, allowing them to allocate resources effectively and design campaigns that resonate with high-value segments. For example, a retail brand might use predictive analytics to identify customers who are likely to purchase seasonal items based on past buying trends and then target them with timely promotions. This proactive approach not only boosts conversion rates but also ensures that advertising budgets are spent efficiently [22, 23].

Personalization and dynamic creative optimization represent a significant leap forward in delivering tailored advertising experiences. Machine learning enables advertisers to personalize ad content by analyzing individual user data points, such as browsing history, purchase records, and social media interactions. This personalization extends beyond static messaging; dynamic creative optimization allows ads to adapt in real time based on user preferences and contextual factors. For instance, an e-commerce platform might display different product recommendations in its ads depending on whether a user is browsing from a mobile device or desktop computer. This level of customization enhances user satisfaction by presenting relevant content that aligns with their immediate needs and preferences, thereby increasing the likelihood of engagement [24].

Real-time campaign optimization is another area where machine learning excels. Traditional advertising methods often relied on post-campaign analysis to refine strategies, but machine learning enables continuous adjustments during the campaign itself. Algorithms monitor performance metrics such as click-through rates, conversions, and user interactions in real time and make automatic modifications to improve outcomes. For example, if an ad format performs exceptionally well with a particular audience segment, machine learning systems can increase its frequency while reducing less effective formats. This dynamic approach ensures that campaigns remain agile and responsive to changing consumer behaviors, maximizing return on investment [7, 25].

Fraud detection and prevention have become critical components of digital advertising due to the prevalence of ad fraud schemes that drain resources and undermine campaign effectiveness. Machine learning plays a pivotal role in combating these issues by identifying anomalies in data patterns that may indicate fraudulent activity. For example, algorithms can detect irregularities such as unusually high click volumes from specific IP addresses or inconsistent engagement metrics across platforms. By flagging these anomalies early, machine learning systems help advertisers avoid wasting budgets on fraudulent impressions or clicks and ensure that their campaigns reach genuine users. This not only protects advertisers' investments but also contributes to a healthier digital advertising ecosystem [26].

The integration of machine learning into targeted advertising has fundamentally transformed how marketers approach audience engagement and campaign management. By leveraging advanced algorithms for audience segmentation, predictive analytics, personalization, real-time optimization, and fraud prevention, advertisers can create highly effective campaigns that resonate deeply with their target audiences. These applications not only enhance the precision and efficiency of advertising efforts but also foster meaningful connections between brands and consumers in an increasingly competitive digital landscape. As machine learning technology continues to evolve, its role in shaping the future of targeted advertising will undoubtedly expand further, driving innovation and delivering unparalleled value for businesses worldwide [27].

1.5 BENEFITS OF MACHINE LEARNING IN ADVERTISING

Machine learning has revolutionized advertising by delivering significant benefits that enhance precision, optimize costs, and improve user experiences. One of its most notable advantages is the ability to achieve enhanced precision and accuracy in ad targeting. Machine learning algorithms analyze vast amounts of consumer data, such as browsing history, purchase patterns, and social media activity, to identify trends and correlations that would be difficult for human analysts to discern. These insights allow advertisers to segment audiences into micro-groups and deliver highly personalized messages tailored to individual preferences. This level of precision ensures that ads reach the right audience at the right time, increasing engagement rates and minimizing wasted impressions. For example, machine learning can predict which users are most likely to respond to a specific product based on their past behavior, ensuring that marketing efforts are both relevant and impactful [28, 29].

Another critical benefit of machine learning in advertising is its ability to optimize costs and improve ad spend efficiency. Traditional advertising often involves trial-and-error methods that can lead to overspending on ineffective campaigns. Machine learning systems, however, continuously analyze performance metrics in real time and make adjustments to maximize return on investment. By identifying high-performing channels and strategies, these systems help advertisers allocate budgets more effectively, reducing overall costs while achieving better results. For instance, machine learning can determine the optimal frequency and timing for ad delivery, ensuring that resources are directed toward opportunities with the highest likelihood of success. This cost efficiency is particularly valuable in competitive industries where maximizing the impact of every dollar spent is essential for maintaining profitability [30, 31].

Improved user experience is another significant advantage brought by machine learning in advertising. By delivering ads that are highly relevant to individual users, machine learning reduces the likelihood of intrusive or irrelevant content that can lead to ad fatigue. Instead, users encounter advertisements that align with their interests and needs, creating a more positive interaction with brands. Dynamic creative optimization further enhances this experience by adapting ad content in real time based on contextual factors such as device type or location. For example, an e-commerce platform might display different product recommendations depending on whether a user is browsing from a mobile device or desktop computer. This personalization fosters a sense of connection between consumers and brands, increasing the likelihood of engagement while building long-term loyalty [32, 33].

The ability of machine learning to process real-time data also contributes significantly to its benefits in advertising. Unlike traditional methods that rely on post-campaign analysis, machine learning systems continuously monitor user interactions with ads, such as clicks, views, and conversions, and make automatic adjustments to improve outcomes. This dynamic approach ensures that campaigns remain agile and responsive to changing consumer behaviors, maximizing their effectiveness over time. For example, if a particular ad format performs exceptionally well among a specific demographic group, machine learning systems can increase its frequency while reducing less effective formats for other groups. This adaptability not only enhances campaign performance but also ensures that advertising remains relevant in an ever-evolving digital landscape [34].

Finally, machine learning plays a crucial role in addressing challenges such as fraud detection and prevention in advertising. Ad fraud schemes, such as click fraud or fake impressions, can drain resources and undermine campaign effectiveness. Machine learning algorithms excel at identifying anomalies in data patterns that may indicate fraudulent activity. For instance, they can detect irregularities such as unusually high click volumes from specific IP addresses or inconsistent engagement metrics across platforms. By flagging these issues early, machine learning systems help advertisers protect their investments and ensure that their campaigns reach genuine users. This capability not only safeguards budgets but also contributes to a healthier digital advertising ecosystem where trust between advertisers and consumers can thrive [35].

1.6 CHALLENGES AND ETHICAL CONSIDERATIONS

The integration of machine learning into advertising has brought about significant challenges and ethical considerations, particularly concerning privacy and data security. Machine learning systems rely heavily on vast amounts of consumer data to deliver personalized advertising experiences, but this dependence raises questions about how data is collected, stored, and used. Consumers are increasingly concerned about the potential misuse of their personal information, especially in cases where data is shared without explicit consent or exposed to breaches. For instance, algorithms that track browsing habits or purchase histories can inadvertently infringe on privacy if they fail to anonymize sensitive information. To address these concerns, businesses must implement robust data protection measures, such as encryption and secure storage protocols, while adhering to regulations like the General Data Protection Regulation (GDPR) and the California Consumer Privacy Act (CCPA), which mandate stringent standards for data handling [36, 37].

Balancing personalization with consumer trust is another critical challenge in machine-learning-driven advertising. While personalized ads can enhance user experiences by delivering relevant content, they can also provoke discomfort if consumers feel that their privacy is being invaded. The fine line between personalization and intrusion often hinges on transparency, consumers must understand how their data is being used and have the ability to opt out of tracking if they choose. For example, machine learning algorithms that predict consumer preferences based on past behavior must ensure that these predictions are accurate and non-invasive. Building trust requires advertisers to prioritize ethical practices, such as obtaining explicit consent for data collection and providing clear explanations of how personalization works. Without this transparency, businesses risk alienating consumers and undermining the effectiveness of their campaigns [38, 39].

Navigating regulatory frameworks like GDPR and CCPA adds another layer of complexity to ethical advertising practices. These regulations establish strict guidelines for data usage, requiring businesses to obtain informed consent from users before collecting or processing their information. They also impose penalties for non-compliance, incentivizing companies to adopt ethical standards in their advertising strategies. For instance, GDPR emphasizes the importance of data minimization, collecting only the information necessary for a specific purpose, and mandates that users have access to their own data with the ability to request its deletion. Machine learning systems must be designed with these principles in mind to ensure compliance while maintaining their functionality. Additionally, regulatory frameworks encourage businesses to invest in technologies that enhance transparency, such as dashboards that allow users to monitor how their data is being utilized [40, 41].

Bias within machine learning algorithms presents another ethical dilemma in advertising. Algorithms trained on skewed or incomplete datasets can perpetuate discriminatory practices by favoring certain demographics over others. For example, an algorithm designed to target high-value customers might inadvertently exclude individuals from underrepresented groups due to biases in the training data. This issue not only undermines fairness but also exposes businesses to reputational risks and potential legal challenges. To mitigate bias, companies must conduct rigorous testing of their algorithms and ensure that training datasets are diverse and representative of all user segments. Additionally, implementing oversight mechanisms can help identify and address biases before they impact advertising outcomes [42, 43].

The ability of machine learning systems to influence consumer behavior introduces concerns about manipulation and transparency. As algorithms become more adept at predicting user preferences, there is a risk that they could exploit vulnerabilities for commercial gain, for instance, by encouraging impulsive purchases or promoting products that may not align with a user's actual needs. This raises ethical questions about the extent to which advertisers should leverage predictive capabilities without crossing into manipulation. Transparency is key in addressing these concerns; businesses must disclose how their algorithms operate and ensure that consumers are aware of the factors influencing their decisions. Providing users with control over their interactions, such as options to limit tracking or customize ad preferences, can help mitigate the risks associated with manipulation [44].

Fraud prevention also remains a significant challenge in machine learning-driven advertising. Ad fraud schemes, such as click fraud or fake impressions, not only drain resources but also compromise the integrity of campaigns by diverting efforts away from genuine users. Machine learning algorithms play a crucial role in detecting fraudulent activity by analyzing patterns and identifying anomalies within datasets. For instance, unusually high engagement rates from specific IP addresses may indicate fraudulent behavior that needs to be addressed promptly. While these systems are effective at flagging potential issues, businesses must remain vigilant in updating their models to adapt to evolving fraud tactics [45].

1.7 FUTURE TRENDS IN MACHINE LEARNING FOR ADVERTISING

The future of machine learning in advertising is poised to be shaped by its integration with AI-powered tools, advancements in contextual targeting, and the evolution of predictive modeling and sentiment analysis. The synergy between machine learning and AI is unlocking new possibilities for advertisers, enabling them to automate complex processes while enhancing precision and efficiency. AI-powered tools such as generative AI platforms are already transforming ad creation, allowing marketers to generate tailored content, optimize creatives, and streamline campaign management. For instance, platforms like Google Ads are testing features that use AI to suggest headlines and descriptions, while startups like Omneky leverage

AI insights to create data-driven ads that maximize engagement. These innovations not only reduce the time and effort required for ad creation but also ensure that campaigns resonate deeply with target audiences [46, 47].

One of the most significant shifts in advertising is the move toward contextual targeting as a response to the phasing out of third-party cookies. As privacy regulations tighten and consumers demand greater control over their data, advertisers are turning to machine learning algorithms to analyze first-party data and unstructured information from sources like social media posts and product reviews. Contextual targeting focuses on delivering ads based on the content of a webpage or app rather than relying on individual user profiles, ensuring compliance with privacy standards while maintaining relevance. For example, AI-powered tools can identify keywords or themes within digital content and match them with appropriate advertisements. This approach not only addresses privacy concerns but also enhances user experience by aligning ads with the context in which they appear [48, 49].

Advancements in predictive modeling are revolutionizing how advertisers anticipate consumer behavior and optimize campaigns. Machine learning algorithms analyze historical data to forecast future trends and preferences, enabling marketers to craft highly targeted strategies that maximize engagement. Predictive analytics allows advertisers to customize bids based on the lifetime value of individual consumers, optimizing performance over time rather than focusing solely on short-term gains. For instance, AI-driven models can predict peak purchasing periods for specific products or services, allowing businesses to allocate resources effectively during high-demand times. This capability ensures that advertising efforts are both timely and impactful, driving higher conversion rates and return on investment [50].

Sentiment analysis is emerging as a powerful tool for understanding consumer emotions and refining advertising strategies. Machine learning algorithms can process vast amounts of textual data from social media platforms, reviews, and customer feedback to gauge public sentiment toward brands or products. By identifying positive or negative trends in consumer attitudes, advertisers can tailor their messaging to address concerns or capitalize on favorable perceptions. For example, sentiment analysis might reveal that consumers associate a particular product with sustainability, prompting marketers to highlight eco-friendly features in their campaigns. This emotional intelligence not only enhances the relevance of advertisements but also fosters stronger connections between brands and their audiences [51].

As machine learning continues to evolve, its role in advertising will expand further into areas such as augmented reality (AR) and programmatic advertising. AR applications powered by machine learning are enabling immersive brand experiences that engage consumers in innovative ways, such as virtual try-ons or interactive product demonstrations. Programmatic advertising is also benefiting from AI-driven automation, which streamlines ad buying processes and enables hyper-targeting based on real-time data insights. With forecasts predicting substantial growth in programmatic ad spending over the next few years, machine learning will remain at the forefront of this transformation by optimizing placements and ensuring campaigns reach the most relevant audiences [52, 53].

1.8 CONCLUSION

The role of machine learning in targeted advertising has revolutionized the way marketers approach campaign strategy, audience engagement, and campaign optimization. By leveraging advanced algorithms to analyze vast datasets, businesses can deliver personalized messages with unprecedented precision, optimize ad spend, and enhance user experiences. However, these benefits come with challenges such as privacy concerns, ethical considerations, and regulatory compliance. As technology continues to evolve, the integration of machine learning with AI-powered tools, contextual targeting, and predictive analytics will further transform the advertising landscape. By embracing these trends while prioritizing ethical practices, advertisers can create impactful campaigns that resonate deeply with their audiences.

REFERENCES

1. Jamal, Z. and I. Khan, The role of advertising in global integrated marketing communications. *Journal of Policy Options*, 2024. **7**(3): pp. 47–53.
2. Lee, H. and C.-H. Cho, Digital advertising: Present and future prospects. *International Journal of Advertising*, 2020. **39**(3): pp. 332–341.
3. Chaudhary, K., et al., Machine learning-based mathematical modelling for prediction of social media consumer behavior using big data analytics. *Journal of Big Data*, 2021. **8**(1): p. 73.
4. Hair Jr, J.F., Knowledge creation in marketing: The role of predictive analytics. *European Business Review*, 2007. **19**(4): pp. 303–315.
5. Choi, J.-A. and K. Lim, Identifying machine learning techniques for classification of target advertising. *ICT Express*, 2020. **6**(3): pp. 175–180.
6. Sharma, A., N. Patel, and R. Gupta, Enhancing ad targeting through AI-powered audience segmentation: Leveraging K-means clustering and random forest algorithms. *European Advanced AI Journal*, 2021. **10**(2): pp. 1–22.

7. Nayyar, G., S. Suman, and T. Lakshmi, Optimizing Ad campaigns with machine learning: Data-driven approaches in modern media. *International Journal of Multiphysics*, 2024. **18**(3): pp. 1746.
8. Mehrotra, D., *Basics of artificial intelligence & machine learning*. 2019: Notion Press.
9. Shah, N., et al., Research trends on the usage of machine learning and artificial intelligence in advertising. *Augmented Human Research*, 2020. **5**: pp. 1–15.
10. Meyer, G., et al., A machine learning approach to improving dynamic decision making. *Information Systems Research*, 2014. **25**(2): pp. 239–263.
11. Yang, W., Beyond algorithms: The human touch machine-generated titles for enhancing click-through rates on social media. *Plos One*, 2024. **19**(7): p. e0306639.
12. Eslami, M., et al. *Communicating algorithmic process in online behavioral advertising*. in *Proceedings of the 2018 CHI conference on human factors in computing systems*. 2018.
13. Eggers, F. and D.B. McCabe, Trial-and-error marketing: The role of the customer in tech start-ups. *International Journal of Technology Marketing*, 2016. **11**(2): pp. 149–164.
14. Leppäniemi, M. and H. Karjaluoto, Exploring the effects of gender, age, income and employment status on consumer response to mobile advertising campaigns. *Journal of Systems and Information Technology*, 2008. **10**(3): pp. 251–265.
15. Grier, S.A. and S. Kumanyika, Targeted marketing and public health. *Annual Review of Public Health*, 2010. **31**(1): pp. 349–369.
16. Singhal, A., Optimizing programmatic advertising: A machine learning approach to predictive ad targeting. *Journal of Knowledge Learning and Science Technology* ISSN: 2959-6386 (online), 2024. **3**(3): pp. 327–339.
17. Mahato, B.K., et al. Algorithmic Analysis and Implementation Strategies For Targeted Advertising on Diverse Social Media Platform. in *2024 15th International Conference on Computing Communication and Networking Technologies (ICCCNT)*. 2024. IEEE.
18. Chaudhuri, N., et al., On the platform but will they buy? Predicting customers' purchase behavior using deep learning. *Decision Support Systems*, 2021. **149**: p. 113622.
19. Gkikas, D.C. and P.K. Theodoridis, Predicting online shopping behavior: Using machine learning and google analytics to classify user engagement. *Applied Sciences*, 2024. **14**(23): p. 11403.
20. Santos, M., Optimizing digital advertising with big data: Analyzing consumer behavior for real-time decision making. *Nuvern Applied Science Reviews*, 2021. **5**(12): pp. 1–8.
21. Ologunebi, J. and E. Taiwo, *Personalized ad Content and Individual User Preference: A boost for Conversion Rates in the UK E-commerce Business*. 2024.
22. Gharibshah, Z. and X. Zhu, User response prediction in online advertising. *aCM Computing Surveys (CSUR)*, 2021. **54**(3): pp. 1–43.

23. Boone, T., et al., Forecasting sales in the supply chain: Consumer analytics in the big data era. *International journal of forecasting*, 2019. **35**(1): pp. 170–180.
24. Singh, B. and C. Kaunert, Future of digital marketing: hyper-personalized customer dynamic experience with ai-based predictive models, in *Revolutionizing the AI-Digital Landscape*. 2024, Productivity Press. pp. 189–203.
25. Kivistö, A., Role of artificial intelligence in promotional campaigns. Master's Degree Programme in Digital Marketing and Corporate Communication, Jyväskylä University School of Business and Economics, 2024. https://urn.fi/URN:NBN:fi:jyu-
26. Zhu, X., et al., *Fraud Prevention in Online Digital Advertising*. 2017: Springer.
27. Arora, S. and S.R. Thota, *Using Artificial Intelligence with Big Data Analytics for Targeted Marketing Campaigns*. Shivkrupa Publications, no. June, 2024.
28. Wang, X. and B. Hu, *Machine Learning Algorithms for Improved Product Design User Experience*. IEEE Access, 2024.
29. Rosener, W., Optimizing website advertising: Exploring Ad types and strategic placement. *Journal of Business Administration Online*, **18**(1): pp. 45–59.
30. Birim, S., et al., The derived demand for advertising expenses and implications on sustainability: a comparative study using deep learning and traditional machine learning methods. *Annals of Operations Research*, 2024. **339**(1): pp. 131–161.
31. Shoushtari, F., et al., Optimization in marketing enhancing efficiency and effectiveness. *International Journal of Industrial Engineering and Operational Research*, 2023. **5**(2): pp. 12–23.
32. Kaponis, A., M. Maragoudakis, and K.C. Sofianos, *Enhancing User Experiences in Digital Marketing through Machine Learning: Cases, Trends, and Challenges*. Preprints, 2024.
33. Huang, M., et al., Dynamic optimization models for displaying outdoor advertisement at the right time and place. *International Journal of Geographical Information Science*, 2021. **35**(6): pp. 1179–1204.
34. Perlich, C., et al., Machine learning for targeted display advertising: Transfer learning in action. *Machine Learning*, 2014. **95**(1): pp. 103–127.
35. Bakumenko, A. and A. Elragal, Detecting anomalies in financial data using machine learning algorithms. *Systems*, 2022. **10**(5): p. 130.
36. Muniratnam, M., K.M. Reddy, and Y. Aavula, Privacy and ethical considerations in data-driven marketing, in *Predictive Analytics and Generative AI for Data-Driven Marketing Strategies*. Chapman and Hall/CRC. pp. 165–182.
37. Park, G., The changing wind of data privacy law: A comparative study of the European Union's General Data Protection Regulation and the 2018 California Consumer Privacy Act. *UC Irvine Law Review*, 2019. **10**: p. 1455.
38. Aishwarya Gowda, A.G., H.-K. Su, and W.-K. Kuo. *Personalized E-commerce: Enhancing Customer Experience through Machine Learning-driven Personalization*. In *2024 IEEE International Conference on Information Technology, Electronics and Intelligent Communication Systems (ICITEICS)*. 2024. IEEE.
39. Stevenson, D.M., *Data, Trust, and Transparency in Personalized Advertising*. 2016.

40. Mbah, G.O., *Data privacy in the era of AI: Navigating regulatory landscapes for global businesses*. 2024.
41. Ayoola, E., et al., *Striking a Balance: Harmonizing Data Minimization and Business Objectives*. NDPC–: p. 122.
42. Akter, S., et al., Algorithmic bias in machine learning-based marketing models. *Journal of Business Research*, 2022. **144**: pp. 201–216.
43. Van Giffen, B., D. Herhausen, and T. Fahse, Overcoming the pitfalls and perils of algorithms: A classification of machine learning biases and mitigation methods. *Journal of Business Research*, 2022. **144**: pp. 93–106.
44. De Marcellis-Warin, N., et al., Artificial intelligence and consumer manipulations: from consumer's counter algorithms to firm's self-regulation tools. *AI and Ethics*, 2022. **2**(2): pp. 259–268.
45. Bello, O., et al., Analysing the impact of advanced analytics on fraud detection: A machine learning perspective. *European Journal of Computer Science and Information Technology*, 2023. **11**(6): pp. 103–126.
46. Vashishtha, S. and P. Sharma, Artificial intelligence and more effective advertising: unlocking the power of data and automation, in *Advances in Digital Marketing in the Era of Artificial Intelligence*. 2024, CRC Press. pp. 162–171.
47. Phay, H., *Creative AI: a data-driven design approach for creative online ad optimisation using artificial intelligence and big data*. 2019.
48. Rafieian, O. and H. Yoganarasimhan, Targeting and privacy in mobile advertising. *Marketing Science*, 2021. **40**(2): pp. 193–218.
49. Thomas, I., Planning for a cookie-less future: How browser and mobile privacy changes will impact marketing, targeting and analytics. *Applied Marketing Analytics*, 2021. **7**(1): pp. 6–16.
50. Mecharla, D., J. Avaldhar, and K. Rukmini, *Predictive Analytics Techniques for Marketing*, in *Predictive Analytics and Generative AI for Data-Driven Marketing Strategies*. Chapman and Hall/CRC. pp. 53–67.
51. Sánchez-Núñez, P., et al., Opinion mining, sentiment analysis and emotion understanding in advertising: A bibliometric analysis. *IEEE Access*, 2020. **8**: pp. 134563–134576.
52. Moreno-Armendáriz, M.A., et al., Deep-learning-based adaptive advertising with augmented reality. *Sensors*, 2021. **22**(1): p. 63.
53. Sharma, A., P. Sharma, and R. Gaur, Artificial Intelligence (AI) and the future of marketing trends: Challenges and opportunities. *Artificial Intelligence in Peace, Justice, and Strong Institutions*, 2025: pp. 23–46.

CHAPTER 2

AI-Enhanced Personalization

Crafting Tailored Experiences for Every Customer

A. Ghayathri and Nirmala Mohan

2.1 INTRODUCTION

Globalization and dynamic technological development have resulted in qualitative transformations in all areas of life, which scholars refer to as the fourth industrial revolution, which is the coexistence of machines and their capability to exchange information. Thus, a key element is the development of artificial intelligence (AI) (Manesh et al., 2020; Verma et al., 2021). The age of AI is upon us. Firms across the globe are leading their recent advances with AI, machine learning, and deep learning, even though the majority of it is a long way short of anything that can be described as a breakthrough (Pearson, 2019). The application of AI to drive personalization strategies has been among the most groundbreaking innovations in the high-speed marketing space in recent years. AI-driven marketing customization is changing the manner in which companies engage with their target audiences by exposing them to tailored experiences that drive conversion rates and foster brand loyalty as well as engage consumers. Companies are increasingly depending on AI to enhance the experience and interaction of their customers. AI can revolutionize the way businesses interact with their customers. It is unlocking new opportunities to enhance results, streamline processes, and evolve practices. It will explore the various ways AI technology can be used to enhance

DOI: 10.1201/9781003625452-2

customer interactions, including chatbots, personalized recommendations, and predictive analytics (Swatman & Chin, 2004). AI-driven personalization is the term used to refer to the application of AI and machine learning algorithms to scrutinize vast amounts of data and present individual consumers with tailored experiences, recommendations, and content. It encompasses a wide spectrum of marketing practices, including targeted email marketing, social media platform recommendations for personalized content, and e-commerce websites with personalized product recommendations. The aim of AI-driven customization is to provide consumers with an individualized marketing experience that makes them feel unique and recognized.

Based on Benbya et al. (2020), the adoption of smart technology solutions for online marketing is driving organizations to leverage new technologies such as AI and big data to improve the consumer experience. AI personalization applies advanced data interpretation and novel machine learning methods to customize experiences, products, and services for individual users in a wide range of domains. The operation of these tailored shopping services is being transformed by generative AI, introducing a new dimension internal operational efficiency and e-commerce personalization. These AI-driven systems continuously improve their accuracy by iterative refinement as more the data is collected (Klaus & Zaichkowsky, 2022). AI redefines learning trajectories and delivers real-time feedback in education, customized treatment, and anticipatory health monitoring in healthcare. The entertainment industry applies the technology to personalize content and craft interactive stories, and the workplace enjoys AI-fueled assistants and customized training programs. AI helps business growth by drawing customers and investors. Nevertheless, the extensive dissemination of different AI technology software makes it difficult to comprehend its concept and minimizes its application in local enterprises (Kotyrloa et al., 2024). The finance, automotive, and connected mobility industries use AI to build behavior-based insights, risk scoring, and in-car personalization experiences. With advances in AI, applications become more targeted toward hyper-personalized digital agents and emotionally intelligent systems that learn to tailor themselves to distinct contexts in real time.

2.2 BENEFITS OF AI-ENHANCED PERSONALIZATION

Because of its benefits, AI was quickly adopted and is still being adopted in many areas, i.e., medicine, economy, education, and transport, which resulted in different kinds of functionality according to the established goal (Borges et al., 2021). The following are the benefits of AI-enhanced personalization.

2.2.1 Enhanced Customer Engagement

AI-driven personalization enhances customer interaction and conversion rates through the provision of hyper-relevant experiences, process automation, and data-driven decision-making. It saves time, enhances retention through communication that is relevant to them, and learns continuously from interactions to best optimize marketing strategies (Harshavardhan, 2024). Companies may draw in and hold the interest of customers by providing tailored content, offers, and product recommendations. Customers who receive personalized experiences are more likely to interact with brands and feel understood and respected.

2.2.2 Enhanced Conversion Rates

AI chatbots and virtual assistants employ natural language processing (NLP) to interpret customer questions and deliver personalized responses in real time. Such personalization not only boosts customer satisfaction but also raises the chances of conversion (Patil, 2025). AI personalization enables companies to offer the appropriate goods or services to the appropriate clients at the appropriate moment. AI algorithms can forecast which goods or deals will appeal to certain customers by examining user data and behavior, therefore boosting the possibility of conversion and promoting income expansion.

2.2.3 Enhanced Customer Retention

This data-centric strategy allows companies to invest resources wisely, targeting channels and messages that speak most to their audiences. Predictive analytics software can even predict customer churn, enabling companies to enact anticipatory retention plans (Babadoğan, 2024). Personalized interactions foster a deep emotional bond between brands and consumers. Customers are more inclined to stick around and make additional purchases when they believe that their unique requirements and preferences are being satisfied.

2.2.4 Enhanced Decision Support

AI-powered personalization uses high-end data analytics, machine learning, and predictive modelling to understand individual consumer behavior and tastes. By looking at past data, AI mechanisms can spot trends and forecast future action, and this helps companies make the right choices (Harshavardhan, 2024). AI can give you customized suggestions and insights that help you make better financial, health, and educational decisions, among others. From monitoring your spending to helping you plan your study schedule these customized insights make and facilitate smarter decisions simpler

2.2.5 Super Relevant Experiences

One of the most important strengths of AI-based personalization is its capacity to provide highly targeted experiences. AI technologies can construct in-depth customer profiles by gathering data from numerous sources, including browsing history, purchasing behavior, and social interactions. These profiles allow companies to develop personalized messages, product recommendations, and promotions that are responsive to individual preferences and requirements (Wijethilak et al., 2024). AI makes things more relevant by learning customer behavior, habits, and interactions to serve up just what is most likely to like or need. Rather than generic recommendations, it serves up filtered recommendations whether a movie, product, or article making the experience more interesting and richer for the user.

2.2.6 Saves Time and Lessens Overwhelm

AI-powered personalization automates marketing and customer service operations, freeing up businesses from precious time. AI-powered email marketing software can automate send times, personalize messages, and dynamically segment audiences, minimizing the need for human intervention (Patil, 2025) (Hemalatha, 2023). With all that content and all those options available out there on the internet, AI helps cut through the noise. By minimizing options to most compatible with users' tastes, it saves time and avoids decision fatigue enabling the user to find what one is searching for more easily without endless scrolling and browsing.

2.2.7 More Engagement and Conversion

AI increases interaction by allowing immersive experiences like augmented reality (AR) and virtual reality (VR). AI, coupled with these technologies, allows customers to engage with products in a more immersive and personalized manner, resulting in higher purchase intent and satisfaction (Patil, 2025). Businesses have a lot to gain from AI personalization since it increases the chances of bringing customers to action. Personalized product recommendations, message relevance, and timely offers are likely to generate more engagement and increased conversions, improving customer satisfaction and revenue.

2.2.8 Smart Automation

Personalization powered by AI makes intelligent automation possible, with companies being able to provide frictionless and efficient customer experiences. AI tools have the ability to automate repetitive tasks, like customer segmentation, email marketing, and recommendations, which in turn release resources for strategic activities (Patil, 2025) (Hemalatha, 2023). AI-based software like virtual assistants and chatbots use personalization to communicate more naturally. They learn to talk like you, remember past conversations, and give suitable advice or recommendations, giving a seamless and natural user experience without any human interaction.

2.2.9 Hyper-Personalized Communication

AI-powered personalization is not just the prerogative of large corporations; it also enables SMEs to provide highly personalized and individualized customer experiences. AI-based systems allow SMEs to blend data-driven insights with customer interaction procedures, transforming business practices (Okeke, 2024). AI personalizes messages based on who you are and what you care about, from the email tone to when it sends. This kind of personalization makes the message more human and timelier and allows brands to create richer, more personal relationships with their users.

2.2.10 Continuous Learning

AI-powered personalization is not a static effort but an ongoing process of learning and enhancement. AI systems study customer interactions and feedback to improve profiles and enhance the accuracy of predictions and recommendations over time (Wijethilak et al., 2024) (Patil, 2025). Unlike static systems, the more you use AI, the better it becomes. It learns as you use it repeatedly, always improving its knowledge of your needs and desires. This ongoing learning means the personalization is constantly improving, getting better and better with each use and more accurate and helpful.

2.3 OBJECTIVES OF THE STUDY

2.3.1 To Analyze the Role of AI in Personalized Marketing

This goal investigates how AI uses customer data to build personalized experiences, allowing companies to address individual needs more efficiently. It looks at the effect of AI on content personalization, suggestions, and customer support.

2.3.2 To Identify AI Techniques and Tools Enabling Personalization

This goal emphasizes the most important AI methods like machine learning, NLP, and deep learning that support personal marketing. It also includes tools like recommendation engines, chatbots, and predictive analytics that allow for AI-powered personalization.

2.3.3 To Assess the Impact of AI-Enhanced Personalization on Customer Engagement and Retention

This goal looks into how personalization through AI expands customer engagement in the form of pertinent content and experiences, alongside long-term loyalty and churn avoidance through predictive guidance.

2.3.4 To Understand the Challenges and Limitations of AI-Enhanced Personalization

This goal examines the difficulties of personalization based on AI, such as data privacy concerns, algorithmic bias, low-quality data, and over-personalization risks, as well as financial and technical impediments to businesses.

2.4 SIGNIFICANCE OF THE STUDY

This study aims to investigate the possibility of transformative change in AI to achieve efficient and scalable personalization in various industries. As businesses work to deliver personalized experiences to ever more diverse and growing customer bases, AI is a powerful driver of automating and optimizing personalized experiences. Using machine learning models and real-time data processing, organizations can offer personalized content, recommendations, and services more closely aligned with customers' wishes and behaviors. The study investigates ways of optimizing personalization efforts, emphasizing the capability of businesses to leverage big data to make better and more effective decision-making. Besides investigating technical and strategic benefits, the study also investigates strong ethical implications. These involve maintaining robust data protection practices, fostering transparency, and promoting responsible use of AI technology. Furthermore, the study investigates the future path of AI development, taking into consideration how subsequent innovations will extend personalization capabilities while also creating new challenges of fairness, accountability, and user trust.

2.5 SCOPE OF THE STUDY

This research is concerned with analyzing and assessing customer-focused personalization strategies across different contexts, including marketing campaigns, product recommendation systems, and customer care services. Essentially, the research seeks to explore how companies are capable of adapting experiences, products, and interactions to meet individual customers' behavior and preferences with the aim of increasing satisfaction, engagement, and loyalty. Nevertheless, successful implementation of personalization is followed by a chain of complicated problems. At the top of these are ethical and technological problems presented by gathering and utilizing customers' information. Data privacy is of utmost importance as customers grow increasingly more sensitive about how their personal data is being gathered, stored, and utilized. Moreover, algorithmic bias possesses the ability to taint personalization results, resulting in biased or deceptive recommendations likely to reinforce existing disparities or discriminate against particular groups of users. Another significant problem is to strike the right balance between automated systems and human touch. Although automation holds the ability to contribute significantly toward efficiency and scalability, overdependence on it can lead to impersonal or infuriating experiences. Thus, the research also explores how companies are capable of implementing human touch in meaningful ways into automated personalization systems effectively to gain authenticity and trust in customer interactions.

2.6 REVIEW OF LITERATURE

Mohammad Shafiquzzaman Bhuiyan (2024) articulates that the AI-based personalization, specifically through virtual assistants and chatbots, affects consumers' experiences in different sectors, such as banking, hospitality, and retail. As AI continues to grow at a faster pace, companies are now utilizing AI to customize their products based on individual customer needs, thus improving customer experience and engagement. Through the processing of customer data, AI has the ability to offer personalized recommendations, simplify services, and produce more focused marketing campaigns. In finance, personalized financial advice and product offerings are assisted by AI, whereas in hotels, virtual assistants can improve the guest experience by anticipating needs and tastes.

Mustafa Ayobami Raji, Hameedat Bukola Olodo, Timothy Tolulope Oke, Wilhelmina Afua Addy, Onyeka Chrisanctus Ofodile, and Adedoyin Tolulope Oyewole (2024) enlighten that the transformative impact of AI on the e-commerce industry, highlighting how AI-based customization is revolutionizing the shopping experience. Through the analysis of huge volumes of consumer data, AI systems can present very personalized product suggestions that match individual tastes and behaviors. This kind of personalization increases customer satisfaction, since customers feel more understood and appreciated, culminating in increased brand loyalty. Also, content curation enabled by AI, ranging from product recommendations to personalized advertisements, enhances consumer interaction by offering suitable choices that appeal to their interest.

Rachid Ejjami (2024) provides a critical examination of how companies in France can use AI to make their marketing more effective and increase customer interactions. It also points out the critical role that AI technologies can play in redefining conventional marketing strategies, allowing companies to offer more personal and effective experiences to customers. Through the integration of AI, businesses can maximize their marketing activities, enhance targeting, and improve customer engagement in a more data-driven and scalable way. The study emphasizes the need to align AI projects with the business's particular needs to make them relevant and effective. It also highlights the necessity for businesses to navigate the regulatory landscape with caution, making sure that their AI strategies are compliant with local regulations and ethical standards. Finally, the research recommends that French companies need to have a strategic way of implementing AI, balancing innovation and compliance in order to achieve long-term growth and competitiveness.

Amit Singhal (2024) describes the processes by which AI facilitates personalization, encompassing predictive analytics and instantaneous data processing, and evaluates the ramifications for both advertisers and consumers. It also suggests that AI-facilitated personalization not only elevates advertisement relevance but also enhances user satisfaction, engagement, and conversion rates. This research presents a holistic overview of AI's function in programmatic advertising, tackling both technological advancements and ethical dilemmas, along with suggestions for prospective research and industry practices.

Sudenaz Ceren Ünlü (2024) articulates the influence of personalization on enhancing user engagement, satisfaction, and operational efficiency across a variety of applications, including e-commerce platforms, healthcare systems, and educational tools. Also, it scrutinizes the challenges associated with the deployment of personalized interfaces, encompassing issues related to privacy, data ethics, and algorithmic bias. The outcomes of this study contribute significantly to the expanding corpus of knowledge regarding AI's transformative capacity in the creation of intuitive, efficient, and user-centric interfaces, ultimately reshaping the benchmarks for digital interactions.

2.7 RESEARCH METHODOLOGY

In order to provide organizations opportunities for improving their adoption of AI, the study aims to provide insightful details regarding how AI influences customer experience and engagement in digital transformation (Romano et al., 2022). The Research methodology describes the systematic approach and procedures employed to gather, analyze, and interpret data pertaining to the objectives of the study. It gives a clear description of the research design (qualitative, quantitative, or mixed methods), the sampling methods, data collection tools (e.g., surveys, interviews, or experiments), and data analysis methods. This section maintains the transparency and reproducibility of the study so that readers can evaluate the validity and reliability of the findings of the research. By precisely describing the methodological decisions, the researcher reflects the rigor of the study and how the applied methods are suitable for the research questions or hypotheses.

2.8 RESEARCH DATA

Both *primary* and *secondary* data are used for the study.

Primary data is information collected directly by a researcher for a specific research study or objective. It is new and never collected or analyzed before. Surveys, interviews, experiments, and direct observation are some of the methods of collecting primary data. The data is highly reliable and tailored to the research requirements, but time-consuming and expensive to obtain. Primary data is collected through *questionnaire.*

Secondary data, on the other hand, is the existing data that others have gathered, processed, and published. One can obtain such data from sources such as books, scholarly articles, government reports, or web-based databases. Secondary data tends to be less expensive and readily available than primary data but might not be suitable to the specific research questions or even outdated and biased depending on the source.

2.9 SAMPLE SIZE

Sample size in research refers to the number of observations or participants in a study. It has important value in the validity and reliability of the research findings. The bigger the sample size, the greater the chances that it will increase the statistical power of a study, and hence, the chances of finding an effect if there is one. Conversely, a very small sample size may lead to misleading or inconclusive results due to greater variability and greater room for random error. The sample size of the study has been limited to *100.*

2.10 SAMPLING TECHNIQUE

Convenient sampling method is used in this study. Convenient sampling or convenience sampling is a non-probability sampling in which researchers select participants who are most accessible or convenient. Convenient sampling is most often employed when time is short, funds are limited, or accessibility is an issue. Convenient sampling provides quick and inexpensive data collection at the cost of restrictions, most importantly, a lack of generalizability because the sample may not be representative of the larger population. Despite this drawback, it is a highly prevalent approach employed in exploratory research, especially in psychology, education, and marketing.

2.11 STATISTICAL TOOLS

In this study, *SPSS* statistical tool has been adopted for analysis purpose. The following tests are used for analysis purpose

- **Cronbach's Alpha reliability test:** Cronbach's Alpha is a measure of a statistical estimate used to calculate the reliability or internal consistency of a collection of scale or test items. It quantifies to what extent a collection of items relates to one another as a collection, in effect whether they all measure the same factor in the same manner. The alpha coefficient ranges from 0 to 1, and the greater the value, the greater the reliability; an appropriate cut-off for reliability is typically 0.70 or higher.

- **Independent sample t-test:** Independent samples t-test is a statistical test used to determine if there is a significant difference between the means of two unrelated samples or groups. It is literally a way of comparing the means of two groups to determine if they are likely to be drawn from the same population or not. The test gives a *p*-value, which is the chance of obtaining the results obtained (or more extreme results) assuming that the null hypothesis is true. A small *p*-value (typically less than 0.05) shows that there is a statistically significant difference between the means, leading to the null hypothesis being rejected.
- **Friedman test:** The Friedman test is a non-parametric test for comparing three or more related groups or time points, often when the data are ordinal or not normally distributed, and it is a non-parametric equivalent to repeated measures ANOVA. The Friedman test ranks the values in each "block" or subject and computes the sum of ranks for each treatment or group. These sums of ranks serve as the basis for the test statistic, which will establish whether the groups significantly differ.
- **Frequency distribution:** Frequency distribution is a form of presenting data to indicate the frequency of every value or a set of values. It offers a concise representation of a set of data as it groups analogous data points into classes and their frequencies, hence making it possible to detect patterns, trends, and outliers. Frequency distributions are represented in table form, in charts, or in graphs in the form of histograms or bar charts to improve the readability of the data. They are widely applied in statistics to examine both qualitative and quantitative data, facilitating improved decision-making and greater understanding of the overall structure of the data.

2.12 HYPOTHESIS OF THE STUDY

- There is no significant difference among the mean rank of the different methods of AI-enhanced personalization strategies.
- There is no significant difference between male and female with regard to ethical concern regarding AI-enhanced personalized marketing.

2.13 DATA ANALYSIS AND INTERPRETATION

The frequency analysis shows that 58.0% of the respondents are male, and 42.0% are female (Table 2.1).

49.0% of the respondents are in the age group of below 20, 30.0% of the respondents are in the age group 21–30, 17.0% of the respondents are in the age group 31–40, 3.0% of the respondents are above 50 years of age, and only 1.0% of the respondents are in the age group 41–50.

64.0% of the respondents are students, 22.0% of the respondents are employees, 11.0% of the respondents are Professionals, 3.0% of the respondents are home maker, and 0% of the respondents are Entrepreneurs.

64.0% of the respondents belong to the income group less than 10,000, 13.0% of the respondents belong to the income group 30,000–60,000, 10.0% of the respondents belong to the income group above 90,000, 7.0%

TABLE 2.1 Frequency Distribution for Demographic Variable

Variables		Frequency	Percentage
Gender	Male	58	58.0
	Female	42	42.0
Age	Below 20	49	49.0
	21–30	30	30.0
	31–40	17	17.0
	41–50	1	1.0
	Above 50	3	3.0
Occupation	Student	64	64.0
	Employee	22	22.0
	Professional	11	11.0
	Entrepreneur	0	0
	Home Maker	3	3.0
Income	Less than 10,000	64	64.0
	10,000–30,000	7	7.0
	30,000–60,000	13	13.0
	60,000–90,000	6	6.0
	Above 90,000	10	10.0
Educational Qualification	SSLC	1	1.0
	HSC	15	15.0
	UG	62	62.0
	PG	20	20.0
	Diploma	2	2.0

Source: Primary Data.

TABLE 2.2 Friedman Test Table Showing the Most Effective Methods of AI-enhanced Personalization Strategies

AI-Enhanced Personalization Methods	Mean Rank	Chi Square	*P* Value
Personalized product suggestions based on customer preferences	3.20		
AI-powered customer support (chatbots)	2.98		
Tailored ads on website or social media	3.17	9.365	0.053
Personalized email or SMS offers	2.92		
Voice assistance or smart devices recommending products	2.74		

Source: Maximize marketing impact with AI! Explore its role in enhancing customer experience and personalization strategies.

of the respondents belong to the income group 10,000–30,000, and 6.0% of the respondents belong to the income group of 60,000–90,000.

62.0% of the respondents are UG graduates, 20.0% of the respondents are PG graduates, 15.0% of the respondents completed HSC, 2.0% of the respondents are diploma holders, and 1.0% of the respondents completed SSLC (Table 2.2).

2.13.1 Interpretation

Since *P* value is more than 0.05, the null hypothesis is accepted. Hence, it is concluded that there is no significant difference among mean toward the different methods of AI-enhanced personalization. Based on mean score personalized product suggestions based on customer preferences (3.20) is the highly noticed method of customer personalization, followed by tailored ads on website or social media (3.17), AI-powered customer support (chatbots) (2.98), personalized email or SMS offers (2.92), and voice assistance or smart devices recommending products (2.74) (Table 2.3).

2.13.2 Interpretation

Since the *P* values are more than 0.05, there is no significant difference between male and female with regard to overall ethical concerns like misuse of personal data, lack of transparency in how AI is used, AI making decisions without human oversight, and unfair targeting or bias with regard to AI-enhanced personalized marketing (Table 2.4).

TABLE 2.3 Independent Sample t-Test for Significant Difference Between Male and Female with Regard to Ethical Concern Regarding AI-Enhanced Personalized Marketing

Ethical Concerns	**Gender**				***t* Value**	***P* Value**
	Male		**Female**			
	Mean	**SD**	**Mean**	**SD**		
Misuse of personal data	4.00	1.043	4.00	0.911	0.000	1.000
Lack of transparency in how AI is used	3.91	0.904	4.02	0.811	0.366	0.532
AI making decisions without human oversight	3.76	.942	3.95	0.854	−1.055	0.294
Unfair targeting or bias	3.72	.988	3.50	0.890	1.167	0.246

Source: AI-Powered Personalization in Marketing: Enhancing Customer Experiences, Elton Mayfield.

TABLE 2.4 Reliability Test

Reliability Statistics	
Cronbach's Alpha	**No. of Items**
0.847	**26**

2.13.3 Interpretation

For basic research purpose, the Cronbach alpha value should be higher than 0.7. The alpha coefficient for the 26 items in this study is 0.847; this suggests that the items in the questionnaire has high internal consistency.

2.14 FINDINGS OF THE STUDY

The results of a research study are the findings obtained from the data analysis that were gathered in the process of research. They are the most important results or conclusions that are obtained from the research, providing information on the research questions, hypotheses, or objectives that were established at the start of the study. From the data analysis, the following findings were derived:

- From the survey, it is found that the majority of the respondents were male.
- The majority of the respondents fall under the age group of below 20 years.

- The majority of the respondents were undergraduate students.
- The majority of the respondents were getting a monthly income of less than 10,000.
- The majority of the respondents have agreed that they have noticed AI-enhanced personalization methods like personalized product suggestions based on customer preferences, AI-powered customer support (chatbots), tailored ads on websites or social media, personalized email or SMS offers, and voice assistance or smart devices recommending products.
- The majority of the respondents have strongly agreed that they perceive benefits in brands using AI to personalize the customer experience, such as making shopping easier and helping to find relevant products or services more efficiently.
- The majority of the respondents have agreed that they recognize benefits in AI-driven personalization by brands, including enhanced customer service interactions and the introduction of innovative features.
- The majority of the respondents have agreed that they have experienced benefits from AI-driven personalized marketing, such as more relevant product recommendations, faster and more efficient customer service, more personalized offers and discounts, and improved website and app experiences.
- The majority of the respondents have strongly agreed that they are concerned about ethical issues in AI-driven personalized marketing, particularly the misuse of personal data.
- The majority of the respondents have agreed that they are concerned about ethical issues in AI-driven personalized marketing, such as a lack of transparency in how AI is used, decisions made without human oversight, and the risk of unfair targeting or bias.
- The majority of the respondents have agreed that they have encountered challenges and limitations with AI-enhanced personalization, including irrelevant product recommendations, chatbots or AI tools not understanding customer needs, perceptions of overly invasive customization, and the absence of human interaction when needed.

2.15 SUGGESTIONS FROM THE STUDY

2.15.1 Real-Time AI-Powered Personalization by Customer Behavior

Companies must focus on harnessing AI to develop real-time, dynamic personalization that reacts dynamically to customer activity. This entails applying machine learning algorithms and behavioral data to decipher customer preferences, browsing patterns, buying history, and context factors like location or hour of day. The aim is to provide appropriate content, offers, and recommendations at a moment's time, increasing engagement, satisfaction, and conversion rates. Real-time personalization is now not a nicety but an imperative to compete in the modern digital-first economy.

2.15.2 Quantifying the Effect of AI Personalization: Cross-Channel Integration and Customer Journey Mapping

To measure AI personalization, organizations must invest in strong cross-channel personalization and customer journey mapping. This involves monitoring the behavior of users across various touchpoints, for example, websites, mobile applications, email programs, and social media and combining these findings to develop an integrated and consistent experience. By mapping the customer journey, businesses can pinpoint where personalization makes the most significant impact, identify drop-off points, and refine their strategies accordingly. This also enables holistic measurement of ROI and customer lifetime value (CLV) derived from AI initiatives.

2.15.3 Determining Effective AI Customization Methods to Engage Consumers

With AI technologies advancing at a fast pace, companies need to determine and implement the most effective AI-based customization methods to enhance consumer engagement. Such methods can be the following:

- Predictive analytics to predict customer requirements.
- Natural language processing (NLP) to drive chatbots and voice assistants.
- Image recognition for customized visual content.

Reinforcement learning to learn from experiences based on real-time feedback. Testing and refining these tools to see what works with different segments enable a more individualized and engaging customer experience driving advocacy and loyalty.

2.15.4 Enforcing Ethical AI Practices in Order to Establish Consumer Trust

Though AI-powered personalization has extensive advantages, there are also concerns about ethics such as data privacy, algorithmic bias, and transparency. Enterprises have to follow responsible AI principles in order to ensure consumer confidence and regulatory compliance (Patil, 2025) (Gungunawat et al., 2024). Trust is the basis of any customer relationship, and AI must be deployed with an explicit ethical framework to uphold and build upon that trust. That involves ensuring the following:

- Transparency regarding how data is used and gathered.
- Fairness in algorithmic decision-making to prevent bias.

Accountability by explicit governance of AI systems. Consumers are increasingly discerning regarding their data, and showing responsible AI practices fosters brand reputation and consumer trust, which are fundamental to sustained loyalty and reputation.

2.15.5 Prioritizing Privacy Compliance to Avoid Legal and Ethical Pitfalls

With increasing privacy regulations worldwide such as GDPR, CCPA, and more becoming more stringent, companies need to prioritize privacy compliance. AI systems must be developed with privacy by design principles such as the following:

- Data minimization (processing only required data) method
- Anonymization method.

Non-compliance can result in significant fines, litigation, and damage to reputations. Maintaining these principles not only steers clear of legal issues but also upholds ethical accountability and builds consumer trust in the dedication of the brand to data safeguarding.

2.16 CONCLUSION

AI-powered personalization in e-commerce provides transformational prospects to promote user interaction and efficiency of operations. But its success hinges on balancing technological innovation with ethical considerations, providing that customer privacy and trust are maintained along with commercial profits (Nwanna et al., 2025). The world of marketing has witnessed a revolutionary change with the advent of AI-based personalization, which is now an asset for brands in terms of customer engagement on an individual and more personalized level. Since AI has the capability of processing huge chunks of consumer information, marketers have the ability to create highly personalized experiences that meet each customer's taste, conduct, and requirement in a specifically designed manner. This shift allows brands to offer personalized recommendations, targeted advertisements, and even dynamic content that resonates with consumers on a deeper level. By utilizing AI's capabilities, companies can significantly enhance customer engagement, improve conversion rates, and foster stronger brand loyalty. As a result, businesses are able to deliver more relevant experiences that feel personal, driving both short-term results and long-term customer relationships. The increasing use of AI in marketing holds the promise of an even more advanced method of customer engagement in which each interaction point is planned to serve individual needs and expectations.

Today, no one can have any doubt that success in business can be achieved only by adopting innovative technologies, therefore, businesses invest in AI technologies. Nevertheless, a wide range of digital marketing offers making it hard to understand the feasibility of different functions of intelligent technologies. This results in unjustified expenses and cuts down on business operations profitability (Potwora et al., 2023). As AI technology continues to develop, the possibility of even more creative and advanced marketing strategies expands exponentially. The future holds exciting possibilities to continue to enrich customer experiences through further personalization, potentially revolutionizing the way brands engage with consumers. With the capacity to predict and respond to individual customer actions in real time, companies will be able to provide highly personalized and effective content that not only engages but also deepens customer relationships. But with these innovations comes an added responsibility for companies to be ethical in their conduct, making transparent AI-based decisions and building trust with their public. In a world where personalization is the key, companies need to walk the thin line between innovation and ethics, making sure that they build a space where technology benefits the customer's best interests while furthering business objectives. The AI-driven future of marketing is limitless, yet it will also need to be carefully weighed for its ethical dimensions to fully realize its potential.

Further study, it's often said, can explore whether companies can have a balance between employing AI and interacting with customers. Implementing AI in the customer service steps can potentially pose a negative influence on customer satisfaction, if done to excess. As a way to achieve a balance, studies may explore how customer service employs AI, identify the situations that require human touch the most, and examine how shoppers feel about AI (Lau & Lee, 2018).

The future direction of this research is to extend the knowledge of AI-powered personalization to different industries, customer bases, and cultural environments. Future studies could investigate real-time and predictive personalization methods, evaluate long-term effects on customer retention via longitudinal studies, and investigate new AI tools like generative models. There is also scope to address ethical and user-focused issues like data privacy, transparency, and user trust. Moreover, exploring the application of human-AI collaboration in marketing strategies and assessing the direct effect of personalization on important business metrics such as ROI and customer lifetime value might be valuable for both the academic community and practitioners.

REFERENCES

Babadoğan, B. (2024). Harnessing AI and predictive analytics to revolutionize customer retention strategies. *Podcast*, *8*(1), 65–65. https://doi.org/10.62802/k2a4gf39

Benbya, H., Davenport, T. H., & Pachidi, S. (2020). Artificial intelligence in organizations: Current state and future opportunities. *SSRN Electronic Journal*, *19*, 1–15.

Bhuiyan, M. S. (2024). The role of AI-enhanced personalization in customer experiences. *Journal of Computer Science and Technology Studies*, 6(1), 162–196.

Borges, A. F., Laurindo, F. J., Spínola, M. M., Gonçalves, R. F., & Mattos, C. A. (2021). The strategic use of artificial intelligence in the digital era: Systematic literature review and future research directions. *International Journal of Information Management*, *57*, art. no. 102225.

Ejjami, R. (2024). Leveraging AI to enhance marketing and customer engagement strategies in the french market, *International Journal for Multidisciplinary Research (IJFMR)* 6(3), 23147.

Gungunawat, A., Khandelwal, N., & Gupta, N. (2024). AI-powered personalization in digital marketing: Transforming consumer engagement and strategy. *Research Review International Journal Of...*, *9*(11), 183–191. https://doi.org/10.31305/rrijm.2024.v09.n11.026

Harshavardhan, M. (2024). Leveraging artificial intelligence in marketing: Case studies on enhancing personalization, customer engagement, and business performance. *Podcast*, *13*(9), 131–136.

Hemalatha, A. (2023). *AI-Driven Marketing: Leveraging Artificial Intelligence for Enhanced Customer Engagement*. 7. https://doi.org/10.47715/jpc.b.978-93-91303-61-7

Klaus, P., & Zaichkowsky, J. L. (2022, March). The convenience of shopping via voice AI: Introducing AIDM. *Journal of Retailing and Consumer Services*, *65*, 102490.

Kotyrloa, O., Nabokab, R., Nestorc, V., Tyshkod, D., & Panasenko, O. (2024). Ways to use artificial intelligence to improve the personalisation of marketing strategies and improve the effectiveness of communication with consumers. *Questionnaires Application*, 8, 2024spe074.

Lau, K. W., & Lee, P. Y. (2018, August 14). Shopping in virtual reality: A study on consumers shopping experience in a stereoscopic virtual reality. *Virtual Reality*, *23*(3), 255–268.

Manesh, M. F., Pellegrini, M. M., Marzi, G., & Dabic, M. (2020). Knowledge management in the fourth industrial revolution: Mapping the literature and scoping future avenues. *IEEE Transactions on Engineering Management*, *68*(1), 289–300.

Nwanna, M., Offiong, E., Ogidan, T., Fagbohun, O., Ifaturoti, A., & Fasogbon, O. (2025). AI-driven personalisation: Transforming user experience across mobile applications. *Journal of Artificial Intelligence, Machine Learning and Data Science*, *3*(1), 1920–1929.

Okeke, N. I. (2024). AI-driven personalization framework for SMES: Revolutionizing customer engagement and retention. *World Journal of Advanced Research and Reviews*, 24(1). https://doi.org/10.30574/wjarr.2024.24.1.3208

Patil, D. (2025). Artificial intelligence-driven customer service: Enhancing personalization, loyalty, and customer satisfaction. *Podcast*. https://doi.org/10.2139/ssrn.5057432

Pearson, A. (2019). Personalisation the artificial intelligence way. *Journal of Digital & Social Media Marketing*, 7(3), 245–269.

Potwora, M., Zakryzhevska, I., Mostova, A., Kyrkovskyi, V., & Saienko, V. (2023). Marketing strategies in e-commerce: Personalised content, recommendations, and increased customer trust. *Financial and Credit Activity: Problems of Theory and Practice*, *5*(52), 562–573.

Raji, M. A., Olodo, H. B., Oke, T. T., Addy, W. A. (2024). Onyeka chrisanctus ofodile, adedoyin tolulope oyewole, E-commerce and consumer behavior: A review of AI-powered personalization and market trends. *GSC Advanced Research and Reviews*, 118(3), 066–077.

Romano, B., Sands, S., & Pallant, J. I. (2022, March 21). Virtual shopping: Segmenting consumer attitudes towards augmented reality as a shopping tool. *International Journal of Retail & Distribution Management*, *50*(10), 1221–1237.

Singhal, A. (2024). The role of artificial intelligence in enhancing Ad personalization: A study on programmatic advertising. *Journal of Artificial Intelligence General Science (JAIGS)*, *3*(1), 431–445.

Swatman, P. M., & Chin, C. Y. (2004). The Virtual Shopping Experience: Virtual Presence as a Motivator for Online Shopping (March 19, 2004). Deakin University School of Information Systems Working Paper No. 2003/24, Available at SSRN: https://ssrn.com/abstract=630061 or http://dx.doi.org/10.2139/ssrn.630061

Ünlü, S. C. (2024). Enhancing user experience through AI-driven personalization in user interfaces. *Human-Computer Interaction* (Taylor & Francis), *8*(1), 19–19

Verma, S., Sharma, R., Deb, S., & Maitra, D. (2021). Artificial intelligence in marketing: Systematic review and future research direction. *International Journal of Information Management Data Insights*, *1*(1), art. no. 100002.

Wijethilak, H. P., Singh, S. K., & Dhand, S. (2024). AI for personalizing customer interactions. *Advances in Marketing, Customer Relation*, 221–244. https://doi.org/10.4018/979-8-3373-0219-5.ch011

BIBLIOGRAPHY

1. https://ermarketing.net/navigate-the-channel/ai-powered-personalization-in-marketing-enhancing-customer-experiences/
2. https://eudoxuspress.com/index.php/pub/article/view/382
3. https://www.algolia.com/blog/ai/how-ai-powered-personalization-is-transforming-the-user-and-customer-experience/
4. https://www.bloomreach.com/en/blog/ai-personalization-5-examples-business-challenges
5. https://www.dypatilonline.com/blogs/role-ai-marketing-enhancing-customer-experience-personalization
6. https://www.medallia.com/blog/how-ai-personalization-is-changing-the-customer-experience/
7. https://www.qualtrics.com/blog/ai-and-personalization/

CHAPTER 3

Marketing-Finance Collaboration in the Age of AI

Toward a Reinvented Era Where Predictive Analysis in Cash Management Drives Marketing Performance

Badrane Nohayla, Barzi Ghizlane, and Badrane Hasnaa

3.1 INTRODUCTION

In a constantly evolving world, where technological breakthroughs unfold at a relentless pace, innovation is no longer merely a means of differentiation but a true strategic imperative. Organizations today face uncertain and volatile environments that demand an unprecedented level of decision-making agility. In this context, digital transformation goes beyond the mere adoption of sophisticated tools; it calls for a complete reconfiguration of collaboration methods and management models.

Historically, the marketing and finance departments have developed sometimes divergent approaches: the former focuses on value creation and market expansion, while the latter emphasizes budgetary discipline and cost control. The boundaries between these two domains, once a source of

DOI: 10.1201/9781003625452-3

tension, are now gradually fading, thanks to the disruptive advances brought by artificial intelligence (AI).

At the heart of this transformation, cash management, long perceived as a mere support function, is emerging as a true strategic pillar in service of marketing performance. AI-driven treasury management is no longer confined to forecasting and optimizing financial flows; it is evolving into a proactive anticipation and decision-making system capable of integrating a multitude of operational and behavioral parameters. Leveraging the power of predictive analytics, treasurers can now anticipate liquidity fluctuations, uncover growth opportunities, and mitigate risks, offering strategic insights that enhance decision-making across the organization. This shift, driven by real-time financial data and advanced scenario modeling, empowers the marketing department with greater clarity on available resources and informed budget allocation.

Against this backdrop, the alignment between marketing and cash management is no longer a tedious compromise between opposing logics; it becomes a strategic partnership where cash management leverages its expertise to enable more precise, profitable, and well-targeted marketing actions.

Given this new reality, it is essential to examine how the integration of AI into cash management redefines the relationship between marketing and finance, facilitating smoother communication and aligning their respective objectives. The central question then arises: To what extent does AI-driven cash management reinvent the Marketing-Finance collaboration and create a lasting impact on marketing performance? Therefore, this chapter aims to explore this profound reinvention of the marketing–finance alliance, fueled by the power of predictive cash management. The objective is to analyze how AI, far from being just another technology, is actively reshaping managerial practices, streamlining information flows, and fostering a shared vision focused on business performance and resilience.

Through a structured theoretical reflection, this chapter highlights the mechanisms underlying this organizational transformation while emphasizing its managerial implications. The ultimate goal is to gain a deeper understanding of an era in which a redefined cash management function emerges as a key catalyst for marketing success. To this end, this chapter is structured into four sections. The first section outlines the research objective and methodology. The second section presents the key findings, beginning with the evolution of the relationship between marketing and finance, followed by an exploration of how AI is reshaping modern finance, then examining AI-augmented cash management, and concluding with the reinvention of the strategic alliance between marketing and cash management. The third section provides a discussion of the results, and the final section offers a conclusion, summarizing the insights and implications of the study.

3.2 OBJECTIVE AND METHODOLOGY

AI has now established itself as an essential driver of organizational transformation, disrupting traditional paradigms in financial and marketing management. While numerous studies have examined the impact of AI on finance and marketing separately, few have explored how AI-driven cash management can become a strategic catalyst for optimizing marketing performance. Yet, in an environment characterized by increasing volatility and intensified competition, understanding this dynamic is crucial for companies seeking to balance financial agility with commercial efficiency.

This chapter thus aims to provide an in-depth examination of how AI, by revolutionizing the cash management function, fosters more informed decision-making and optimizes the allocation of marketing resources. It seeks to analyze how the automation of financial flows, the anticipation of liquidity risks, and the use of predictive models contribute to establishing a more seamless and integrated governance framework between these two strategic functions. Through this analysis, the objective is to highlight the mechanisms underpinning this convergence and the operational benefits it generates.

To investigate this relationship and provide a comprehensive analysis, a rigorous review of scientific literature and institutional reports was conducted. Various academic databases were consulted, including EBSCO, Cairn, Springer, ScienceDirect, and Journal Storage (JSTOR), to identify major studies addressing AI's impact on cash management and marketing. Additionally, reports from international organizations such as Société Générale, Wholesale Banking, Deloitte, and the World Economic Forum were analyzed to integrate a macroeconomic and managerial perspective into the study. This documentary methodology enables the cross-examination of theoretical and empirical perspectives, offering a holistic view of the challenges associated with AI integration in financial flow management and its impact on marketing performance.

Through this analytical and exploratory approach, this chapter aims to demonstrate that AI does not merely automate cash management; it transforms it into a genuine strategic lever. AI-driven cash management enhances coordination between finance and marketing, reduces budgetary uncertainties, and optimizes overall commercial investments, ultimately positioning itself as a key enabler of corporate performance.

3.3 RESULTS ANALYSIS

3.3.1 Evolution of the Relationship between Marketing and Finance: From Divergence to Convergence

The collaboration between marketing and finance departments has long been characterized by structural tensions and divergent objectives. While marketing focuses on value creation through customer acquisition and retention, finance prioritizes strict cost management and short-term profitability optimization. This historical disconnect, often a source of friction, highlights the need to develop mechanisms that foster strategic alignment between these two functions.

In an ever-evolving economic and technological landscape, this interface has become essential for maximizing organizational performance. The ability to reconcile marketing's growth-driven strategies with finance's emphasis on financial discipline is now a critical success factor, requiring new approaches that promote synergy and shared objectives between these traditionally distinct domains. In this vein, Morvan and Le Gall-Ely (2021) highlight that this opposition often results in a reductive perception of marketing investments, with finance viewing them more as uncertain operational expenses rather than as a strategic lever for long-term performance. However, the digital era presents new opportunities to rethink and strengthen this cross-functional collaboration. The authors demonstrate that digital tools and advanced analytical methods now enable the integration of marketing performance indicators directly into financial models, bridging the gap between these two functions. The rise of customer relationship management (CRM) technologies and real-time consumer behavior tracking platforms has significantly improved the ability to measure the impact of marketing actions on overall business performance. By contextualizing these insights within a financial framework, organizations can more tangibly demonstrate the profitability of marketing initiatives, thereby reducing tensions and misunderstandings with finance.

Along the same lines, the work of Edeling et al. (2021) provides a structured analysis of the evolving relationship between marketing and finance, shedding light on its key challenges. The authors identify major obstacles, such as differing priorities and the absence of shared metrics to measure the impact of marketing investments on financial performance.

This limitation undermines marketing's credibility among financial decision-makers and hinders decision-making processes aligned with broader strategic priorities.

Furthermore, the study explores how emerging technologies, particularly AI, offer promising avenues to strengthen the synergy between finance and marketing. By introducing advanced analytical capabilities and enhancing collaborative decision-making, AI opens new possibilities for overcoming traditional barriers. Building on this perspective, Edeling et al. (2021) emphasize the transformative impact of AI on the interconnection between marketing and finance. According to them, AI provides unique opportunities to redefine this synergy by leveraging powerful analytical tools capable of processing vast and complex data sets. By transcending the limitations of traditional approaches, AI enables organizations to establish clear links between marketing efforts and financial indicators, fostering a deeper mutual understanding between these two strategic domains. With its predictive capabilities and real-time analytics, AI facilitates informed and collaborative decision-making, aligning marketing and finance objectives around shared priorities. Additionally, it enhances the credibility of marketing initiatives among financial executives by providing precise, tangible evidence of their impact on overall business performance.

By eliminating historical barriers related to the lack of common metrics and conflicting priorities, AI ushers in a new era of close collaboration between marketing and finance, driving sustainable value creation. This data-driven, insight-rich approach positions AI as an indispensable catalyst for reinventing the harmony between these two disciplines.

Historically marked by opposing perspectives, the relationship between finance and marketing has long operated as a delicate balance between budgetary prudence and strategic boldness. However, in an era where data has become the primary driver of business decisions, the focus is no longer on arbitrating between financial discipline and commercial creativity but on merging them within an agile and interconnected decision-making ecosystem.

AI, by enhancing financial management, is revolutionizing this dynamic by integrating cash management into a global predictive cycle, with effects that extend well beyond financial indicators. Through its advanced analytical capabilities, AI transforms liquidity management into a major strategic lever, deeply redefining how businesses allocate their resources and manage their marketing investments. Thus, the transition toward proactive and intelligent cash management holds the key to a renewed synergy between these two strategic functions.

Before exploring these transformations, it is essential to examine in depth how AI is redefining the very foundations of cash management, ushering in an era of augmented financial management. This thorough exploration will provide a better understanding of the systemic effects of this innovation on marketing strategies. However, this transformation of cash management cannot be fully grasped without a comprehensive understanding of the evolving financial ecosystem driven by AI. By restructuring analytical, forecasting, and risk management mechanisms, AI is shaping a new financial paradigm, in which cash management stands as one of the strategic pillars.

3.3.2 When AI Redraws Modern Finance: A New Horizon for Cash Flow Management and Decision-Making

Generative artificial intelligence (GAI) is redefining the landscape of modern finance, revolutionizing data analysis, risk modeling, and strategic decision-making. Through advanced models such as large language models (LLMs) and generative adversarial networks (GANs), AI enables an unprecedented exploitation of financial information, facilitating market trend forecasting, audit automation, and investment strategy optimization (Lee et al., 2024). By enhancing data quality through the generation of synthetic scenarios, AI strengthens the resilience of economic simulation models, thereby reducing the inherent uncertainty in financial decision-making. Furthermore, in an environment marked by increasingly sophisticated financial threats, AI's advanced anomaly detection and proactive risk management capabilities serve as a strategic lever, enabling financial institutions to enhance their resilience against market turbulence. However, this technological revolution comes with major challenges, particularly in ethics and regulation. The reliability of algorithms and the transparency of AI-assisted decisions raise critical concerns about their impact on financial system stability. It is therefore imperative to establish rigorous control mechanisms that balance technological innovation with responsible governance, ensuring a sustainable and well-regulated adoption of these advancements (Lee et al., 2024).

In the same spirit, Castanet and Planes (2018), in their book *Finance and Artificial Intelligence: A Revolution in Progress*, highlight that AI, through tools such as big data and machine learning, serves as a strategic driver for transforming corporate economic models.

By effectively leveraging vast volumes of available data, these technologies enhance decision-making analysis, introduce new macroeconomic indicators, and significantly improve risk forecasting capabilities. They thus pave the way for more agile and optimized management of production, distribution, and cost processes, strengthening corporate competitiveness in an ever-evolving business environment.

In a similar vein, Barzi and Bamousse (2023a) emphasize that the current environment is highly conducive to development, innovation, and change. The intensification of competition, ongoing crises, digitalization, economic and technological advancements, environmental challenges, and social transformations have led to a significant renewal of corporate financial activities. In this context, AI has positioned itself at the core of the financial industry, driving personalized customer experiences, improved risk management, and a closer alignment of prices with economic realities. Furthermore, this technological advancement is closely linked to risk management. Indeed, AI enables the faster and more precise identification and quantification of potential threats associated with financial product holdings (Lehalle, 2019). By providing more refined analyses and reducing uncertainty, AI enhances the stability and efficiency of financial strategies adopted by the companies.

Thus, while generative AI is revolutionizing risk modeling and financial decision optimization, it also represents a profound shift in how finance leverages knowledge and data. As Desbiolles (2019) highlights, AI is not merely about automating existing processes; it introduces a new form of augmented intelligence, where analytical, reasoning, and forecasting capabilities are enhanced by advanced algorithms. This transformation extends beyond traditional figures and forecasts: AI enables the exploitation of unstructured information sources, such as market signals, behavioral trends, and even customer interactions, to refine decision-making and strengthen the relevance of investment strategies.

AI no longer merely enhances investment analysis and optimization tools; it reinvents how financial flows are anticipated and managed. While Desbiolles (2019) highlights its role in expanding the cognitive and decision-making capabilities of financial actors, Maple et al. (2023) underscore an even more striking advancement: AI no longer simply provides recommendations, it fundamentally alters the dynamics of risk and liquidity management.

Through machine learning and real-time analysis of transactional data, AI improves the accuracy of financial forecasts and mitigates the impact of unexpected economic fluctuations. This transformation ensures a more efficient allocation of resources, providing businesses with greater stability against macroeconomic shocks. From this perspective, AI does not just optimize processes; it creates a new financial paradigm where decision-making becomes proactive and adaptive. Moving beyond traditional statistical analyses, AI integrates complex signals from markets and economic behaviors, refining the assessment of opportunities and risks. This dynamic grants financial institutions a significant strategic advantage, enabling them to anticipate disruptions well before they fully materialize in the markets.

Based on these insights, AI is profoundly restructuring the entire financial ecosystem, redefining traditional approaches and enhancing businesses' adaptability. However, beyond its impact on global financial mechanisms, it is in cash management that AI unfolds its full strategic potential. By transforming this function into a key driver of financial stability and optimization, AI compels a rethinking of liquidity and cash flow management paradigms, where anticipation and automation reshape established practices. Moreover, this evolution extends beyond the financial sphere, directly impacting the performance of other strategic business functions, particularly marketing. By improving the fluidity and predictability of available resources, AI enables a more coherent and better-aligned management of marketing investments with financial objectives, thereby integrating these two functions into a more synergistic and high-performing dynamic.

3.3.3 AI-Augmented Cash Management: Toward Intelligent and Proactive Financial Management

In a globalized environment where uncertainty has become a constant, optimized cash management is crucial for businesses, which are increasingly urged to embrace digital transformation (Badrane & Bamousse, 2023b). In this context, the integration of AI into cash management represents a profound transformation of this function, which was traditionally limited to reactive liquidity management.

As highlighted in the article "Shaping the Future of Treasury" published by Treasury Management International (TMI), AI is revolutionizing cash flow management by introducing advanced predictive capabilities, enabling more precise and frequent cash flow forecasting. By analyzing real-time historical data, AI enhances the accuracy of financial forecasts and reduces the uncertainties that previously hindered cash managers' decision-making. Thanks to this anticipatory capability, businesses can optimize their liquidity management, avoiding excessive capital immobilization while securing long-term investments (TMI, 2024). These promising advances in capital optimization are particularly crucial in a constantly evolving world, where access to financing remains a persistent challenge for businesses of all sizes and across all sectors (Badrane & Bouzahir, 2023).

However, this revolution extends beyond improved cash flow visibility. Cuervo (2023) highlights the crucial role of AI in predictive cash modeling, where advanced neural models, such as feedforward neural networks (FNNs), surpass traditional techniques by reducing the error margin in operational cash flow forecasting. This enhanced accuracy transforms cash management into a proactive function, where financial decisions no longer rely on static estimates but on dynamic scenarios, continuously adjusted based on updated data.

By integrating financial ratios derived from cash flows and macroeconomic indicators, AI enhances corporate financial resilience, minimizing liquidity deficit risks and optimizing resource allocation (Cuervo, 2023).

Beyond liquidity risks, AI at the core of cash management enables businesses to anticipate foreign exchange risks, predict customer insolvency risks, and foresee potential defaults to which they may be exposed. In this regard, the integration of AI into cash management marks a decisive shift toward more strategic and predictive financial flow management. By capitalizing on AI, companies can accurately forecast financial default risks, anticipate customer insolvency, and optimize inventory and supply chain management. This transformation is particularly critical in an uncertain economic environment, where market volatility and payment risks can severely jeopardize financial stability. By analyzing vast amounts of real-time data on customer solvency and economic trends, AI enables companies to adopt proactive strategies to secure cash flow, adjust credit policies, and avoid imbalances that could affect their working capital needs (Badrane & Bamousse, 2023).

Within this same risk management perspective, AI shapes cash management into a function capable of driving sustainable financial transformation, where risk control is coupled with a forward-looking vision that integrates ecological and societal imperatives. In this respect, cash management that combines efficiency and innovation serves as the cornerstone of financial performance while also fostering inclusive and sustainable growth.

In this framework, AI emerges as a strategic catalyst, optimizing resource allocation toward investments that balance profitability with social responsibility (Badrane & Bamousse, 2023). By incorporating environmental criteria into predictive analysis models, AI enables cash managers to anticipate not only traditional financial risks but also emerging threats related to climate change, new sustainability regulations, and fluctuations in green markets. This proactive approach strengthens corporate resilience to environmental shocks, while ensuring financial decision-making is aligned with ESG (environmental, social, and governance) objectives.

Beyond sustainability considerations, AI plays a key role in optimizing working capital (WCR) by streamlining procurement decisions and inventory management. More precise stock level management helps prevent shortages that affect profitability while also avoiding overstock situations that tie up valuable financial resources. This strategic oversight enhances companies' ability to free up liquidity, providing them with greater flexibility for investment and expansion decisions (Badrane & Bamousse, 2023).

Moreover, beyond risk management and financial forecasting, AI is redefining the operational efficiency of cash management departments through intelligent automation. Machine learning algorithms and robotic process automation (RPA) solutions handle repetitive tasks such as bank reconciliation, payment processing, and regulatory compliance, freeing up time for higher-value strategic activities (TMI, 2024). This digital revolution, combined with the increasing digitalization of financial processes, is propelling cash management into a new era, where financial decisions are made in real time, based on precise and dynamic data. Thus, AI does not merely automate cash management; it reinvents its strategic role. By providing decision-makers with advanced predictive analytics tools, AI transforms cash management into a true financial optimization lever. Companies no longer simply react to financial constraints; they anticipate them, ensuring greater stability and decision-making grounded in a deep understanding of trends and risks. Alongside its role in optimizing financial processes, the integration of AI into cash management enhances corporate resilience against economic uncertainties and market fluctuations. From this perspective, resilience at the core of cash management remains the vital oxygen for maintaining financial stability. It is built upon effective risk management, aimed at boosting the performance of Moroccan firms, mitigating potential risks, and securing their future in these uncertain times (Barzi & Bamousse, 2023b).

From this perspective, it is worth noting that an innovative cash management function has the potential not only to initiate but also to orchestrate the transformation of businesses toward enhanced performance. As a result, the adoption of innovative practices in financial flow management is no longer a choice but an imperative necessity for any organization seeking to overcome the uncertainties of an ever-evolving environment (Badrane & Bamousse, 2025).

By combining technological innovation with risk management expertise, businesses can ensure their long-term sustainability, secure their future, and turn challenges into opportunities for sustainable growth.

Building on these insights, by redefining cash flow management through advanced analytics and enhanced risk anticipation, AI is propelling cash management beyond its traditional role. It is no longer merely a function for liquidity optimization; it is now established as a strategic lever driving the company's overall performance. However, this transformation is not confined to the financial sphere alone; it creates bridges between different business functions, fostering a more integrated and agile approach to organizational management.

Among these cross-functional synergies, the interaction between cash management and marketing is taking on a new dimension in the AI era. Long viewed as a relationship shaped by budgetary trade-offs, this alliance is now being reinvented under the influence of intelligent technologies. This shift frames the exploration of : Marketing and Cash Management in the AI Era: A Reinvented Strategic Alliance, highlighting the new opportunities AI offers to synchronize financial management with marketing initiatives more effectively.

3.3.4 Marketing and Cash Management in the AI Era: A Reinvented Strategic Alliance

Far from merely automating financial processes, AI is shaping a new ecosystem where cash management becomes a true catalyst for performance and cross-functional synergies. As highlighted in a study by Deloitte in collaboration with the World Economic Forum, AI does not just optimize financial operations; it generates collaborative solutions capable of transcending organizational silos, thereby enhancing the relevance and responsiveness of other business functions (Deloitte & WEF, 2018).

This transformation goes beyond the traditional boundaries of cash management; it also flows into other strategic functions, particularly marketing. In this regard, more precise, agile, and well-anticipated cash flow management creates an environment where marketing investments can be managed with greater efficiency. No longer just a budgetary constraint, AI-augmented cash management becomes a strategic lever, aligning financial resources with market opportunities and optimizing marketing performance proactively.

In the era of digital transformation, AI is significantly expanding the role of cash management, turning it into a lever for strategic innovation. Now, with real-time processing capabilities, cash managers have access to advanced analytical tools that enable them to anticipate financial fluctuations with greater accuracy, optimize hedging strategies, and secure investments. The integration of emerging technologies such as blockchain further strengthens this evolution by ensuring greater transparency and traceability of financial flows. Moreover, the automation of routine tasks frees cash managers from operational constraints, allowing them to focus on high-value strategic activities, including financial resource optimization and strategic planning. In this context, cash management evolves into a true financial control center, solidifying its role as a key contributor to the organization's overall success (JDN, De Félix Grévy, 2025). However, in a company, performance cannot be assessed in isolation. Each function's efficiency inevitably influences the others. As a result, the strategic elevation of cash management, empowered by AI, has a direct and profound impact on marketing decisions. An agile and predictive cash management system enhances the synchronization between financial resources, advertising investments, and customer acquisition strategies. By providing real-time visibility into financial flows, AI-driven cash management enables marketing teams to fine-tune their campaigns with precision, capitalizing on peak profitability periods while minimizing budget inefficiencies. No longer merely a support function, AI-enhanced cash management emerges as a true growth catalyst. It fosters more informed, agile, and strategically aligned marketing decisions, ensuring that financial and commercial objectives move in tandem to drive sustainable success.

Similarly, AI and predictive analytics do not merely refine cash management; they also transform how marketing decisions are made and optimized. By leveraging vast amounts of real-time data, these technologies enable companies to anticipate financial fluctuations while aligning marketing strategies more effectively with economic cycles and consumer behavior. Al Khaldy et al. (2023) highlight AI's crucial role in optimizing marketing investments, emphasizing that predictive analytics helps identify with greater accuracy the periods and customer segments offering the highest profitability potential. With this augmented intelligence, businesses can allocate resources more strategically, avoiding budget inefficiencies while maximizing the return on investment of advertising campaigns. Furthermore, by cross-referencing financial transaction data with consumer trends, AI fosters a more agile and proactive marketing approach, where each action is designed based on the company's actual financial capacity and emerging market opportunities.

Within this framework, AI no longer simply enhances forecast accuracy and budget optimization; it becomes a true strategic anticipation tool, transforming resource management into a dynamic and evolving process. By integrating advanced predictive models, businesses can optimize campaign targeting and segmentation while gaining greater capacity to detect market shifts in advance. This approach allows them to rapidly adjust marketing strategies in response to emerging trends and economic fluctuations (Muhajir, 2024).

Such responsiveness is essential in an environment of heightened volatility, where marketing decisions must be aligned not only with commercial opportunities but also with actual cash availability and projected investment profitability. From this perspective, with augmented intelligence, marketing campaigns are no longer based on approximate projections, but on precise forecasts that enhance targeting, segmentation, and offer personalization. This ability to identify the most profitable customer segments and high-receptivity periods maximizes return on investment by reducing costs associated with ineffective actions. Moreover, by integrating weak market signals, predictive analytics enables businesses to anticipate demand fluctuations, adapt strategies in real time, and mitigate risks linked to sudden shifts in purchasing behavior.

From this perspective, AI does not merely connect marketing and finance; it establishes a more fluid and integrated governance model, where every budgetary decision is based on a deep understanding of the interactions between financial flows and commercial performance. This approach enables businesses to secure their investments while maximizing their impact, thereby strengthening a more resilient and well-managed growth dynamic.

3.4 DISCUSSION

The analysis of the results highlights a profound transformation in the role of cash management, driven by AI, thereby redefining organizational dynamics and their impact on marketing performance. Traditionally perceived as a support function, cash management has evolved in the AI era into a central pillar of organizational strategy, enabling more agile budgetary decisions and optimized resource allocation. This shift goes beyond merely enhancing financial efficiency; it establishes an integrated governance model, where marketing decisions are now informed by real-time financial data and robust analytical forecasts.

One of AI's major contributions to cash management lies in its ability to transform liquidity management into a dynamic and predictive process. By providing accurate cash flow projections, AI enables businesses to anticipate periods of high and low profitability, allowing them to adjust budgetary decisions more strategically. This financial fluidity directly enhances marketing performance by ensuring better synchronization between resource availability and advertising or promotional investments. Unlike traditional approaches, where marketing budgets were often determined based on static estimates, AI introduces a level of flexibility that optimizes campaign profitability while minimizing financial risks.

Moreover, AI plays a key role in optimizing capital allocation by enabling decision-making based on simulated scenarios and advanced behavioral analyses. By leveraging real-time data, AI allows businesses to identify the most profitable market segments and adapt marketing strategies according to economic trends and available financial capacity. This convergence between cash management and marketing not only ensures greater responsiveness to market fluctuations but also enhances the relevance of business decisions by relying on solid analytical foundations.

The automation of financial processes is another fundamental driver of this transformation. By reducing the time spent on repetitive and administrative tasks, AI frees up valuable resources that can be redirected toward strategic initiatives. This agility enhances coordination between financial and marketing teams, fostering better collaboration and enabling faster execution of business decisions. Furthermore, the integration of AI into cash management significantly improves risk management, whether related to liquidity risks, market volatility, or payment defaults. By anticipating these threats with greater accuracy, AI helps secure investments and ensure continuity in marketing initiatives, preventing budget disruptions that could negatively impact commercial performance.

AI also plays a crucial role in preventing customer insolvency, a key responsibility of cash managers. With its advanced analytical capabilities, AI enables businesses to identify at-risk customers early by analyzing behavioral, transactional, and macroeconomic data.

This proactive monitoring strengthens financial stability, thereby serving as a valuable source of insights for marketing teams. By gaining visibility into customer solvency, marketers can adjust their strategies accordingly. For instance, for high-risk customers, companies can offer flexible payment solutions, targeted promotional offers, or customized loyalty programs to minimize the risk of non-payment while maintaining profitable customer relationships. Conversely, low-risk segments can be offered more attractive incentives, ensuring a more secure return on investment. Amidst this backdrop, this shared intelligence between cash management and marketing optimizes commercial performance by aligning marketing actions with strategic financial parameters.

Beyond financial aspects, AI also contributes to better resource governance and harmonization of objectives across different business functions. By establishing a decision-making framework based on unified indicators, AI fosters a shared vision between cash management and marketing, enabling more coherent and efficient budget management. This ability to align strategic priorities through shared data enhances the fluidity of interactions between departments, reducing traditional tensions associated with budgetary trade-offs.

Another fundamental area where AI enhances marketing efficiency lies in working capital management (WCR) by streamlining procurement decisions and inventory management.

A more precise stock level management helps prevent stockouts that harm profitability while also avoiding overstock situations that tie up valuable financial resources. This optimized inventory management not only benefits cash management but also has direct implications for customer perception and marketing effectiveness. A stockout leads to customer dissatisfaction and negatively affects customer retention, while overstocking can project an image of a company that lacks agility and operational efficiency. With AI, businesses can adjust orders in real time, based on consumer trends and demand forecasts, ensuring continuous product availability while minimizing storage costs. Furthermore, better logistics flow management allows businesses to align marketing campaigns with actual product availability, preventing ineffective promotions on limited stock or, conversely, excessive inventory accumulation that is difficult to sell. The alignment between cash management and marketing thus becomes a key factor in customer satisfaction and profitability, ensuring that each campaign is synchronized with the company's operational capacity. In this vein, this strategic coordination not only optimizes financial performance but also enhances brand credibility and market positioning.

Along similar lines, AI enables a more refined personalization of marketing strategies by cross-referencing financial data with consumer behavior and market dynamics. Through predictive analytics, it facilitates the identification of the most profitable business opportunities and allows companies to adjust campaigns according to the most favorable investment periods. This direct link between cash management and marketing creates an integrated management model, where every business decision is based on a rigorous evaluation of available resources and expected economic returns.

Ultimately, AI at the core of cash management transcends its initial role to become a driver of marketing performance. It does not merely optimize financial processes; it shapes a new decision-making dynamic, where budgetary flexibility and analytical precision align financial and commercial objectives. By streamlining resource allocation, improving cash flow visibility, and strengthening risk management, AI transforms cash management into a key enabler of marketing success. As a result, far from being a mere budgetary constraint, it becomes a lever for innovation and competitiveness, equipping businesses with the means to anticipate, adapt, and optimize their marketing strategies in an ever-evolving environment.

3.5 CONCLUSION

In the era of digital transformation, where AI is reshaping decision-making, this chapter has examined how AI, by revolutionizing cash management, drives a new dynamic in the collaboration between finance and marketing. Far from being a mere technological evolution, its integration into cash management goes beyond optimizing financial flows; it shapes a new strategic governance model, where data becomes the driving force behind a more agile and efficient coordination between these two essential functions.

The exploration of this transformation has highlighted a fundamental reality: AI-augmented cash management is no longer merely a guarantor of financial stability but a key player in shaping the company's strategic decisions. By enhancing predictive capabilities, AI transforms liquidity management into a decision-making lever, directly driving the responsiveness and efficiency of marketing actions. This reconfiguration extends far beyond mere budget synchronization. It ushers in a new era where marketing investments are no longer constrained by static limitations but evolve fluidly, adapting to financial realities and market opportunities. At the heart of this revolution, predictive analytics emerges as a central element in the convergence between cash management and marketing. By leveraging advanced machine learning and AI models, cash management shifts from a reactive approach to a proactive one, capable of precisely anticipating financial flow fluctuations and their impact on marketing decisions.

AI no longer simply provides a snapshot of available resources; it projects future scenarios, enabling businesses to adapt their advertising and commercial strategies based on projected profitability trends. This ability to forecast and adjust in real time optimizes the budget planning of marketing campaigns, ensuring that investments are made at the most opportune moments to maximize their impact.

More broadly, the insights presented highlight a strategic convergence between cash management and marketing, driven by more refined data utilization, enhanced risk management, and optimized resource allocation. By streamlining interactions between these two functions, AI enables more coherent decision-making, based on reliable forecasts and a shared understanding of financial and commercial imperatives. Marketing performance no longer relies solely on creativity or strategic boldness but also on the ability to anticipate cash flow cycles, adjust investments based on projected profitability, and strengthen financial resilience in the face of market uncertainties.

The integration of predictive analytics into cash management revolutionizes risk management by enabling businesses to anticipate demand fluctuations, price variations, and emerging consumer trends with unprecedented accuracy. This proactive approach transforms budget allocation strategies, ensuring that marketing investments are optimized, avoiding wasteful expenditures during periods of low liquidity while maximizing promotional impact when economic conditions are most favorable.

As a result, cash management is no longer a passive financial function, it evolves into a strategic enabler, equipping decision-makers with reliable predictive intelligence to drive more agile, data-driven marketing strategies.

At its core, this study underscores a fundamental shift: AI is not merely a tool for financial optimization; it is a transformative force that reshapes organizational structures and decision-making dynamics. By breaking down the traditional divide between financial caution and commercial ambition, AI fosters an integrated governance model, where marketing and finance no longer operate in silos but in synergy, feeding each other with real-time insights to maximize value creation.

The enterprise of the future will not only be more digitalized but also smarter, more agile, and deeply interconnected. It will thrive on augmented intelligence, where finance and marketing are seamlessly aligned, driving sustainable growth, enhanced competitiveness, and long-term performance in an increasingly volatile business landscape.

REFERENCES

Al Khaldy, M. A., Al-Obaydi, B. A. A., & al Shari, A. J. (2023, May). The impact of predictive analytics and AI on digital marketing strategy and roi. In *Conference on Sustainability and Cutting-Edge Business Technologies* (pp. 367–379). Cham: Springer Nature Switzerland.

Badrane, H., & Bouzahir, B. (2023). Le Crowdfunding: Outil crucial pour la démocratisation de l'accès au financement et la promotion de l'inclusion financière au Maroc. *International Journal of Accounting, Finance, Auditing, Management and Economics*, 4(5–1), 298–318.

Badrane, N., & Bamousse, Z. (2023a). Chapter 7: Green finance and cash management: An innovative alliance for a prosperous and sustainable future in Africa. In B.L. Salvador Bizotto (Ed.), *Academic Research & Reviews in Social, Human, and Administrative Sciences-III* (pp. 208–227). Ankara, Türkiye: Global Academy Publishing House.

Badrane, N., & Bamousse, Z. (2023b). L'intelligence artificielle au cœur des métiers du trésorier: Ressort clé de la croissance vers une performance pérenne. *International Journal of Advanced Research in Innovation, Management & Social Sciences*, 6(2). DOI: 10.57109/33

Badrane, N., & Bamousse, Z. (2023c). Le lancement des virements instantanés : Quels apports pour la gestion de la trésorerie des entreprises au Maroc ? *International Journal of Accounting, Finance, Auditing, Management and Economics*, 4(4–1), 669–683. https://doi.org/10.5281/zenodo.8298904

Badrane, N., & Bamousse, Z. (2025). Les Nouvelles Voies de Financement Novatrices : Vecteur de Changement Transformateur vers la Performance Financière des Entreprises au Maroc. *Revue Française d'Economie Et De Gestion*, 6(2).

Barzi, G., & Bamousse, Z. (2023a). L'intelligence artificielle dans la fonction financière : Un levier de développement face aux défis futurs. *International Journal of Advanced Research in Innovation and Social Sciences*, 6(2).

Barzi, G., & Bamousse, Z. (2023b). La résilience au cœur de la fonction financière des entreprises: Levier de pérennité contre les effets des crises au Maroc-Cas du Covid-19. *Economic and Management Review*, 1(1).

Bataineh, A. Q., Abu-AlSondos, I. A., Frangieh, R. H., Salameh, A. A., & Alnajjar, I. A. (2024). Predictive modeling in marketing analytics: A comparative study of algorithms and applications in e-commerce sector. *Kurdish Studies*, 12(1), 499–515.

Castanet, C., & Planes, C. (2018). Finance et intelligence artificielle: Une révolution en marche. *Enjeux Numériques*, N°1, Annales des Mines.

Cuervo, R. (2023). Predictive AI for SME and large enterprise financial performance management. arXiv preprint arXiv:2311.05840.

De Félix Grévy, C. (2025). L'intelligence artificielle dans les services financiers: Transformer la trésorerie pour l'avenir. JDN. https://www.journaldunet.com/fintech/1538977-l-intelligence-artificielle-dans-les-services-financiers-transformer-la-tresorerie-pour-l-avenir/

Deloitte, World Economic Forum. (2018). *The New Physics of Financial Services Understanding how artificial intelligence is transforming the financial ecosystem*, Deloitte &World Economic Forum.

Desbiolles, J. (2019). Finance et Intelligence artificielle (IA): d'une révolution industrielle à une révolution humaine… tout est à repenser… *Annales des Mines – Réalités industrielles, Février*, 2019(1), 5–8. https://doi.org/10.3917/rindu1.191.0005

Edeling, A., Srinivasan, S., & Hanssens, D. M. (2021). The marketing– finance interface: A new integrative review of metrics, methods, and findings and an agenda for future research. *International Journal of Research in Marketing, Elsevier*, 38(4), 857–876.

Lee, D. K. C., Guan, C., Yu, Y., & Ding, Q. (2024). A comprehensive review of generative AI in finance. *FinTech*, 3(3), 460–478. https://doi.org/10.3390/fintech3030025

Lehalle, C. A. (2019). La finance de marché à l'ère de l'intelligence bon marché dans. *Revue d'économie financière*, 135(3), 67–84

Maple, C., Porter, J., & Stewart, H. (2023). The AI revolution: Opportunities and challenges for the finance sector. ArXiv. https://arxiv.org/abs/2308.16538

Morvan, J., & Le Gall-Ely, M. (2021). « Arguments en faveur d'une recherche à l'interface Marketing-Finance »: Commentaire. *Recherche et Applications En Marketing*, *36*(4), 48–57. https://www.jstor.org/stable/27287516

Muhajir, A. (2024). Predictive analytics in marketing: contribution to marketing performance. *Management Studies and Business Journal (PRODUCTIVITY)*, 1(3), 447–460.

Société Générale Wholesale Banking (2024). AI: An opportunity for treasurers in search of performance. *Société Générale*. https://wholesale.banking.societegenerale.com/fr/actus-opinions/toutes-publications/news-details/news/ai-an-opportunity-for-treasurers-in-search-of-performance/

Treasury Management International (TMI). (2024, September). *AI: An Opportunity for Treasurers in Search of Performance*. In *Shaping the Future of Treasury*. Treasury Management International (TMI).

CHAPTER 4

Data-Driven Decision-making and Predictive Analytics

Mostafa Ahmadi

4.1 INTRODUCTION

In today's digital world, data play a key role in evolving the decision-making and operation processes of enterprises. Organizations can forecast their needs, such as optimizing services, personalizing recommendations, and tailoring advertising, by leveraging available datasets.

Ocient (2022) evaluated a sample of 500 pioneering companies in technology and data and found that enterprises have shifted beyond big data frameworks and encounter datasets of remarkably larger sizes and complexity. Thus, organizations are well-positioned to effectively understand customer behavior and market dynamics, enabling them to optimize supply chains, accurately predict customer decisions and emerging trends, and personalize marketing practices.

Davenport and Harris (2007) believed that data-driven decision-making was in fact born when statistical analysis was employed to perform operations in organizations in the mid-20th century. The evolution of technologies, including the Internet of Things (IoT), artificial intelligence (AI), and cloud computing, has further enhanced data analytics capabilities in recent decades (McAfee et al., 2012). As a result, enterprises can exploit a variety of sources to obtain data, for example, transactions, sensor networks, and social media platforms, to structure the data and comprehensively identify consumer preferences, behavior, and market trends.

DOI: 10.1201/9781003625452-4

AI identifies complicated patterns within complex and large datasets. Machine learning (ML) is an AI approach that can be utilized to shift from descriptive to prescriptive and predictive analytics in which data-driven algorithms and approaches drive strategic decision-making (Jordan & Mitchell, 2015). Organizations can adopt ML-based marketing to personalize their efforts and enhance consumer involvement, leading to higher consumer loyalty and profitability. The recommendation system of Amazon accounts for almost one-third of its sales (McKinsey & Company, 2021). The personalized content recommendation system of Netflix is also a major example (Gomez-Uribe & Hunt, 2015).

Manyika et al. (2011) reported that enterprises with data-driven decision-making systems mostly have larger market shares, profitability, and productivity. AI frameworks, including user-friendly platforms (e.g., Azure ML, Google Cloud AI, and AWS), have been democratized and used to enable small and medium enterprises (SMEs) to perform complicated analytics and acquire competitive advantages in today's competitive markets. Organizations can exploit such resources to remain competitive and streamline operations and foster rapid innovation.

This chapter is focused on exploring AI-based analytics, AI-driven marketing approaches, and AI ethics. Furthermore, the contributions of new trends (e.g., real-time decision-making and generative AI) to predictive analytics progress are discussed. In sum, the contributions of AI and data to the establishment of innovative and customer-centered environments are highlighted.

4.2 EVOLUTION OF AI IN PREDICTIVE ANALYTICS

4.2.1 Growth of Data and Advanced Analytics

Several technological factors, for example, ubiquitous mobile devices and increasing IoT sensors and social media platforms, are involved in the substantial rise in data. Digital footprints are produced by a massive number of interactions (e.g., on social networks and online shops) every day, and such data are potential drivers of organizations. Major retailing companies obtain huge quantities of data on consumer transactions continuously so that their pricing and logistics can be optimized (Manyika et al., 2011). For example, Walmart's supply chains are regularly refined to ensure the temporal and spatial availability of goods.

The assessment of review data for relevant and personalized content recommendations has played a major role in the subscriber retention strategies of Netflix (Gomez-Uribe & Hunt, 2015). Finding the favorite shows in a short time would increase customer satisfaction and engagement and, therefore, decrease the churn rate. The diversity, size, and velocity of modern data remain challenging to conventional statistical techniques, necessitating the manual engineering of features and data distribution assumptions. AI, including ML, may learn complex connections within large datasets, minimize labor costs, and offer valuable insights.

Google DeepMind has achieved a 40% reduction in costs by optimizing cooling systems in data centers through ML algorithms (Evans & Gao, 2016). This suggests that data-driven decision-making helps significantly save back-end and infrastructural costs while boosting customer-end tasks. AI-driven analytics help organizations improve their proactivity when responding to resource limitations and market volatility by predicting customer demands, optimizing delivery systems, and scheduling manufacturing.

Market basket analysis is a major application of ML algorithms in the retailing sector. It can identify the most frequent baskets of products and enables firms to develop optimal shelf layouts and targeted cross-selling recommendations. Amazon has utilized large-scale data to find "frequently bought together" products. This demonstrates the contribution of targeted product recommendations to enhancing shopping experiences and order values (Smith & Linden, 2017). Market basket analysis is also used by grocery shops to develop targeted recommendations and product bundles so that marketing efforts can be aligned with consumers' changing preferences more effectively.

Loyalty programs have enjoyed improved responsiveness and dynamics through ML. Firms may offer precise rewards and/or recommendations using real-time analytics to respond effectively to consumer behavior. Starbucks monitors and evaluates the purchase preferences and frequency of consumers through its loyalty application to enhance consumer retention using personalized recommendations (Renascence, 2024). This would not have been imagined in early static segmentation years when demographic grouping was the basis of marketing.

4.3 RISE OF ML ALGORITHMS

ML became popular during the mid-20th century when the Checkers-playing Program was proposed by Arthur Samuel and demonstrated that machines are capable of learning from experience (Samuel, 1959). Rosenblatt (1958) studied perceptrons and laid the ground for neural network development. Initial models faced limitations in computing power, simplistic frameworks, and a lack of sufficient data. A dramatic rise in computational power and the emergence of huge training datasets induced a shift from rule-based expert models to data-driven learning models.

The growing adoption of support vector machines (SVMs) (Cortes & Vapnik, 1995) and the introduction of decision tree (DT) algorithms (mostly related to the random forest [RF] algorithm of Breiman and other ensemble methods) were the major drivers of embracing ML models. Such advancements remarkably improved accuracy in, for example, medical diagnostics and fraud detection. There are several learning strategies for ML models:

> Supervised learning refers to the prediction of certain outcomes by training an ML model using labeled data. It is often employed in recommendation systems, loan default risk analysis, and credit scoring. For instance, financial institutions predict default probabilities using historical data on borrowers for information on interest rates and approvals.

Unsupervised learning involves ML models to find hidden patterns in an unlabeled dataset for applications such as dimensionality reduction and clustering. Retailing enterprises categorize their consumers using their purchase behavior through clustering models to develop segment-tailored marketing (Aguiar & Waldfogel, 2018).

Reinforcement learning allows ML algorithms to use trial and error to learn optimal strategies. This learning strategy promotes dynamic pricing and utilizes demand elasticity to adjust recommendations (Influencer Marketing Hub, 2024).

Deep learning models are utilized for sentiment analysis, language translation, and image recognition. These algorithms are used by social media platforms in order to measure the sentiments of consumers and direct brand management policies.

Predictive maintenance in production plants represents a key application of ML models. These models analyze the real-time sensor data of machines and detect forthcoming defects to minimize maintenance costs and downtime. Predictive analytics is used in the aviation division of General Electric to monitor jet engines for maintenance schedule optimization (McKinsey & Company, 2021). Financial institutions utilize ML-based algorithms to detect transaction fraud in a short time and minimize institutional and customer losses.

Generative AI offers capabilities beyond simple text generation. For example, GPT, as demonstrated by Brown et al. (2020), can generate synthetic news articles that are nearly indistinguishable from human-written text. This ability highlights its potential for producing high-quality synthetic data, which can be used to evaluate predictive algorithms, thereby helping to manage privacy concerns and reducing reliance on sensitive real-world data. Moreover, by simulating realistic natural language dialogues, GPT paves the way for applications that enhance training programs through the creation of authentic conversational scenarios, ultimately accelerating internal training processes while safeguarding confidential information.

Overall, predictive AI has enjoyed major efficiency enhancements and increased ranges in light of ML evolution and the rapid increase in high-quality datasets, and algorithms have shifted beyond basic predictions and today encompass fully autonomous decision-making, real-time optimization, and accurate personalization in multiple fields.

4.4 AI APPLICATIONS IN MARKETING AND PREDICTIVE ANALYTICS

4.4.1 Customer Segmentation

Effective marketing requires insights into the similarities and differences of customers. AI-based customer segmentation involves not only demographics but also psychological traits, real-time interactions, and behavioral factors. Spotify provides playlists with algorithmic tailoring to effectively cluster users through their music behavior and preferences (Aguiar & Waldfogel, 2018). Such personalization helps further increase the engagement of users, leading to higher loyalty and promoting exploration.

Likewise, ML-tailored advertisements in Starbucks' loyalty application recommend items to frequent morning coffee customers differently from those sent to late afternoon customers (Renascence, 2024). Micro-level pattern-based segmentation helps optimize lifetime value and satisfaction for consumers. Financial institutions segment customers to identify risk factors in loans, enabling the development of products that balance responsible lending with profitability.

4.4.2 Customer Behavior Prediction

Organizations may use predictive AI to predict customer behavior, for example, the probability of buying certain products or churn risk. Historical data, for example, social interactions, spanning transactions, and online behavior, can be modeled to develop proactive policies. Target has employed predictive AI to evaluate purchase behavior changes and find recently pregnant customers. This demonstrates that relevant items can be predicted and marketed (Duhigg, 2012). These advantages with ethics and transparency help promote not only trust but also brand relations.

Streaming media, for example, Netflix, predict the content preferences of their viewers through well-structured ML models. Netflix provides title recommendations to ensure continuous viewer engagement through the analysis of viewer's ratings, time spent, and view history (Gomez-Uribe & Hunt, 2015). A decrease in time-to-content (i.e., the searching time) has a direct association with viewer retention enhancement. E-commerce enterprises identify cross-selling or up-selling opportunities using recommender systems so that the average transaction size can be enlarged (Smith & Linden, 2017).

4.4.3 Personalization and Campaign Optimization

AI-personalized marketing provides users with dynamically customized recommendations, online experiences, and emails. For example, Amazon uses full homepage personalization through users' favorite items, buying behavior, and browsing history to provide unique storefronts. Likewise, Netflix shows different thumbnails for a given movie, based on the preferred genres of each user (Gomez-Uribe & Hunt, 2015).

The process of optimizing campaigns includes monitoring key performance indicators (KPIs) and adjusting marketing spend through real-time analytics. For example, AI models may realize that a social media advertisement is efficient and effective for a certain demographic group and bring additional financial resources in a short time. The social media analytics of Coca-Cola assesses engagement criteria and implements swift campaign pivoting through AI models (Keyhole, 2023). This allows for designing a marketing strategy based on tailored dynamic dialogues rather than static broadcasts.

4.4.4 Customer Relationship Enhancement

Long-term relationships can be fostered using efficient customer relationship management through AI algorithms. Natural language processing (NLP) has been efficiently exploited in chatbot development; a chatbot may fulfill troubleshooting, handle queries, and utilize product discovery to guide customers. Sephora has developed a chatbot that incorporates skincare preferences into the process of finding cosmetic/health products.

It recommends relevant items using personal data and purchase history, enabling the enterprise to obtain competitive advantages in a competitive market of beauty products.

CRM strategies may use sentiment analysis to capture social media users' attitudes toward brands. Rapid identification of negative sentiments helps enterprises promptly intervene and offer clarifications/resolutions to cope with negative feedback. Enterprises can possess a major competitive advantage through real-time feedback and receive customers' criticism and suggestions.

4.5 DYNAMIC PRICING STRATEGIES

The real-time prediction capabilities of AI models enable dynamic pricing and help adjust service/product prices based on factors such as customer segments, inventory, competitive pricing, and current demands. This idea was initially implemented by airline companies to change seat prices frequently during the day, depending on seat availability and booking rate. E-commerce organizations later adopted similar strategies and optimized margins using AI algorithms to preserve their competitive advantages (Influencer Marketing Hub, 2024).

For example, Airbnb uses dynamic nighttime host pricing based on previous occupancies, special events, seasonality, and location (Airbnb, 2024). Hosts receive pricing recommendations so that their revenue and occupancy can be maximized. Such dynamic pricing provides help to hosts with peak-demand prices and to travelers with budget accommodation.

4.5.1 AI-Driven Content Generation

It is difficult to generate relevant, effective content under marketing message saturation. AI-generated content can cope with such difficulties and helps with email campaigns, social media captions, blog posts, and short videos optimized through user preferences and brand voice. Preserving creative and authentic content requires human intelligence, while AI algorithms can significantly reduce the cost and time needed to draft baseline materials. Generative AI (GenAI) has emerged as a transformative tool in marketing, allowing firms to automate content creation while maintaining a level of personalization and relevance (Cillo & Rubera, 2024).

Enterprises may also use automatically customized advertisements for particular groups of audiences. Marketing professionals may use AI algorithms to produce several items rather than a single advertisement to meet the preferences of various demographic categories. As a result, organizations can create efficiently appealing messages. These approaches have enjoyed dramatic efficiency improvements through AI algorithms. Research indicates that firms such as Coca-Cola and Unilever (2022) have already started leveraging GenAI to co-create marketing content and advertising, demonstrating its increasing role in modern marketing strategies. (Cillo & Rubera, 2024).

4.5.2 Real-Time Sentiment Analysis

Users on social media, for example, Instagram, Twitter, and Facebook, can share their positive and negative ideas about campaigns and products/services. AI-based sentiment analysis leverages this feedback to identify potential crises and emerging trends. Real-time sentiment analysis enables enterprises to remain responsive to complaints and address shortcomings, adapting messages to dynamic customer attitudes (Barunaha et al., 2023).

The sentiment analysis system of H&M may reveal criticism of a recently launched group of fashion items for sustainability or fitness. Timely responses help organizations cope with such challenges effectively by providing further clarification concerning manufacturing or revealing product details. Enterprises that fail to manage feedback on social media platforms risk significant reputational challenges stemming from minor complaints. (Barunaha et al., 2023)

4.5.3 AI in Predictive Supply Chain Management

Supply chain disruptions can be costly, both financially and reputationally. Predictive analytics enhance the stability and reliability of supply chain operations by forecasting demand, anticipating bottlenecks, and suggesting optimal resource allocation. By tracking factors such as weather patterns, geopolitical risks, and real-time sales data, AI systems can help companies like Zara adjust production runs to match shifting consumer tastes.

Advanced analytics and large-scale data integration are the drivers of the nearly real-time inventory management of Walmart (Manyika et al., 2011). The automation of logistics, purchase orders, and replenishment minimizes overstocks and stockouts and refines the efficiency of operations. Likewise, AI-enabled route optimization has helped DHL incorporate package volumes and road and traffic conditions, improve timeliness, and minimize emissions.

TABLE 4.1 Summary of AI Applications in Marketing

AI Application	Description
Predictive Analytics in Marketing	Utilizing AI to predict market trends, customer preferences, and optimize marketing strategies.
Customer Behavior Forecasting	Analyzing past transactions and behaviors to anticipate customer needs and prevent churn.
AI-Driven Personalization	Leveraging AI to deliver customized recommendations, tailored advertisements, and personalized content.
Real-Time Decision-Making	Using AI models to react swiftly to customer interactions, optimizing engagement in real time.
Sentiment Analysis	Extracting customer sentiment from social media and reviews to shape marketing strategies and responses.
AI in Supply Chain Optimization	Optimizing inventory management, supplier relations, and demand forecasting through AI analytics.
Dynamic Pricing Strategies	Adjusting product and service pricing dynamically based on demand, competition, and market factors.
Customer Relationship Management (CRM)	Enhancing customer relationships through AI-driven chatbots, automated responses, and loyalty programs.
AI-Generated Content	Using generative AI to create relevant, engaging marketing content such as blog posts and ad copies.

4.5.4 AI in Customer Retention Strategies

Customer retention is more affordable than customer acquisition. As a result, customer retention is an essential approach. AI algorithms can identify at-risk customer patterns; at-risk customers are those with interactions that signal dissatisfaction or declining engagement. Telecommunication enterprises implement churn prediction algorithms to find potentially canceling customers and develop retention strategies such as bundled service offers and data plan discounts.

Likewise, the predictive AI of the Starbucks loyalty application provides occasional rewards to preserve customer engagement (Renascence, 2024). Enterprises can assess visit frequencies, product preferences, and order sizes to provide customized recommendations and remind their customers of their competitive advantages over other companies efficiently (Table 4.1).

4.6 ETHICAL CONSIDERATIONS IN AI-DRIVEN MARKETING

AI-powered marketing is required to meet several ethical standards, for example, accountability, algorithmic fairness, and privacy, as AI algorithms are increasingly used in many fields for many purposes.

4.6.1 Privacy Concerns

Detailed user data, including geographic location and browsing history, are typically crucial in AI-assisted systems. The California Consumer Privacy Act (CCPA) and European General Data Protection Regulation (GDPR) strictly regulate the collection, storage, and sharing of personal data (European Parliament, 2016). Lack of informed consent and inefficient handling of sensitive data have reputational and legal consequences for firms.

Privacy by design has been adopted by technology giants, for example, Apple, and mechanisms such as differential privacy have been implemented to protect user data privacy (Dwork, 2008). Despite the preservation of aggregate analytics advantages through such methods, personal identifiers are not exposed. Robust privacy measures are essential for preserving customer trust, considering concerns about intrusive data collection and data breaches.

4.6.2 Algorithmic Bias

AI algorithms are trained using certain data, and imbalance or impartiality in such datasets can lead to biased outputs and perpetuation (Buolamwini & Gebru, 2018). Biased models may appear in applications such as targeted advertisement, credit scoring, and recruitment. An advertisement platform could unintentionally display job positions of higher payments more frequently to male audiences than to females.

Bias correction includes analyzing datasets to ensure diversity and applying fairness criteria in the development of AI algorithms. Fairness constraints were introduced for classification (Zafar et al., 2017). The reweighting of data samples for bias neutralization was discussed (Kamiran & Calders, 2011). Zhang et al. (2018) coped with inadvertent biases through an adversarial learning approach. Coupled with the interdisciplinary collaboration of ethicists, domain experts, and data scientists, such techniques may minimize negative consequences and enhance fairness in user treatment.

4.6.3 Transparency and Explainability

A large number of AI models are black boxes, and those who lack expertise may not realize the detailed procedures of decision-making and prediction. This could diminish customer trust in marketing, particularly under manipulative or invasive AI-generated suggestions. In this respect, explainable AI (XAI) offers human-interpretable reasoning for AI outputs. A number of methods, including feature importance scoring, surrogate modeling, and model distillation, explain the denial of a loan or the targeting of a specific advertisement (Jordan & Mitchell, 2015).

Regulations require healthcare professionals and financial institutions to provide sufficient transparency for AI-generated decisions. Certain transparency degrees can be expected to be required by regulations in the future, particularly in systems where pricing or customer choice are strongly dependent on algorithms.

4.7 ETHICAL IMPLICATIONS OF DATA OWNERSHIP

AI algorithms are developed based on owned data. These data are traditionally considered to be generated by corporations that use user data with minimal control or compensation provided to individuals. Regulatory organizations or public sentiments require that higher degrees of control and direct compensation be granted to individuals. Novel technologies, such as blockchain-based wallets, provide greater decentralization and enable users to control the use of their data; users can be micro-paid for their shared personal ideas.

Therefore, digital marketing can be reshaped, and enterprises could implement trust-based data transactions of higher transparency rather than passive user data collection.

4.8 CONSUMER TRUST AND BRAND REPUTATION

Failure to meet ethical requirements may diminish the credibility of brands in AI contexts. It is to be mentioned that rebuilding damaged trust might be a dramatic challenge. Recent publicized scandals, for example, the Cambridge Analytica scandal, demonstrate regulatory scrutiny and customer backlash can be the consequences of controversial data exercises. In contrast, prioritizing AI ethics, for example, bias mitigation and privacy protection, enables organizations to stand out in a competitive marketplace. The IBM-Harris Poll Survey (2019) found that 78% of U.S. consumers are more likely to trust companies that prioritize the protection of their personal data. Furthermore, the report highlights that transparency in data handling and robust privacy practices significantly enhance customer trust and loyalty, encouraging positive word-of-mouth and long-term engagement.

4.9 FUTURE DEVELOPMENTS IN AI AND PREDICTIVE ANALYTICS

4.9.1 Generative AI in Marketing

GPT-based algorithms have triggered a content creation revolution. They could generate social media posts, product descriptions, and marketing copies to remarkably shorten the production time for large campaigns. GPT-based frameworks are expected to gain higher popularity and capture customer sentiment and detailed brand guidelines. Next-generation models shall adapt their writing approaches rather than merely generating large generic text quantities in order to meet the demands of particular groups of audiences. Despite the key role of human intelligence in quality assurance, GPT-based models contribute to the reshaping of marketing strategies in light of their adaptability and speed.

The applications of GPT algorithms are not limited to texts. Images, videos, and interactive chatbots generated by AI promote immersive consumer experiences. With the growth of AR/VR technologies, GPT-based models can help produce 3D demos of products or virtual store layouts and redefine consumer engagement.

4.9.2 Collaboration between Marketing and Technical Teams

Data scientists and marketing experts are to collaborate to effectively exploit AI. Marketing centers should understand market positioning, brand identity, and customer psychology, and data scientists are to help through technical implementation and algorithmic expertise. Cross-disciplinary groups align high-level analytics with organizational goals to promote the adoption of AI; for example, the collaboration of data scientists with marketing professionals at Procter & Gamble for product launch strategy refining to ensure the inclusion of relevant customer ideas into prediction algorithms (McKinsey & Company, 2021).

Hybrid roles such as marketing data scientists may emerge as AI continues to increasingly penetrate competitive marketing approaches. This, in turn, connects ML knowledge and customer insights. Enterprises that promote these collaborations can achieve innovation and adaptability in a short time.

4.9.3 Ethical AI Adoption

AI ethics represent a core parameter in sustainable organizational operations as customer awareness and regulatory scrutiny continue to increase.

Bias audits, transparent reporting, and fairness metrics can be expected to be standardized. Considering the growth of XAI technologies, higher disclosure transparency may be required for the impacts of automated systems on user experiences, content, and pricing by regulatory organizations.

Furthermore, the current quality standards could manifest in third-party certifications and audits for ethical AI, for example, LEED and ISO certifications, representing external validation for the responsible use of AI. These systems may offer guidelines on allowable data collection, allowable personal data use, and enforced accountability systems in the case of standard violation by organizations. The adoption of such systems could be a competitive advantage for organizations that aim to promote public trust.

4.9.4 AI and Real-Time Decision-Making

Large quantities of real-time data are generated by IoT devices and online interactions. AI models that can process such large datasets enable enterprises to make rapid reactions. The consequences are beyond automated consumer support, personalized web content, and dynamic pricing. Retailers may utilize real-time consumer motion data to adjust in-store layouts or advertisements, and restaurants could be expected to embrace dynamic supply reorders and predict demand growth for specific items. Uber has deployed the surge pricing strategy to update based on rider demand and driver availability in a short time (Influencer Marketing Hub, 2024).

Scalable infrastructures and effective data systems are required for real-time analytics. Edge computing (e.g., data processing near the data generation location) can contribute to the acceleration of time-sensitive task fulfillment in a short time using AI.

4.9.5 Future-Proofing Businesses through AI

Apart from tackling enterprise challenges, organizations can exploit AI algorithms to cope with potential disruptions in the future. They can implement prediction systems to predict market shifts, measure economic fluctuation risks, and detect new customer preferences. Tesla has incorporated AI into its vehicle software updates, self-driving vehicle research, and battery management, which highlights the exploitation of predictive AI by enterprises to effectively tackle societal and technological challenges (McKinsey & Company, 2021).

Apart from product innovation, AI has been used by organizations to meet environmental sustainability standards. AI-driven climate algorithms contribute to minimizing greenhouse gas (GHG) emissions and maximizing energy saving, leading to greener practices. The data centers of Google are equipped with AI to decrease their carbon footprint (Evans & Gao, 2016).

4.10 CONCLUSION

AI and ML have revolutionized predictive analytics and helped organizations exploit huge datasets to obtain real-time and practical insights. Data-driven decision-making is utilized in many contexts, for example, the tailored recommendations of streaming services and inventory optimization in retailing enterprises. Many corporations, for example, Amazon and Netflix, exploit predictive analytics to raise their profitability and customer loyalty and transform customer experiences (Gomez-Uribe & Hunt, 2015; Smith & Linden, 2017).

The maturity of AI is not limited to technological knowledge. AI ethics, such as algorithmic fairness and user privacy, are essential for reputation and customer trust. Regulatory bodies, such as GDPR (European Parliament, 2016), require data use transparency, and fairness-oriented methods emphasize unbiased training data (Kamiran & Calders, 2011; Zafar et al., 2017; Zhang et al., 2018). Furthermore, the collaboration of legal, technical, and marketing professionals contributes to meeting ethics and long-term organizational values in the use of AI models.

Real-time analytics is also expected to boost decision-making, adaptation to market fluctuations, customer feedback, and competitor actions swiftly. Enterprises where such tools are effectively deployed are likely to succeed. They are future-proofed against disruptions and implement supply chains with higher resilience while developing engaging consumer experiences that lead to loyalty enhancement.

Finally, predictive analytics is a paradigm in which decision-making is performed not only based on intuition but also on AI-identified data patterns. Organizations increasingly realize the capabilities of AI, and data-driven methods are expected to play a key role in preserving competitive advantages in the business world. Integrating data science frameworks with effective marketing practices can revolutionize not only customer interactions but also products and services, fostering collaboration, innovation, and ethical standards. Enterprises adopting AI can achieve sustainable growth and build consumer trust in a data-centered world.

REFERENCES

Aguiar, L., & Waldfogel, J. (2018). *Platforms, Promotion, and Product Discovery: Evidence from Spotify Playlists.* National Bureau of Economic Research Working Paper No. 24713 https://papers.ssrn.com/sol3/papers.cfm?abstract_id=3198015

Airbnb. (2024). *Smart Pricing Overview.* https://www.airbnb.com/help/article/1163/what-is-smart-pricing

Barunaha, A., Prakash, M. R., & Naresh, R. (2023). Real-Time Sentiment Analysis of Social Media Content for Brand Improvement and Topic Tracking. *Proceedings of the 6th International Conference on Intelligent Computing (ICIC-6 2023)*, 26–31. https://doi.org/10.2991/978-94-6463-250-7_6

Brown, T., Mann, B., Ryder, N., Subbiah, M., Kaplan, J. D., Dhariwal, P., Neelakantan, A., Shyam, P., Sastry, G., Askell, A., Agarwal, S., Herbert-Voss, A., Krueger, G., Henighan, T., Child, R., Ramesh, A., Ziegler, D. M., Wu, J., Winter, C., Hesse, C., Chen, M., Sigler, E., Litwin, M., Gray, S., Chess, B., Clark, J., Berner, C., McCandlish, S., Radford, A., Sutskever, I., & Amodei, D. (2020). Language models are few-shot learners. *Advances in Neural Information Processing Systems, 33,* 1877–1901. https://papers.nips.cc/paper_files/paper/2020/file/1457c0d6bfcb4967418bfb8ac142f64a-Paper.pdf

Buolamwini, J., & Gebru, T. (2018). Gender shades: Intersectional accuracy disparities in commercial gender classification. In *Proceedings of the Conference on Fairness, Accountability, and Transparency* (Vol. 81, pp. 77–91). https://proceedings.mlr.press/v81/buolamwini18a.html

Cillo, P., & Rubera, G. (2024). Generative AI in innovation and marketing processes: A roadmap of research opportunities. *Journal of the Academy of Marketing Science.* https://doi.org/10.1007/s11747-024-01044-7

Cortes, C., & Vapnik, V. (1995). Support-vector networks. *Machine Learning, 20*(3), 273–297. DOI: 10.1007/BF00994018

Davenport, T. H., & Harris, J. G. (2007). *Competing on analytics: The new science of winning.* Harvard Business Press. https://www.researchgate.net/publication/275712863_Competing_on_Analytics_The_New_Science_of_Winning

Duhigg, C. (2012). *The power of habit: Why we do what we do in life and business.* Random House. https://ia803102.us.archive.org/35/items/CharlesDuhigg.ThePowerOfHabit_201808/Charles-Duhigg.The-Power-of-Habit.pdf

Dwork, C. (2008). Differential privacy: A survey of results. In *Proceedings of the 5th International Conference on Theory and Applications of Models of Computation* (pp. 1–19). Springer. DOI: 10.1007/978-3-540-79228-4_1

European Parliament. (2016). General Data Protection Regulation (GDPR). *Official Journal of the European Union.* https://eur-lex.europa.eu/legal-content/EN/TXT/?uri=CELEX%3A32016R0679

Evans, J., & Gao, J. (2016). DeepMind's approach to energy optimization. *Nature Energy, 2*(1), 1–3. https://www.scirp.org/reference/referencespapers?referenceid=2912003

Gomez-Uribe, C. A., & Hunt, N. (2015). The Netflix recommender system: Algorithms, business value, and innovation. *ACM Transactions on Management Information Systems*, 6(4), 13. DOI: 10.1145/2843948

IBM and Harris Poll. (2019). *Consumer Attitudes Toward Data Privacy*. IBM. Retrieved from https://newsroom.ibm.com/Survey-Consumer-Attitudes-Towards-Data-Privacy

Influencer Marketing Hub. (2024). *The Ultimate Guide to Amazon Dynamic Pricing Strategy*. https://influencermarketinghub.com/amazon-dynamic-pricing/

Jordan, M. I., & Mitchell, T. M. (2015). Machine Learning: Trends, perspectives, and prospects. *Science*, *349*(6245), 255–260. https://www.cs.cmu.edu/~tom/pubs/Science-ML-2015.pdf

Kamiran, F., & Calders, T. (2011). Data preprocessing techniques for classification without discrimination. *Knowledge and Information Systems*, *33*(1), 1–33. https://www.researchgate.net/publication/228975972_Data_Pre-Processing_Techniques_for_Classification_without_Discrimination

Keyhole. (2023). *Coca-Cola's Social Media Strategy: A Deep Dive Into A Gripping Campaign*. https://keyhole.co/blog/coca-cola-social-media-strategy/

Manyika, J., Chui, M., Brown, B., Bughin, J., Dobbs, R., Roxburgh, C., & Byers, A. H. (2011). Big data: The next frontier for innovation, competition, and productivity.

McAfee, A., Brynjolfsson, E., & Davenport, T. H. (2012). Big data: The management revolution. *Harvard Business Review*, *90*(10), 60–68. https://hbr.org/2012/10/big-data-the-management-revolution

McKinsey & Company. 2021. Retrieved from https://www.mckinsey.com/~/media/mckinsey/business%20functions/mckinsey%20digital/our%20insights/big%20data%20the%20next%20frontier%20for%20innovation/mgi_big_data_exec_summary.pdf

Ocient. (2022, August 9). *The world is moving beyond big data, according to Ocient survey of 500 data and technology leaders*. Press Release. Retrieved from https://www.businesswire.com/news/home/20220809005494/en/The-World-Is-Moving-Beyond-Big-Data-According-to-Ocient-Survey-of-500-Data-and-Technology-Leaders

Renascence. (2024). *How Starbucks Builds Loyalty and Enhances Customer Experience with Rewards Programs*. https://www.renascence.io/journal/how-starbucks-builds-loyalty-and-enhances-customer-experience-cx-with-rewards-programs

Rosenblatt, F. (1958). The perceptron: A probabilistic model for information storage and organization in the brain. *Psychological Review*, *65*(6), 386. https://www.ling.upenn.edu/courses/cogs501/Rosenblatt1958.pdf

Samuel, A. L. (1959). Some studies in machine Learning using the game of checkers. *IBM Journal of Research and Development*, *3*(3), 210–229. https://people.csail.mit.edu/brooks/idocs/Samuel.pdf

Smith, J., & Linden, G. (2017). Two decades of recommender systems at Amazon.com. *IEEE Internet Computing*, *21*(3), 12–19. https://assets.amazon.science/76/9e/7eac89c14a838746e91dde0a5e9f/two-decades-of-recommender-systems-at-amazon.pdf

Unilever. (2022). Annual report and accounts 2022. Unilever Press. Retrieved from https://www.unilever.com/annual-report-2022

Zafar, M. B., Valera, I., Gomez-Rodriguez, M., & Gummadi, K. P. (2017). Fairness constraints: Mechanisms for fair classification. In *Proceedings of the 20th International Conference on Artificial Intelligence and Statistics* (Vol. 54, pp. 962–970). https://proceedings.mlr.press/v54/zafar17a.html

Zhang, B. H., Lemoine, B., & Mitchell, M. (2018). Mitigating Unwanted Biases with Adversarial Learning. *Proceedings of the 2018 AAAI/ACM Conference on AI, Ethics, and Society*. Association for Computing Machinery. https://arxiv.org/abs/1801.07593

CHAPTER 5

AI-Driven Finance Function and Marketing

A Close Partnership for Performance

Barzi Ghizlane, Badrane Nohayla, and Badrane Hasnaa

5.1 INTRODUCTION

In an environment where technological innovation has become a fundamental pillar redefining every sector, artificial intelligence (AI) is emerging as a crucial tool for transformation, influencing companies' internal and external processes. Its adoption is revolutionizing the way organizations collect, analyze, manage, and exploit their data, replacing conventional, traditional approaches with a more predictive analysis based primarily on precise insights.

Indeed, among the many areas impacted, the convergence of the two departments, finance and marketing, opens new avenues where data, automation, and predictive analysis become the pivots of more agile and informed decision-making. Traditionally, these have been two distinct functions, one focused on profitability and cash flow management, the other on customer engagement and loyalty. However, the emergence of new technologies is creating synergies and strong links between them. This innovative era unites these two fields, drawing on the in-depth analysis of complex data to optimize decision-making strategy.

DOI: 10.1201/9781003625452-5

From a financial point of view, the finance function is primarily concerned with managing the profitability of investments and optimizing budgets. Its role is based on the efficient allocation of financial resources to maximize profits and ensure the long-term viability of companies. On the other hand, from a marketing point of view, it is considered a cost center rather than a strategic axis of value creation. In addition, spending on advertising campaigns, brand image development, brand awareness, and sales strategies was often seen as investments whose profitability and performance remained uncertain. However, technological innovation has profoundly altered this dynamic by integrating advanced modeling, forecasting, and automation tools, offering a more rational and efficient approach to marketing investments. Today, thanks to tools such as advanced algorithms and predictive analysis, financial managers have at their disposal advanced systems for optimizing the allocation of marketing resources, considering changes in consumer behavior and expectations, return on investment, expected financial performance, and market trends. The aim of this study is to explore the different aspects of this change, highlighting the new dynamics it creates and the opportunities it presents for financial and marketing activities.

5.2 METHODOLOGY

The methodology of this chapter is mainly based on a systematic literature review that aims to study the contributions of AI in the financial sector and its role in the evolution of marketing strategies (Table 5.1). This approach is based on an in-depth analysis of existing literature through a review of articles published in various recognized academic and professional journals. This methodological approach essentially enables us to identify the following points:

- Current trends in the adoption of innovative tools such as AI in the financial sector, highlighting technological developments and their implications.
- The theoretical frameworks mobilized by various scientific researchers to analyze the integration of AI in the finance and marketing department.
- The main challenges, opportunities, and implications that may affect these two strategic pillars of the organization.

TABLE 5.1 Method for Selecting Scientific Articles

Selection Criteria	Method
Literature search	The selected databases for the literature review include the following: • Scopus • Google Scholar • Elsevier • Cairn • Web of Science, etc.
Keywords used in search	The literature search was carried out using a combination of relevant keywords to ensure a comprehensive exploration of the subject. The keywords selected were the following: • AI in finance and marketing • AI-driven financial decision-making and digital transformation • Finance function and AI • AI on marketing • AI on finance • Marketing analytics and predictive AI models • Digital innovation on marketing • Digital innovation on finance
Inclusion criteria	• Articles published between 2015 and 2025 • Articles addressing the application of innovative tools in the financial field • Articles addressing the application of innovative tools in the marketing field • Articles published in English • Scientific studies exploring the interaction between finance and marketing, highlighting the synergies enabled by AI.
Exclusion criteria	Certain articles have been excluded from the analysis to ensure the relevance of the results presented: • Articles published before 2015, except for essential or theoretical references • Publications lacking a defined methodology or not peer-reviewed • Studies dealing with the application of AI, but not related to finance or marketing • Documents that are too general and do not detail the use of AI.
Classification of Articles	The selected articles are classified according to key concepts: • Applications of AI in finance and marketing • The synergy between "finance and marketing" • The transformation of the financial function activities • AI in relation to financial and marketing performance • The challenges and issues of this digital transformation.

Source: authors.

Indeed, the choice of scientific articles was not random. However, it is based primarily on certain criteria to perfect the scientific information presented.

5.3 RESULTS

The aim of this analysis is to examine how the technological revolution is impacting the evolution of the finance function, while supporting the transformation of marketing activities in a constantly changing environment. In terms of evolution, synergies between company departments become an important step in a context where digitalization imposes data analysis and new management practices.

5.3.1 Toward a More Agile, Automated, Intelligent, and Strategic Finance Function

The transformation of the finance function stems from a context marked by increased market volatility, growing regulatory constraints, and new stakeholder expectations. Faced with these challenges, organizations can no longer be content with traditional, conventional financial management. Instead, they need to adopt a more innovative and agile approach that draws on advanced analytical tools and methods to help them make relevant strategic decisions. The main objective is to move from a reactive finance function to a lever for forecasting, guidance, and strategic steering.

Indeed, the advent of digital technologies has profoundly transformed the financial activity of all organizations. This digital evolution in corporate financial activity covers a wide range of new financial products, systems, and software that improve connectivity and speed of information processing (Gomber, P., Koch, J. A., & Siering, M., 2017). The adoption of advanced technologies offers companies the opportunity to reinvent their operational models and enhance decision-making agility by leveraging predictive analytics and sophisticated algorithms. It is changing financial management by making cash flows more responsive, secure, and automated (Badrane, N., & Bamousse, Z., 2023a). By automating accounting and financial tasks, finance managers can focus on more strategic activities such as risk management, budget, and cost optimization.

Technological evolution has been marked by the integration of AI into business activities. The adoption of this innovative tool has represented a decisive revolution and a major change in the financial field (Eisfeldt, A. L., & Schubert, G., 2024). Thanks to these algorithms, processes are automated with great precision and speed, eliminating the need for human intervention in repetitive, standardized processes (Roozen, F., Steens, H. B. A., & Spoor, L. L., 2019). This automation not only improves operational efficiency but also reduces errors and increases productivity.

AI plays a fundamental role in the transformation of the corporate finance function through the integration of intelligent models to strengthen financial processes, automate accounting and reporting operations, improve cash flow management, and optimize cost structuring through advanced analytics (Cao, L., 2020). What is more, AI brings a new dimension to financial system modeling, by including essential tools for understanding and anticipating market trends. Thanks to these advances, companies can simulate different economic scenarios and measure their impact on their financial performance. This plays a fundamental role in the evolution of the financial sector, providing decision-making support to improve corporate profitability (Badrane, N., & Bamousse, Z., 2023b).

5.3.2 Importance of Artificial Intelligence in Financial Activities

Much more than a process optimization tool, AI profoundly transforms a company's financial activities by improving data analysis, anticipating market developments, and accelerating decision-making. This innovative tool facilitates the automation of complex tasks such as auditing, cost management, and accounting analysis (Desbiolles, J. P., 2019). Thanks to machine learning algorithms and natural language processing technologies, AI solutions make it possible to analyze large quantities of data in a minimum of time.

When it comes to cost management, AI enhances the implementation of target costing by providing fine-grained analyses of profitability, identifying opportunities and margins for optimization, and adjusting pricing strategies in line with market trends and consumer behavior (Fähndrich, J., 2023). This method is relevant in competitive sectors, where cost control and value maximization are essential. In addition, AI improves the management of financial resources by facilitating a more efficient allocation of capital and reducing operational costs (Barzi, G., & Bamousse, Z., 2024).

Moreover, AI improves financial risk management by optimizing fraud detection and vulnerability identification through advanced learning techniques (Farahani, M. S., & Ghasemi, G., 2024). It also simplifies compliance with financial services regulations by automating transaction monitoring and producing accurate, up-to-date reports on risk and performance. In addition, it plays a key role in improving consumer confidence and facilitating digital transactions, thus promoting a more stable and inclusive financial system (Badrane, H., & Bouzahir, B., 2023).

The integration of intelligent systems provides executives with relevant tools in the form of interactive dashboards that integrate real-time data for better analysis of financial trends. In this regard, CFOs must anticipate these developments by developing AI, digital transformation, and data management skills at the heart of their teams to better meet market needs (Roozen, F., Steens, H. B. A., & Spoor, L. L., 2019).

5.3.3 The Evolution of the Marketing Department in an Intelligent Environment

In an environment described as "intelligent," companies need to modernize their marketing strategies to meet the new expectations of consumers, who demand more immersive and personalized experiences. In this respect, marketing is no longer simply a means of competitive differentiation, but a driver of innovation and organizational transformation.

Digital transformation is a major driver of change in marketing activities. The rise of intelligent technologies, notably AI, is profoundly redefining marketing practices. The integration of this tool has contributed to the evolution of the marketing department, enabling advanced data management and optimized interaction between companies and consumers (Haleem, A., Javaid, M., Qadri, M. A., Singh, R. P., & Suman, R., 2022). This ability to process large quantities of data has changed the way companies target and interact with their customers.

This evolution is driving the shift from product-centric to consumer-centric marketing, leveraging big data and advanced behavioral analytics (Mrhari, A., & Dinar, Y., 2018). AI is transforming companies' financial decisions by optimizing marketing investments and streamlining advertising budgets via tools like marketing automation and programmatic buying. What is more, through big data and machine learning, companies now have powerful tools for in-depth analysis and interpretation of consumer behavior (Dimitrieska, S., Stankovska, A., & Efremova, T., 2018). By harnessing a wide range of data from social networks, online transactions, customer interactions, and purchase histories, these technologies identify consumer trends and preferences with great precision. Machine Learning enhances this analysis by automating data processing and perfecting predictions based on self-learning algorithms. This fine-tuned market analysis enables companies to make more informed and enlightened decisions, strengthening their competitiveness and capacity for innovation in a dynamic economic context.

Thanks to predictive analytics and machine learning algorithms, companies can anticipate customer needs, personalize their offers, improve their advertising campaigns, and boost their competitiveness (Kumar, V., Rajan, B., Venkatesan, R., & Lecinski, J., 2019; Ma, L., & Sun, B., 2020). This ability to predict trends and adjust offers according to individual expectations enhances the customer experience, promotes loyalty, and maximizes the effectiveness of marketing campaigns.

AI is also helping to streamline time-consuming tasks such as social network management, customer service via chatbots and market segmentation (Haleem, A., Javaid, M., Qadri, M. A., Singh, R. P., & Suman, R., 2022; Ma, L., & Sun, B., 2020). This transformation is not limited to simply improving operational efficiency but also rethinks the synergy between the brand and its consumer, creating a more personalized, flexible, agile, and engaging form of communication.

5.3.4 The Interaction between the Financial Function and Marketing through AI

AI is revolutionizing organizational practices, impacting both marketing strategies and financial management. In an ecosystem dominated by digital transformation and process optimization, companies need to reinvent the synergy between these two essential functions. Traditionally perceived as separate functions, finance and marketing today tend to articulate more closely, thanks to AI models. This synergy aligns marketing decisions with financial requirements, with the aim of maximizing efficiency and return on investment. Indeed, AI is transforming marketing into a highly automated, data-driven system, with a direct impact on corporate financial management (Chintalapati, S., & Pandey, S. K., 2022). It optimizes budget allocation, enhances the ability to forecast marketing investments and promotes better resource management.

AI optimizes the budget management of marketing campaigns, providing a dynamic and rational allocation of resources. This advanced tool enables real-time analysis of advertising performance across all channels, identifying market dynamics, measuring performance gaps and dynamically adapting budget allocation according to measured performance. From a financial point of view, this gives the finance function a better view of the real impact of marketing spend and enables it to adjust investments according to the most profitable customer segments

(Nalini, M., Radhakrishnan, D. P., Yogi, G., Santhiya, S., & Harivardhini, V., 2021; Ma, L., & Sun, B., 2020).

Leveraging these advances, companies are developing artificial agents capable of making marketing decisions by analyzing customer data, competition, and internal trends (Overgoor, G., Chica, M., Rand, W., & Weishampel, A., 2019; Chintalapati, S., & Pandey, S. K., 2022). This personalization increases customer loyalty, which has a positive impact on profitability and revenue stability.

Technological advances help reduce the costs associated with repetitive tasks. In financial terms, this optimization improves expense management, as savings can be reinvested in key investments (Shaik, M., 2023). Finance departments can thus promote budget allocation by directing investments toward higher value-added actions, such as improving the customer experience, developing new marketing strategies or in-depth analysis of sales performance. What is more, freeing human resources from routine tasks enhances employees' skills, enabling them to concentrate on more complex, strategic tasks.

Technological innovation has the potential to improve the accuracy of financial decisions associated with marketing strategies. By improving the ability to analyze market trends and consumer behavior, it makes financial and marketing decisions more accurate and efficient (Frimousse, S., & Peretti, J. M., 2019). It helps finance and marketing teams to better allocate the advertising budget by identifying the most profitable channels and adjusting investments according to the results achieved (Marinchak, C. M., Forrest, E., & Hoanca, B., 2018; Stone, M., Aravopoulou, E., Ekinci, Y., Evans, G., Hobbs, M., Labib, A., ... & Machtynger, L., 2020). At the same time, it facilitates the selection of distribution channels by assessing their profitability and impact on sales. AI enables intelligent pricing by considering variables such as demand, competition, and consumer expectations, guaranteeing optimal profitability while remaining competitive.

Through AI, the finance function can accurately assess the impact of each marketing action on profitability by analyzing campaign performance and revenue contribution in real time (Magableh, I. K., Mahrouq, M. H., Ta'Amnha, M. A., & Riyadh, H. A., 2024). Recommendation systems based on advanced algorithms facilitate the optimal allocation of resources and strategic orientation toward actions with high profitability, thus promoting sales growth and customer loyalty (Huang, M. H., & Rust, R. T., 2021). In this respect, these algorithms have become a key player in digital transformation and a marketing partner for aligning financial and sales strategies (Barzi, G., & Bamousse, Z. 2024).

5.3.5 Challenges and Issues of Artificial Intelligence in Financial and Marketing Activities

Although AI is profoundly transforming the financial and marketing landscape of companies, revolutionizing their traditional processes, and opening a window onto an innovative, promising, and efficient way forward. Its adoption raises several major challenges and gives rise to complex issues that touch on several dimensions – technological, ethical, and regulatory.

The integration of innovative tools into the financial activity of organizations raises important questions in terms of transparency and regulation. AI models often present a significant barrier to their adoption in financial operations. Errors made by these systems can lead to major financial losses, especially for companies that rely on them to make strategic decisions (Maple, C., Szpruch, L., Epiphaniou, G., Staykova, K., Singh, S., Penwarden, W., … & Avramovic, P., 2023). If AI is not properly adjusted or learns from biased data, it can produce errors in analysis and incorrect results, leading to financial losses and reduced efficiency for businesses.

Indeed, the integration of intelligent systems into a company's financial activity means that finance managers must now take on additional responsibility for managing technological risks and data quality (Wallon, C., 2019). The rapid evolution of AI also represents a challenge for finance managers. These technologies are characterized by constant evolution and can quickly become obsolete (Singh, K., Hasan, M., & Rajendran, R. P., 2023). An AI model that is effective at a given point in time can become less effective if the training data is not regularly updated, or if the economic environment changes. Therefore, it is important for financial managers to keep abreast of technological developments and incorporate adaptive mechanisms to guarantee the effectiveness and relevance of the models they use.

Unlike traditional financial instruments, AI models, specifically deep neural networks, operate like "black boxes," making it difficult to explain or interpret their decisions transparently (Singh, K., Hasan, M., & Rajendran, R. P., 2023). This ambiguity can lead to analysis errors, biased decision-making, or undetectable anomalies. This poses a problem of trust and regulation, as it is difficult for financial managers to verify the validity of algorithmic decisions. It can also lead to systemic risks and damage investor confidence.

In this respect, financial managers need to integrate rigorous monitoring and auditing systems to ensure that decisions made with the help of algorithms are justified and in line with corporate objectives.

What is more, the quality of the data provided by these tools is a central issue for companies. In this respect, financial managers are faced with a variety of challenges, such as incomplete data, data heterogeneity between different departments within the company, and compliance with current regulations. If data is of poor quality, financial forecasts can be inaccurate, leading to inappropriate decisions and exposing the company to compliance or management risks.

The evolution of AI in the financial sector requires significant investment in research, technological infrastructure, and data management, favoring large companies with the resources to acquire these advanced technologies and integrate them effectively into their processes (Singh, K., Hasan, M., & Rajendran, R. P., 2023). These large companies can invest in specialized data science teams, use cutting-edge cloud technologies, and integrate advanced AI tools to refine market analysis, automate financial decisions and better manage risk. However, these dynamic risks reinforcing the dominance of large companies, to the detriment of smaller ones. With reduced budgets and a lack of specialized personnel, the latter find it harder to keep up with the pace imposed by this technological evolution. This situation could also stifle innovation in the financial sector.

In marketing, AI enables companies to target consumers with extreme precision and harness vast amounts of behavioral data to analyze their preferences, emotions, and even psychological weaknesses (German, S., O'Sullivan, S., & Raworth, K., 2019; Kumar, D., & Suthar, N., 2024). With advanced machine learning algorithms, companies can tailor their advertising strategies very precisely, personalizing their messages and offers according to customers' emotions and needs. While this technology improves the customer experience and makes marketing campaigns more effective, it raises important ethical questions, particularly in terms of manipulating purchasing choices. AI exploits cognitive biases and psychological strategies to influence consumers, leading them to make impulse or unnecessary purchases, which in turn encourages over-consumption and dependence on online platforms. If this power is not strictly regulated, it can exacerbate inequalities and limit the freedom of individuals in their purchasing decisions.

Although AI algorithms are black boxes, this can reduce the trust of consumers, who do not understand why they receive specific offers or why their online behavior influences automated decisions (Darling, J., & Truebenbach, A. E., 2018; Kumar, D., & Suthar, N., 2024). This lack of transparency raises concerns about algorithmic biases, which could discriminate against consumers on implicit factors such as gender, ethnicity, or socio-economic status (Buolamwini, J., & Gebru, T., 2018).

AI mechanisms collect and analyze vast amounts of personal data in order to improve performance and adapt marketing strategies. However, this massive use of data entails privacy risks, as many consumers are unaware of how their information is collected, stored, and used. Companies must comply with regulations such as the General Data Protection Regulation (GDPR) in Europe, to prevent sanctions while ensuring consumer trust (Rahman, J., Raihan, A., Tanchangya, T., & Ridwan, M., 2024; Kshetri, N., Dwivedi, Y. K., Davenport, T. H., & Panteli, N., 2024).

5.4 DISCUSSION

Technological evolution is having a significant impact on the internal workings of companies, by redefining the interactions between the finance function and marketing activities. Digital transformation and the emergence of AI are accelerating the process of strategic transformation, making interdepartmental collaboration essential to maximize efficiency.

The automation and integration of intelligent tools into corporate financial management not only optimize costs and anticipate challenges and risks but also ensure more flexible and transparent resource management. This shift represents an evolution toward intelligent, strategic finance, where decisions are based on predictive analysis and advanced algorithms to master business models and adjust financing in line with market dynamics.

In the marketing sector, the exploitation of data via predictive models is transforming customer relations. In-depth behavioral analysis enables us to adjust offers and adapt campaigns in real time to maximize their effectiveness. The personalization of exchanges becomes a key loyalty-building tool, while the automation of marketing actions improves team efficiency by reducing repetitive tasks. The speed of execution offered by digitalization is a major strategic advantage for organizations capable of exploiting these innovations.

One of the main challenges of this transformation is the convergence of finance and marketing departments. These departments, once considered separate functions, are now moving toward a common approach thanks to AI tools. One of the main benefits of this interconnection is the ability of organizations to adjust their strategies in line with changes in the market and economic environment. The integration of intelligent technologies into financial and marketing processes requires companies to adapt their skills and organizational strategy. Managers need to invest in employee training in technological tools, as mastery of technological innovations is becoming a necessity for both financial players and marketing experts, to take full advantage of the tools available.

The emergence of digital technology in finance and marketing represents a decisive turning point in corporate management. Much more than just a trend, this evolution is part of a structural dynamic that is redefining the interactions between internal functions, with the aim of increasing overall efficiency and fostering sustainable growth in an ever-changing economic environment. Companies that succeed in integrating these technologies effectively will gain a significant competitive advantage by controlling costs, making decisions more quickly, and improving customer relations.

Despite its many advantages, AI raises several major challenges that impact every organization's activity. Rapidly evolving technological advances require companies to develop adaptation strategies and provide ongoing training. When it comes to financial data management, companies must meet the challenges of quality, security, and regulatory compliance. The adoption of the latter requires reliable, well-structured databases, as well as careful attention to the protection of sensitive information. In marketing, the massive use of consumer data raises ethical and regulatory challenges. Companies need to use these algorithms carefully and responsibly to avoid abuse and protect users' privacy. Regulations such as the General Data Protection Regulation (GDPR) are needed to frame these practices and strike the right balance between technological progress and consumer protection.

5.5 CONCLUSION

Against a backdrop of increasing technological transformation and ever-changing market expectations, AI is emerging as a cornerstone of every organization's business development. The integration of AI into business services is redefining traditional and conventional practices, while offering advanced automation capabilities, accurate predictive analysis, and increased optimization of resources.

On the one hand, the finance function is taking advantage of AI to consolidate risk management, refine budget forecasts, and boost the profitability of investments. This requires a reconfiguration of skills and professions in terms of integrating intelligent processes that facilitate faster, more accurate decisions, better aligned with the strategic objectives of organizations. In marketing, on the other hand, AI is transforming customer relationship management, enabling advanced personalization and optimization of advertising strategies. The exploitation of massive data, combined with machine learning algorithms, enables companies to anticipate customer needs and adapt their offers to market expectations. This ability to adjust marketing strategies in line with consumer trends and behaviors translates into stronger customer loyalty and improved returns on promotional actions.

While the convergence of finance and marketing through AI promotes more coherent and efficient decision-making, it requires complex organizational adaptation. The development of new synergies between finance and marketing departments requires the evolution of internal processes, rigorous resource management and the progressive integration of technological innovations to improve their efficiency.

AI opens the way to a new era of performance and agility for finance and marketing, but its successful integration is essentially based on a balanced strategic approach. Companies must not only master technological tools but also anticipate their impact on people, governance, and long-term competitiveness.

This work highlights the impact of AI on the transformation of corporate finance and marketing functions, facilitating decision-making and optimizing operational efficiency. It demonstrates how AI enables better resource management by aligning budgetary and commercial decisions through advanced technologies. In addition, it highlights the new skills required of finance managers and proposes a useful theoretical framework for analyzing the digital transformation of organizations and its impact on strategic management.

Although this research provides an in-depth analysis, it relies solely on a theoretical approach without validation by case studies and concrete examples, which limits the identification of real difficulties encountered when adopting AI. To deepen this research, an empirical analysis of companies using these technological advances would offer a more precise view of their impacts and the challenges encountered, particularly by comparing large companies and small medium-sized enterprises. In addition, an analysis of technological innovations and their role in corporate strategies, particularly in sectors such as fintech or e-commerce, would enable us to refine our recommendations and anticipate market trends.

REFERENCES

Badrane, H., & Bouzahir, B. (2023). Le Crowdfunding: Outil crucial pour la démocratisation de l'accès au financement et la promotion de l'inclusion financière au Maroc. *International Journal of Accounting, Finance, Auditing, Management and Economics*, 4(5-1), 298–318.

Badrane, N., & Bamousse, Z. (2023a). L'intelligence artificielle au cœur des métiers du trésorier: Ressort clé de la croissance vers une performance pérenne. *International Journal of Advanced Research in Innovation, Management & Social Sciences*, 6(2), 1–18.

Badrane, N., & Bamousse, Z. (2023b). Le lancement des virements instantanés: Quels apports pour la gestion de la trésorerie des entreprises au Maroc? The introduction of instant transfers: What benefits for corporate cash management in Morocco?. *International Journal of Accounting, Finance, Auditing, Management and Economics*, 4(4–1), 669–683.

Barzi, G., & Bamousse, Z. (2024). L'innovation Dans La Fonction Financière: Une Allure Vers La Performance. *Economics and Management Review*, (2), 1–19.

Buolamwini, J., & Gebru, T. (2018, January). Gender shades: Intersectional accuracy disparities in commercial gender classification. In *Conference on Fairness, Accountability and Transparency* (pp. 77–91). PMLR.

Cao, L. (2020). AI in finance: A review. Available at SSRN 3647625.

Chintalapati, S., & Pandey, S. K. (2022). Artificial intelligence in marketing: A systematic literature review. *International Journal of Market Research, 64*(1), 38–68. https://doi.org/10.1177/14707853211018428

Darling, J., & Truebenbach, A. E. (2018). All transverse motion is peculiar: Connecting the proper motions of galaxies to the matter power spectrum. *The Astrophysical Journal*, 864(1), 37.

Desbiolles, J. P. (2019, February). Finance et Intelligence artificielle (IA): d'une révolution industrielle à une révolution humaine … tout est à repenser … In *Annales des Mines-Réalités Industrielles* (No. 1, pp. 5–8). Cairn/Softwin.

Dimitrieska, S., Stankovska, A., & Efremova, T. (2018). Artificial Intelligence and Marketing. *Entrepreneurship* (6)2, 298–304

Eisfeldt, A. L., & Schubert, G. (2024). AI and Finance (No. w33076). National Bureau of Economic Research.

Fähndrich, J. (2023). A literature review on the impact of digitalisation on management control. *Journal of management control*, 34(1), 9–65.

Farahani, M. S., & Ghasemi, G. (2024). How AI Changes the Game in Finance Business Models. *International Journal of Innovation in Management, Economics and Social Sciences*, 4(1), 35–46.

Frimousse, S., & Peretti, J.-M. (2019). *L'apprenance au service de la performance.* Académie des Sciences de Management de Paris. EMS Éditions. p.264

German, S., O'Sullivan, S., & Raworth, K. (2019). Communicating AI. *The Lancet Digital Health*, 1(2), e51–e52.

Gomber, P., Koch, J. A., & Siering, M. (2017). Digital Finance and FinTech: Current research and future research directions. *Journal of Business Economics*, 87, 537–580.

Haleem, A., Javaid, M., Qadri, M. A., Singh, R. P., & Suman, R. (2022). Artificial intelligence (AI) applications for marketing: A literature-based study. *International Journal of Intelligent Networks*, 3, 119–132.

Huang, M. H., & Rust, R. T. (2021). A strategic framework for artificial intelligence in marketing. *Journal of the Academy of Marketing Science*, 49(1), 30–50. https://doi.org/10.1007/s11747-020-00749-9

Kshetri, N., Dwivedi, Y. K., Davenport, T. H., & Panteli, N. (2024). Generative artificial intelligence in marketing: Applications, opportunities, challenges, and research agenda. *International Journal of Information Management*, 75, 102716.

Kumar, D., & Suthar, N. (2024). Ethical and legal challenges of AI in marketing: An exploration of solutions. *Journal of Information, Communication and Ethics in Society*, 22(1), 124–144.

Kumar, V., Rajan, B., Venkatesan, R., & Lecinski, J. (2019). Understanding the role of artificial intelligence in personalized engagement marketing. *California Management Review*, *61*(4), 135–155.

Ma, L., & Sun, B. (2020). Machine learning and AI in marketing: Connecting computing power to human insights. *International Journal of Research in Marketing*, 37(3), 481–504.

Magableh, I. K., Mahrouq, M. H., Ta'Amnha, M. A., & Riyadh, H. A. (2024). The role of marketing artificial intelligence in enhancing sustainable financial performance of medium-sized enterprises through customer engagement and data-driven decision-making. *Sustainability*, 16(24), 11279.

Maple, C., Szpruch, L., Epiphaniou, G., Staykova, K., Singh, S., Penwarden, W., … & Avramovic, P. (2023). The ai revolution: Opportunities and challenges for the finance sector. arXiv preprint arXiv:2308.16538.

Marinchak, C. M., Forrest, E., & Hoanca, B. (2018). The impact of artificial intelligence and virtual personal assistants on marketing. In M. Khosrow-Pour (Ed.), *Encyclopedia of Information Science and Technology* (4th ed., pp. 1–9). Information Resources Management Association.

Mrhari, A., & Dinar, Y. (2018). Intelligence artificielle: quel avenir pour le marketing? *Public & Nonprofit Management Review*, 3(1).

Nalini, M., Radhakrishnan, D. P., Yogi, G., Santhiya, S., & Harivardhini, V. (2021). Impact of artificial intelligence (AI) on marketing. *The International Journal of Aquatic Science*, 12(2), 3159–3167.

Overgoor, G., Chica, M., Rand, W., & Weishampel, A. (2019). Letting the computers take over: Using AI to solve marketing problems. *California Management Review*, *61*(4), 156–185. https://doi.org/10.1177/0008125619859318

Rahman, J., Raihan, A., Tanchangya, T., & Ridwan, M. (2024). Optimizing the digital marketing landscape: A comprehensive exploration of artificial intelligence (AI) technologies, applications, advantages, and challenges. *Frontiers of Finance*, 2(2), 6549.

Roozen, F., Steens, H. B. A., & Spoor, L. L. (2019). Technology: Transforming the finance function and the competencies management accountants need. *Management Accounting Quarterly*, 2019 (Fall), 1–14.

Shaik, M. (2023). Impact of artificial intelligence on marketing. *East Asian Journal of Multidisciplinary Research*, 2(3), 993–1004.

Singh, K., Hasan, M., & Rajendran, R. P. (2023). Opportunities and challenges of AI/ML in finance. *The Impact of AI Innovation on Financial Sectors in the Era of Industry* 5.0, 238–260.

Stone, M., Aravopoulou, E., Ekinci, Y., Evans, G., Hobbs, M., Labib, A., ... & Machtynger, L. (2020). Artificial intelligence (AI) in strategic marketing decision-making: A research agenda. *The Bottom Line*, 33(2), 183–200.

Wallon, C. (2019). Artificial intelligence applications in corporate finance.

CHAPTER 6

AI-Driven Content Creation and Curation

Mitra Madanchian, Alireza Rafiee, and Hamed Taherdoost

6.1 INTRODUCTION

Artificial intelligence (AI) technology scans enormous amounts of information in an attempt to give marketers profound knowledge of customers' inclinations and conduct, so they can create content that is personalized and engaging. In addition to enhancing the customer experience, this level of personalization increases engagement and conversion rates. AI simplifies repetitive functions like keyword research, content strategy, and performance monitoring, allowing marketers to work more on the creative aspects of their work. The process of content marketing is significantly powered by productivity and reduced cost through these advancements [1–3]. AI-powered tools enhance the quality of content by assessing user interests and offering suggestions for the creation of relevant and interesting content. In addition, they optimize content for search engines by predicting algorithm changes, studying competitor strategies, and identifying trending keywords. This guarantees higher visibility and improved rankings on search engine results pages (SERPs). AI ensures a uniform brand voice in the production of high-volume content, thereby improving audience engagement and reinforcing the brand identity [4–6].

Content creation processes are being revolutionized by generative AI technology, i.e., machine learning and natural language processing (NLP). They are able to create video or audio content, create visuals, and write articles in large quantities. By automating these tasks, marketers can fulfill

DOI: 10.1201/9781003625452-6

the increasing need for new content while also ensuring high-quality standards simultaneously. AI facilitates brainstorming through providing creative ideas that are cultivated from data analysis and hence are able to bridge creative barriers and rationalize the ideation process [7]. AI simplifies the decision-making regarding content marketing with the aid of sophisticated data analysis. Metrics of engagement and ROI are measured through key performance indicators (KPIs) with AI-powered solutions to provide actionable insights. These results allow for more effective planning of resources and refining of strategies. Predictive analytics, for example, can predict audience behavior, hence ensuring the content appeals to the target audience. These data-driven strategies are vital when it comes to refining campaigns and delivering more results [7, 8].

For releasing human producers from doing mundane things in order to concentrate on strategy and creativity, early AI innovations here automated day-to-day jobs like data processing and initial content generation. Mechanizing text creation, drawing conclusions from data, and adapting content to audience inclinations have all been made easier by technologies like machine learning and NLP. This transition is arguably most exemplified by computer-intensive applications like AI-fueled software Canva for graphics design and Jasper.ai for composition that illustrate how the capabilities of the computer enhance human ingenuity [9–11]. Words, images, audiovisual content, and music are but a sampling of various kinds of content whose processing can be facilitated by algorithms.

AI has transformed content curation beyond production by sorting through massive datasets to determine the most relevant topics and trends. To provide personalized content recommendations, AI-based systems can sort through user interests, historical data, and social media trends. By making experiences personalized to each user's interests, this feature increases user engagement [1, 12, 13]. For instance, automated journalism or "robo-journalism" uses algorithms to write financial reports and news stories quickly, but raises issues of human journalists' role in upholding ethical and quality standards [14, 15].

Marketers can create extremely interactive and personalized content based on audience interests with AI-based content strategies. AI technologies can determine personal tastes by studying user behavior, and therefore, one can provide content that strongly appeals to specific audiences. As audiences are likely to interact more with content that reflects their interests, personalization stimulates engagement and conversions [16, 17]. They are likely to be engaged with because they know that what they see, they will like it. AI supports brand recognition and builds confidence through offering consistency of voice brand across extended operations [18]. By automating time-consuming processes like content scheduling, keyword research, and performance monitoring, AI software greatly increases productivity. Marketing teams can concentrate on strategic planning and innovation since this automation saves time and reduces operating expenses. AI offers timely creation of quality content through ideation of content, article writing, and optimizing images at scale [19]. Marketers can discover high-performing content in addition to future tweaks with AI-powered analytics. AI provides actionable insights that inform the creation of authoritative content by monitoring metrics like click-through rates and conversions. Through trending keywords and the optimization of on-page features like meta tags and headlines, AI approaches boost search engine optimization (SEO) and promote greater search engine rankings [20, 21].

In addition to increased visibility, this feature brings organic traffic onto digital platforms. By examining massive collections of data like social media trends, search queries, and customer reviews, AI is particularly good at detecting content themes. It helps marketers create timely ideas that resonate with people by pointing out emerging themes and gaps in the information that already exists. This process ensures originality and relevance in content generation and speeds up the ideation process [22, 23]. By offering concise summaries of applicable studies, technologies such as Semantic Scholar also augment research efforts, saving researchers' and marketers' time [24, 25]. AI helps make content generation scalable by eliminating the need for manual work in the generation process without dropping the consistency or quality. NLP technologies produce human-like content to be applied to blogs, articles, and social network updates at scale. NLP consistency addresses increasing demand for new content while allowing the same marketing message to reach many channels [26].

As AI evolves, its capacity to maintain coherence in high-level campaigns becomes a vital tool for companies that wish to expand their reach. With increased advancement of AI, its contribution to content marketing is even more significant. AI-driven strategies are revolutionizing the way marketers interact with audiences through automated content generation, increased customization, and greater efficiency. Yet the use of AI in content marketing also poses strategic, ethical, and legal issues that need to be resolved. This chapter discusses the various uses of AI in content generation and curation, taking into account both its advantages and disadvantages.

6.2 AI-POWERED CONTENT CREATION

6.2.1 AI-Generated Blogs and Articles

AI-generated content has grown common in a wide range of fields, particularly advertising and journalism. Tools like Anyword utilize NLP in order to more effectively make websites, social media, and ad copy, pointing to the potential uses of AI in content development [27]. The ability of AI to generate long-content that imitates human writing behaviors has established itself as a utility for organizations to use in attempts to increase web presence. Recent developments in deep learning have also greatly improved the performance of NLP models. A well-known option for content writing with automation is the Generative Pre-trained Transformer 3 (GPT-3), which has demonstrated impressive results in producing text that is virtually indistinguishable from a human [28]. The approach enables easy incorporation of AI-produced content across a variety of platforms by producing articles that are rich in context as well as grammatically correct.

6.2.2 Product Descriptions and Marketing Content

In response to the demand for useful product descriptions, there have been advances in AI software that can create effective narratives about products using available product information and consumer feedback to come up with descriptions that appeal to potential customers. Using NLP technology, these websites can personalize content in a bid to attract a particular market, thus enhancing the effectiveness of marketing. Use of AI in marketing content creation goes beyond the generation of text alone but also entails analyzing consumer behavior and preference to deliver personalized marketing experiences that trigger engagement and conversion levels [29]. Such capability is crucial in the contemporary digital world where consumers require content personalized according to their specific needs.

6.2.3 AI in Video, Image, and Audio Content Generation

The incorporation of AI in audiovisual content generation has created new opportunities for innovation and accessibility. Through the integration of NLP with computer vision and audio processing, AI can create complex, multimodal content to augment user experience across a range of platforms. Significant progress has been made in AI-generated video content, especially in the domain of video description generation. Combining visual and audio cues can result in more accurate and interesting video descriptions [30]. Beyond the generation of higher quality information, a multimodal approach like this increases accessibility for people with disabilities, including the blind. The potential of AI for automating content creation processes is demonstrated by developing automated summarization tools for video content, such as in sports broadcasting [31]. The systems can generate brief summaries that capture the substance of the content by analyzing visual cues and audio narrative, addressing the needs of viewers who wish to watch summary highlights.

AI has achieved considerable advancement in image captioning. Deep learning models have been used in more complex methods to produce textual descriptions based on images [32]. The ability of these models to comprehend context, as well as to identify objects in images, allows for the creation of descriptive captions that aid the viewer in making sense of the visual data. In parallel, progress in audio description generation has used computer vision and NLP technology to create content accessible to people with visual disabilities [33]. AI has the potential to cut down the time and effort it takes to make multimedia content accessible by automating the generation of audio descriptions, which will promote inclusiveness.

6.3 AI IN CONTENT CURATION AND PERSONALIZATION

To make a choice on content that will have the greatest influence on consumers, AI algorithms search into a tremendous amount of data such as user interaction, user preferences, and behavior. This feature is best seen on social media sites, online shopping websites, and internet streaming, where recommendation algorithms retain users as well as attract users. AI recommendations, for example, analyze the data of a user and proceed to suggest things accordingly based on machine learning algorithms. Since users are more likely to engage with content that aligns with their interests, these systems not only make users happier but also drive engagement rates higher [9, 34]. The ability of these algorithms to adapt in real time, learning from user interactions to make better recommendations later, speaks to their effectiveness [35]. The major components of AI in social media content curation include data collection, personalization, recommendations, scheduling, and optimization to improve user engagement and content performance (Figure 6.1).

The philosophy of marketing initiatives in contemporary times is personalization, and employing AI has the capabilities of offering experiences which are personalized according to the requirement of customers. Organizations are capable of segmenting their consumers in a better

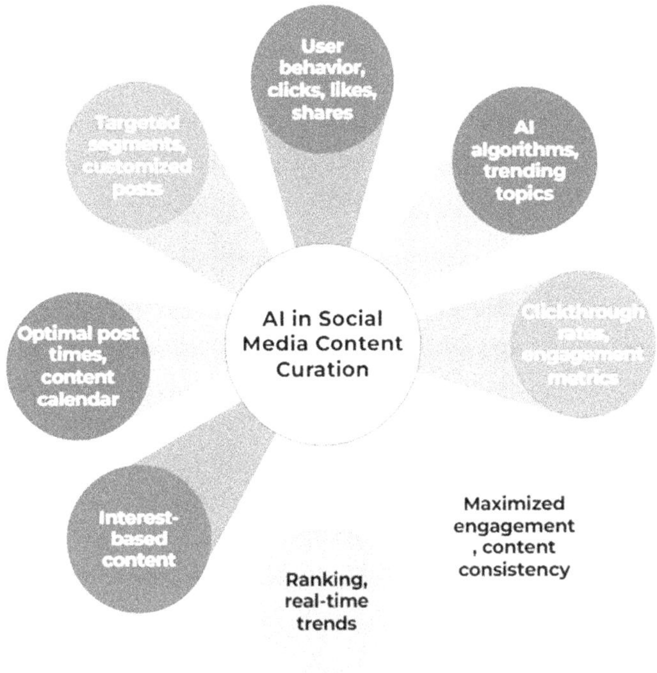

FIGURE 6.1 AI-driven social media content curation process.

manner and providing content that responds to specific needs and desires through implementing AI-driven insights. This tactic is helpful for increasing brand loyalty as well as customer satisfaction. Studies say that AI can analyze customer information and determine likes and trends so that marketers can make targeted offers and communications for each individual [29]. AI software, for instance, can improve email marketing by optimizing subject lines and content based on user behavior to enhance open and conversion rates [36]. In addition, marketers can proactively post relevant content and anticipate requests beforehand because AI can predict buyers' behavior, which improves the overall customer experience [37, 38].

Email marketing has been revolutionized because AI can change dynamic content. Marketers are able to personalize subsequent messages through the use of machine learning algorithms to examine user interaction with past emails, such as segmenting audiences by behavior and interests, send time optimization, and content personalization. Use of AI in email marketing increases the efficiency of the process as well as making it more effective. AI, for example, can calculate when to send emails to certain users to maximize the chances of engagement [39]. AI-driven solutions can mechanize the development of customized email content so that each recipient gets messages that speak to their interests and requirements [40, 41]. In a cluttered digital world where customers are being bombarded with marketing communications, this kind of personalization is essential. Social media platforms are increasingly leveraging AI technologies to improve user engagement and content curation. To curate information based on individual interests and make users happier and retained more, AI algorithms scan users' behavior, likes, and trends [42].

In a time when people are overwhelmed with information, it is especially important. Brands can adjust their content strategy based on audience sentiment and liking through AI-driven social media listening tools [43]. Social media platforms such as TikTok, for instance, use AI to customize users' experiences, allowing users to personalize content curation algorithms to better match their tastes [42]. In addition to increasing interaction, this partnership of user and machine agency creates a more interactive and personalized social media experience. Table 6.1 summarizes recent studies on AI-driven approaches in education and content creation.

6.4 ENHANCING CREATIVITY AND EFFICIENCY WITH AI

6.4.1 AI-Assisted Brainstorming and Idea Generation

The use of AI in ideation processes has transformed the way content creators generate ideas. Traditional ideation methods depend on human creativity alone, which can be restrictive. Yet the potential for high-speed idea generation has been significantly enhanced by the development of generative AI tools such as ChatGPT. Research shows that the combination of AI and human creativity produces more than either approach alone [49]. This collaboration is particularly beneficial to content marketing because it not only improves the quality of the ideas but also promotes a greater diversity of concepts. AI tools can analyze big data to identify trends and generate content ideas that would engage their target audiences. AI, for example, can recommend topics that are consistent with current market trends, audience interests, and seasonal fluctuations, thereby simplifying brainstorming and ensuring that content is pertinent and engaging [50].

TABLE 6.1 Applications and Challenges of AI in Content Creation

Study	Year	Focus	Key Findings	Challenges
Khosravi et al. [44]	2023	Learnersourcing in Education	Framework for collaboration between students, educators, and AI in content generation.	Enhancing existing systems with AI for interactivity.
Speth et al. [45]	2023	ChatGPT for Programming Course Exercises	Highlights effective practices for generating exercises for beginners and intermediate learners.	Balancing AI support with traditional teaching.
Faccia et al. [46]	2023	Generative AI in Higher Education	Discusses personalized content creation and improved assessment strategies through generative AI.	Training educators and developing pedagogical frameworks.
Singh and Ram [47]	2024	Educator Preparation for AI-Driven Learning	Focuses on preparing educators for personalized and adaptive AI systems in education.	Ensuring effective educator training for AI adoption.
Begemann and Hutson [48]	2025	AI in Game Design and Legal Challenges	Examines AI tools in game development and related copyright issues.	Addressing copyright complexities in multimodal content.
Rouabhia	2024	ChatGPT in Educational Material Generation	Emphasizes the potential for efficient and accessible course material generation.	Managing quality and relevance of AI-generated content.

6.4.2 AI-Driven Content Optimization Tools

AI-powered solutions are able to evaluate current content and offer suggestions for enhancements, guaranteeing that it satisfies search engine and user requirements. These tools evaluate elements, including readability, keyword density, and overall engagement potential using machine learning algorithms and NLP [51]. Marketers can swiftly determine which content variations work best by using AI to automate A/B testing procedures. In addition to saving time, this automation yields insights based on data that might guide future content plans [52]. Rapid content testing and iteration guarantees that marketing initiatives are continuously improved and maximized for impact.

6.4.3 Automated A/B Testing for Marketing Content

While addressing digital marketing, automated A/B testing is breakthrough. By using AI, marketers are able to easily test multiple content iterations to learn which one works best for the audience. Displaying two or more variations of content to different segments of audiences and then comparing performance data like click-through rates, engagement, and conversion rates are all part of it [53]. AI can augment this process by rapidly examining the findings and offering useful insights. It can pick up on patterns of user behavior that might go unnoticed by human analysts initially, enabling the ability to make better-informed decisions [54]. This is especially helpful for small and medium-sized businesses (SMEs), who cannot afford to carry out extensive market research. An efficient process that enhances overall marketing effectiveness can be designed by combining AI-powered A/B testing with other marketing automation tools. Companies can prevent themselves from getting overwhelmed with manual testing and focus more on strategic planning and creative development by automating these processes [55].

6.4.4 Role of AI in Improving SEO and Content Discoverability

To make it possible for target consumers to access the information, search engine optimization, or SEO, plays an important role. Through the evaluation of user behaviors and search algorithms, AI highly amplifies SEO practices by personalizing content. In relation to past experiences, AI applications are able to forecast upcoming trends, evaluate competing strategies, and provide corresponding keywords [56]. For example, by making available information on term usage and article structure in a search engine-friendly format, AI can be used to help create SEO-friendly content. In addition, by making available information that is relevant and valuable, this not only increases the likelihood of appearing good in search results but also improves the user experience overall [57]. AI can help create chapter-level metadata for online content, making it easier to find on multiple platforms. AI increases the value of online content by more precisely classifying content, thus making it easier for users as well as scholars to find particular information [58]. Businesses' approaches to content development, optimization, and discoverability are changing because of the adoption of AI in marketing strategies. Marketers can produce more effective and compelling content that speaks to their customers by leveraging AI-driven ideation, content optimization tools, automated A/B testing, and improved SEO practices. The ability of AI technology to fuel marketing innovation will only increase as it continues to develop, and it is thus a vital part of any contemporary marketing strategy.

6.5 AI IN VISUAL AND MULTIMEDIA CONTENT MARKETING

Technological advancements in AI are revolutionizing visual content creation, such as graphics and movies. Deep learning is providing a robust alternative to conventional techniques of video compression, which have been "laboriously hand designed and hand optimized" [59]. From the theory that "Video compression is repeated image interpolation," deep learning codecs already outperform existing codecs like H.261 and MPEG-4 Part 2, and the performance comes close to H.264 [59]. In an era where video watching and content production are on the rise, this improvement in efficiency is imperative. AI is facilitating the creation of totally original visual material as well as compression. In order to create realistic and engaging 360-degree experiences, models such as Latent Diffusion Models for 3D (LDM3D) [60] are able to create both image and depth map data from text prompts. Some of the possible applications are AI-powered video content tools that assist creators in producing and editing videos [61] and even using AI to produce high-fidelity video content in an open-source platform like Open-Sora [62]. AI-powered interactive and immersive content apps enable dynamic user experiences with AR/VR, tailored content, and real-time adaption (Figure 6.2).

Deep learning is also being used to create content, yet it might also be used in advanced recognition. To support more user engagement for browsing large collections of video, early research for the Informedia Digital Video Library showed the way speech recognition might be integrated with information retrieval, image analysis, and NLP. By using speech recognition-created transcripts to search multimedia content [63], the study showed the strength of synergy from the use of several AI

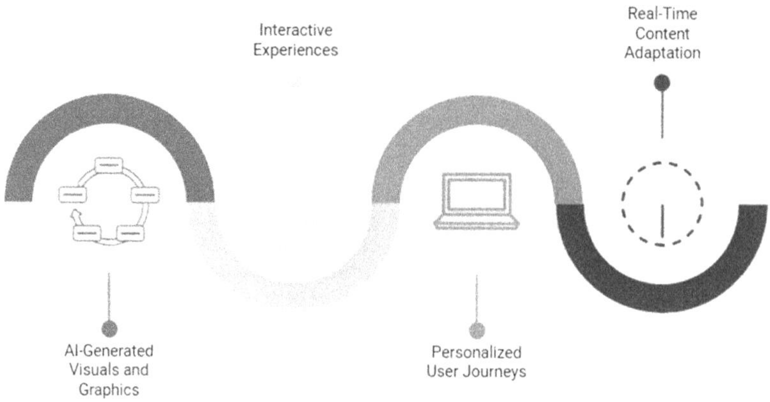

FIGURE 6.2 AI-powered interactive and immersive content applications.

techniques to bypass restrictions of single technologies. More recent studies have centered on utilizing AI for increasing accessibility to media for people with disabilities. With advances in computer vision, speech recognition, and NLP, AI-based accessibility technologies are also being created to empower individuals with disabilities [64]. Because of their potential to be used for harmful purposes, detection of deepfakes and manipulated pictures and videos created using the computer is also becoming important [65, 66]. Although detection of deepfakes is still difficult [65, 66], deep learning models are currently used for their detection [67]. A number of applications, such as speech-to-text translation, content policy compliance, and even celebrity and logo recognition for targeted marketing, are facilitated by AI's capacity to assess media content. Besides creating and identifying content, AI is also enhancing its interactivity and immersiveness. With text inputs, DepthFusion software and the LDM3D model produce interactive 360-degree experiences [60], showing that AI has the potential to revolutionize digital experiences and content creation. AI is also revolutionizing the adult entertainment market [68], creating highly personalized experiences allowing users to interact with artificial agents and customize content. As illustrated by high-accuracy creation of 3D models from a single photo for VR applications, blending AI-generated content and VR technology is creating more interactive experience options [69].

By explaining how the AI came to its conclusions, explainable AI (XAI) is improving user experience in such applications [64]. The landscape of user-generated content (UGC) social media is drastically evolving with the arrival of generative AI. AI technology for creating different forms of media is increasing engagement and speeding up content creation [61]. AI is also drastically revolutionizing the creation of audio content. Significant progress has been achieved in voice production and voice control, and AI-powered voice clones are becoming ever more realistic [70]. Although this skill is multi-purpose, the detection of AI-generated voice is very difficult since research demonstrates that human participants fail to accurately identify AI-generated speech [70]. To help people with autism spectrum disorder, AI-driven emotion detection assistants that can identify emotions from audio and video are also being developed [71]. AI is fueling the mass usage that is driving innovation in content consumption and creation. But despite its advantages, there are also issues of its potential for abuse and ethical considerations, such as the creation of deepfakes and substitution of human labor [65].

6.6 ETHICAL AND LEGAL CONSIDERATIONS IN AI-DRIVEN CONTENT

Legal and ethical concerns have emerged as a growing issue with businesses more and more using AI-driven strategies. In order to unlock the full power of AI for content marketing while upholding credibility and trust, these issues need to be solved. AI algorithms can create incredibly authentic output that strongly resembles human communication, especially when used to create text or multimedia material. Although this ability makes processes more effective, it also poses a great risk if incorrect or misleading information is inadvertently conveyed. AI-generated news stories, synthetic audio clips, and deepfake films can all mislead public opinion and spread misinformation on a large scale. To make sure that AI-generated content honors ethical standards and factuality, marketers must implement strong verification processes.

Intellectual property (IP) and copyright concerns are another complicating factor in the authenticity dilemma. AI-generated content is frequently produced from large databases, some of which contain protected content. It is at times difficult to determine the ownership of AI-generated content, particularly when algorithms combine existing works to create new ones. In addition to rendering copyright claims more difficult, this ambiguity regarding authorship subjects corporations to legal issues. Companies must proactively adopt procedures to properly credit and cite sources so that they can reduce the risk of infringement and promote openness in information creation. Disclosure and transparency are similarly significant issues.

It becomes harder to tell the difference between machine and human-generated content as AI advances. The customer is entitled to know if the content they are viewing was generated by a human or an AI system. Non-disclosure of AI use can be dangerous to customer trust and create authenticity-related ethical issues. Credibility and accountability can be ensured by using transparent labeling techniques and being transparent regarding the use of AI tools in content generation.

AI systems can produce biased or prejudiced outcomes because they are trained on past data, which might be biased.

For example, content recommendation systems have been found to inadvertently amplify certain viewpoints or silence minority views, which would reinforce echo chambers or biases.

There has to be multiple data sets and ongoing algorithmic testing to address these biases. Inclusion and fairness have to be of prime concern in moral AI processes to guarantee content curation is an extensive range of opinions and not unintentionally excluding underrepresented communities. Organizations have to address these risks with a multi-pronged approach with ethical, legal, and technical frameworks to combat them. Some of the key steps include establishing AI governance principles, bias testing, and transparency in labeling content. Integration of AI into content marketing responsibly can also be facilitated through cooperation between marketers, lawyers, and developers of AI.

Additionally, educating customers about the application of AI in content creation will enable them to question the information they receive more intensely. The legal and ethical issues of AI applications in content marketing will become more of a concern as technology develops. Firms can construct a better online world by meeting these challenges ahead of time and striking a middle path between responsibility and innovation. Through the integration of human monitoring within AI processes, legal compliance and maintaining ethical marketing practices are assured.

6.7 AI AND THE FUTURE OF CONTENT MARKETING

Firms wishing to remain competitive in a world where there is so much content have to be aware of the new trends and change accordingly. Among the most noticeable trends is the increase in reliance on AI-based content tools. These more recent, machine learning- and NLP-based technologies can create multimedia content, create prose that resembles human writing, and even design personalized advertising messages. AI-driven video scripts and automated podcast transcripts, for example, are assisting marketers in keeping pace with the demand for varied content formats. AI-driven recommendation engines are also improving the way that marketers connect with their target markets. AI can create content that speaks to some customers based on their behavior, interests, and interaction patterns. This promotes greater engagement and brand loyalty. This trend emphasizes the need for data-driven content strategies that change according to up-to-date insights.

AI is assisting marketers in optimizing their strategy, from augmenting SEO through bot-driven keyword research to dynamically refining content layouts for improved user experience. Furthermore, AI plays a vital role in creating responsive content strategies adjusting to shifting audience expectations by being able to monitor and forecast content performance. AI is definitely making its mark on content marketing in the future, though, not making human marketers obsolete. Rather, it is redefining their work so they can spend more time on strategy and innovation. Human intuition and context sense are still invaluable, especially when telling stories that resonate emotionally with people. Although AI can generate content, human marketers have to bring personality and subtle storytelling. By eliminating routine work, collaborative AI solutions are also allowing marketers.

AI, for instance, is capable of executing straightforward copywriting, performance monitoring, and content serving, leaving marketers to play with creative ideas. Campaigns combining AI and human creativity have the potential to be more innovative, effective, and targeted. As marketers use AI tools as part of their workflows, they are getting more strategic. They are now concentrating on using data insights created by AI to create more compelling and richer marketing stories rather than just producing content. This dance between machine efficiency and human ability is setting a new benchmark for content marketing strategies. The greatest content marketing strategies will be those that beautifully balance human-driven creativity with AI-powered automation. Hybrid content strategies are one of the promising solutions, where humans maintain contextual relevance and quality control while AI handles data analysis and content creation.

This method guarantees brand messaging integrity while optimizing efficiency. Using AI to provide content at scale with personalization will be essential as customers increasingly demand personalized experiences. This entails applying AI algorithms to scan user preferences, forecast content requirements, and make relevant information easily accessible. To maintain customers' trust, marketers must strike a balance between automation and human touch. Multimedia content strategies driven by AI are set to be utilized by brands. AI technologies that can produce movies, interactive infographics, and immersive experiences will be at the forefront because visual and interactive content continues to dominate digital platforms. If marketers are able to successfully integrate these tools into their strategies, they will stand out from the crowded digital space as leaders.

Subsequent content strategies will also have to deal with AI concerns like data privacy, openness, and validity of content in order to preserve ethical standards. Customer trust will be gained through the transparency of AI-generated content and upholding ethical data principles as AI is more deeply integrated into marketing.

6.8 CONCLUSION

AI has amplified the efficiency and reach of content marketing initiatives by using automated content software driven by NLP and AI-driven content ideas. It allows marketers to search-optimize content, automate repetitive tasks, and provide users with personalized experiences. These developments not only make production more efficient but also encourage stronger brand-consumer relationships through personalization of content to the individual's unique preferences. Utilization of AI in content marketing is not without challenges, though. The biggest threat is excessive dependency on automation, and it can result in loss of emotional engagement and sincerity of content. In a bid to ensure that the identity of their brand remains authentic and personal, marketers have to tread the fine line between AI-generated efficiency and human creativity. To avoid loss of consumer trust and compliance with regulatory frameworks, there is a need to address ethical issues, such as data privacy, AI bias, and transparency in content. Marketers have to stay abreast of such issues and find ways that keep responsible use of AI at top priority as tools of AI improve.

Marketers are being presented with a wealth of opportunities in spite of these challenges. AI will be called upon to take content marketing further, from crafting compelling experiences to real-time personalization of content. AI can be leveraged by marketers to create new avenues for engaging with audiences, raising the overall efficiency of their campaigns, and fostering brand loyalty. Human marketers will have more time to concentrate on strategy, innovation, and establishing genuine relationships with their target markets while AI takes care of data-driven tasks and insights. The future of content marketing will be determined by the convergence of human knowledge and technology. To meet the shifting needs of consumers and the digital landscape, AI-driven content curation and creation will keep on evolving.

It is probably the case that in the future there will be more seamless integration of AI tools, and that will allow marketers to roll out more sophisticated and personalized content at mass scale. Nevertheless, the function of human touch will continue to be predominant in guiding AI applications and in enabling content to engage individuals at a deeper level. The future of content marketing will rest on how skillfully its professionals can leverage the best use of strengths of AI while preserving the quintessential features of authenticity, empathy, and imagination.

REFERENCES

1. Haleem, A., et al., Artificial intelligence (AI) applications for marketing: A literature-based study. *International Journal of Intelligent Networks*, 2022. **3**: pp. 119–132.
2. Huang, M.-H. and R.T. Rust, A strategic framework for artificial intelligence in marketing. *Journal of the Academy of Marketing Science*, 2021. **49**: pp. 30–50.
3. Boulos, M., *The Intersection of Artificial Intelligence and Digital Marketing: Balancing Automation with the Human Touch. Assessing the effects on Productivity, Cost, Quality, and their Implications for Employment in the Industry*. Assessing the effects on Productivity, Cost, Quality, and their Implications for Employment in the Industry (January 04, 2024), 2024.
4. Najafov, E., Using ChatGPT for marketing tasks, in *ChatGPT for Marketing: Learn Practical Applications of ChatGPT for Marketing*. 2024, Springer. pp. 49–75.
5. Samal, A., et al., *Measuring Brand Performance With AI Tools*, in *Strategic Brand Management in the Age of AI and Disruption*. 2025, IGI Global Scientific Publishing. pp. 279–302.
6. Rathore, B., Usage of AI-powered marketing to advance SEO strategies for optimal search engine rankings. *Eduzone: International Peer Reviewed/Refereed Multidisciplinary Journal*, 2016. **5**(1): pp. 30–35.
7. Mariani, M.M., R. Perez-Vega, and J. Wirtz, AI in marketing, consumer research and psychology: A systematic literature review and research agenda. *Psychology & Marketing*, 2022. **39**(4): pp. 755–776.
8. Ziakis, C. and M. Vlachopoulou, Artificial intelligence in digital marketing: Insights from a comprehensive review. *Information*, 2023. **14**(12): pp. 664.
9. Subha, M.N., M. Akshay, and M. Mohaneshwar, The influence and integration of artificial intelligence in social media platforms: A comprehensive examination of user engagement, content creation and future implications

for the digital landscape. *Digitalization in the Marketing and International Trade*. **91**: pp. 91–96.
10. Mayer, G., *Inspired by Data: AI's Transformative Role in Corporate Communication*. 2024: EGEA spa.
11. Pratschke, B.M., *Generative AI and Education: Digital Pedagogies, Teaching Innovation and Learning Design*. 2024: Springer.
12. Wijethilak, H.P., S.K. Singh, and S. Dhand, AI for Personalizing Customer Interactions: Improving Engagement and Satisfaction, in *AI, Corporate Social Responsibility, and Marketing in Modern Organizations*. 2025, IGI Global Scientific Publishing. pp. 221–244.
13. Cherukuri, B.R., *AI-Powered Personalization: How Machine Learning is Shaping the Future of User Experience*. 2024.
14. Tousignant, B., *A Hybrid Analysis of the State of Automated Journalism in Canada: Current Impact and Future Implications for Journalists and Newsrooms*. 2020, Concordia University.
15. Sholola, Y.A., et al., Perceived effect of artificial intelligence on ethical journalism among journalists in Kwara State. *International Journal of Research and Innovation in Social Science*, 2024. **8**(2): pp. 2051–2063.
16. Manoharan, A., Enhancing audience engagement through ai-powered social media automation. *World Journal of Advanced Engineering Technology and Sciences*, 2024. **11**(2): pp. 150–157.
17. Prakash, G. and D. Sabharwal, *AI Revolution in Online Media: Transforming Content Creation, Distribution, and Consumption*. Media and Al: Navigating, 2024. 179.
18. Sajan, A. and P. Giri, Understanding artificial intelligence and its major role in branding, in *Strategic Brand Management in the Age of AI and Disruption*. 2025, IGI Global Scientific Publishing. pp. 127–154.
19. Lively, J., J. Hutson, and E. Melick, Integrating AI-generative tools in web design education: Enhancing student aesthetic and creative copy capabilities using image and text-based AI generators. *Journal of Artificial Intelligence and Robotics*, 2023. **1**(1): pp. 23–33.
20. Macumber, R. and V.D. Eswar Pagadala, Google, SEO and helpful content: How artificial intelligence can be helpful for e-commerce websites. *Journal of Digital & Social Media Marketing*, 2024. **12**(3): pp. 206–226.
21. Guelailia, R. and M. Bouziane, Enhancing search engine optimization through artificial intelligence. *Beam Journal of Economic Studies*, 2024. **8**(2): pp. 489–500.
22. Garbuio, M. and N. Lin, Innovative idea generation in problem finding: Abductive reasoning, cognitive impediments, and the promise of artificial intelligence. *Journal of Product Innovation Management*, 2021. **38**(6): pp. 701–725.
23. Baltà-Salvador, R., et al., Empowering engineering students through artificial intelligence (AI): Blended human–AI creative ideation processes with ChatGPT. *Computer Applications in Engineering Education*, 2025. **33**(1): pp. e22817.

24. Bairagi, M. and D. Lihitkar. Revolutionizing research writing and publishing by using AI-powered tools and techniques. in *International Conference on AI-Driven Advancements in Research and Publications: Intellectual Property Rights, Knowledge Management, and Beyond, Ashok Goel Library*, Rishihood University, NCR of Delhi, Sonipat, Haryana, India. 2024.
25. Patel, A. and S. Jain, Present and future of semantic web technologies: a research statement. *International Journal of Computers and Applications*, 2021. **43**(5): pp. 413–422.
26. Hartmann, J. and O. Netzer, Natural language processing in marketing, in *Artificial Intelligence in Marketing*. 2023, Emerald Publishing Limited. pp. 191–215.
27. Srivastava, A.P. and S. Agarwal, *Utilizing AI Tools in Academic Research Writing*. 2024: IGI Global.
28. Aydın, N. and O.A. Erdem. *A research on the new generation artificial intelligence technology generative pretraining transformer 3. in 2022 3rd International Informatics and Software Engineering Conference (IISEC)*. 2022, Türkiye, IEEE.
29. Babatunde, S.O., et al., The role of AI in marketing personalization: A theoretical exploration of consumer engagement strategies. *International Journal of Management & Entrepreneurship Research*, 2024. **6**(3): pp. 936–949.
30. Jin, Q. and J. Liang. *Video description generation using audio and visual cues. in Proceedings of the 2016 ACM on International Conference on Multimedia Retrieval*, New York City, USA, 2016.
31. Gautam, S., et al. *Soccer game summarization using audio commentary, metadata, and captions. in Proceedings of the 1st Workshop on User-centric Narrative Summarization of Long Videos*. Lisbon, Portugal, 2022.
32. He, X. and L. Deng, Deep learning for image-to-text generation: A technical overview. *IEEE Signal Processing Magazine*, 2017. **34**(6): pp. 109–116.
33. Gao, Y., et al., Audio description generation in the Era of LLMs and VLMs: A review of transferable generative AI technologies. arXiv preprint arXiv: 2410.08860, 2024.
34. Bag, S., et al., Journey of customers in this digital era: Understanding the role of artificial intelligence technologies in user engagement and conversion. *Benchmarking: An International Journal*, 2022. **29**(7): pp. 2074–2098.
35. Raji, M.A., et al., E-commerce and consumer behavior: A review of AI-powered personalization and market trends. *GSC Advanced Research and Reviews*, 2024. **18**(3): pp. 066–077.
36. Soni, V., Leveraging artificial intelligence and machine learning for data-driven marketing strategy: A framework for marketing managers. *International Journal of Computer Trends and Technology*, 2024. **72**(8): pp. 208–220.
37. Kumar, V., A.R. Ashraf, and W. Nadeem, AI-powered marketing: What, where, and how? *International Journal of Information Management*, 2024. **77**: p. 102783.
38. Gkikas, D.C. and P.K. Theodoridis, AI in consumer behavior, in *Advances in Artificial Intelligence-based Technologies: Selected Papers in Honour of Professor Nikolaos G. Bourbakis—Vol. 1*. 2021, Springer. pp. 147–176.

39. Priyanga, G., The effects of artificial intelligence on digital marketing. *ShodhKosh: Journal of Visual and Performing Arts*, 2023. **4**(10.29121): pp. 158–167.
40. Vetrivel, S., V. Sabareeshwari, and K. Sowmiya, *Artificial Intelligence in Communications, in Convergence of Antenna Technologies, Electronics, and AI*. 2025, IGI Global. pp. 209–238.
41. Yadav, S. and J. Kaur, Personalized communication: AI-driven solutions for enhanced collaboration, in *Convergence of Antenna Technologies, Electronics, and AI*. 2025, IGI Global. pp. 269–294.
42. Kang, H. and C. Lou, AI agency vs. human agency: Understanding human–AI interactions on TikTok and their implications for user engagement. *Journal of Computer-Mediated Communication*, 2022. **27**(5): p. zmac014.
43. Buhas, V., et al. *AI-Driven Sentiment Analysis in Social Media Content*. in *Digital Economy Concepts and Technologies Workshop 2024*. 2024. Germany.
44. Khosravi, H., et al., Learnersourcing in the age of AI: Student, educator and machine partnerships for content creation. *Computers and Education: Artificial Intelligence*, 2023. **5**: p. 100151.
45. Speth, S., N. Meißner, and S. Becker. *Investigating the use of AI-generated exercises for beginner and intermediate programming courses: a ChatGPT case study. in 2023 IEEE 35th International Conference on Software Engineering Education and Training (CSEE&T)*. 2023, Tokyo, Japan, IEEE.
46. Faccia, A., et al. *Advancements and Challenges of Generative AI in Higher Educational Content Creation A Technical Perspective. in Proceedings of the 2023 8th International Conference on Information Systems Engineering*. 2023, Bangkok, Thailand.
47. Singh, V. and S. Ram, Impact of artificial intelligence on teacher education. *Shodh Sari-An International Multidisciplinary Journal*, 2024. **3**(01): pp. 243–266.
48. Begemann, A. and J. Hutson, Navigating copyright in AI-enhanced game design: Legal challenges in multimodal and dynamic content creation. *Journal of Information Economics*, 2025. **3**(1): pp. 1–14.
49. Schmidt, L., A. Piazza, and C. Wiedenhöft, *"Augmented Brainstorming with AI"–Research Approach for Identifying Design Criteria for Improved Collaborative Idea Generation Between Humans and AI*, in *HHAI 2023: Augmenting Human Intellect*. 2023, IOS Press. pp. 410–412.
50. Whig, P., A.B. Bhatia, and N. Yathiraju, AI-Driven innovations in service marketing transforming customer engagement and experience, in *AI Innovations in Service and Tourism Marketing*. 2024, IGI Global. pp. 17–34.
51. Yadav, A.R., S.S. Yadav, and S. Kamoji. *Artificial intelligence enhanced content management systems: Integration, considerations, and useful examples. in 2023 3rd International Conference on Pervasive Computing and Social Networking (ICPCSN)*. 2023, Salem, Tamil Nadu, India, IEEE.
52. Simion, P.C. and M.A.M. Popescu. *Assessing the Use of Artificial Intelligence in Digital Marketing. Evidence from Romanian Companies. in Proceedings of the International Conference on Business Excellence*. 2023, Romania, Sciendo.

53. Arviani, H., et al., *ChatGPT For Marketing Communications: Friend or Foe?* Kanal: Jurnal Ilmu Komunikasi, 2023. **12**(1): pp. 1–7.
54. Islam, M.A., et al., Artificial intelligence in digital marketing automation: Enhancing personalization, predictive analytics, and ethical integration. *Edelweiss Applied Science and Technology*, 2024. **8**(6): pp. 6498–6516.
55. Kedi, W.E., et al., AI software for personalized marketing automation in SMEs: Enhancing customer experience and sales. *World Journal of Advanced Research and Reviews*, 2024. **23**(1): pp. 1981–1990.
56. Tardaskina, T., Artificial intelligence in marketing: Modern trends and development prospects. *Science, Technologies, Innovation*, 2024. https://doi.org/10.35668/2520-6524-2024-2-06
57. Ijomah, T.I., et al., Innovative digital marketing strategies for SMEs: Driving competitive advantage and sustainable growth. *International Journal of Management & Entrepreneurship Research*, 2024. **6**(7): pp. 2173–2188.
58. Banerjee, B., W.A. Ingram, and E.A. Fox. *Automating chapter-level classification for electronic theses and dissertations. in 2024 IEEE International Conference on Big Data (BigData)*, Washington, D.C., USA, 2024. IEEE.
59. Wu, C.-Y., N. Singhal, and P. Krahenbuhl. *Video compression through image interpolation. in Proceedings of the European conference on computer vision (ECCV)*, Munich, Germany, 2018.
60. Stan, G.B.M., et al., *Ldm3d: Latent diffusion model for 3d.* arXiv preprint arXiv:2305.10853, 2023.
61. Hua, Y., et al. *Generative AI in user-generated content. in Extended Abstracts of the CHI Conference on Human Factors in Computing Systems*, Honolulu, Hawaii, USA, 2024.
62. Zheng, Z., et al., Open-sora: Democratizing efficient video production for all. arXiv preprint arXiv:2412.20404, 2024.
63. Witbrock, M.J. and A.G. Hauptmann, Speech recognition for a digital video library. *Journal of the American Society for Information Science*, 1998. **49**(7): pp. 619–632.
64. Eziamaka, N.V., T.N. Odonkor, and A.A. Akinsulire, AI-Driven accessibility: Transformative software solutions for empowering individuals with disabilities. *International Journal of Applied Research in Social Sciences*, 2024. **6**(8): pp. 1612–1641.
65. Singh, P. and D.B. Dhiman, *Exploding AI-Generated Deepfakes and misinformation: A threat to global concern in the 21st century.* Available at SSRN 4651093, 2023.
66. Khichi, M. and R.K. Yadav. *A threat of deepfakes as a weapon on digital platform and their detection methods. in 2021 12th International Conference on Computing Communication and Networking Technologies (ICCCNT).* 2021. Kharagpur, India, IEEE.
67. Ashani, Z.N., et al., Comparative analysis of deepfake image detection method using vgg16, vgg19 and resnet50. *Journal of Advanced Research in Applied Sciences and Engineering Technology*, 2024. **47**(1): pp. 16–28.

68. Lapointe, V.A., et al., The present and future of adult entertainment: A content analysis of AI-generated pornography websites. *Archives of Sexual Behavior*, 2025: pp. 1–19.
69. Fu, J., S. Fu, and M. Grierson, *Coral Model Generation from Single Images for Virtual Reality Applications*. arXiv preprint arXiv:2409.02376, 2024.
70. Barrington, S., E.A. Cooper, and H. Farid, People are poorly equipped to detect AI-powered voice clones. *Scientific Reports*, 2025. **15**(1): p. 11004.
71. Wang, M. and N. Yang, EmoAsst: emotion recognition assistant via text-guided transfer learning on pre-trained visual and acoustic models. Frontiers in Computer Science, 2024. **6**: p. 1304687.

CHAPTER 7

Optimizing Marketing Campaigns with AI Automation

T. Shirley Devakirubai

7.1 INTRODUCTION

Marketing has undergone a significant change from traditional to modern. Modern marketing functions are more focused on technological advancements. The majority of the marketing activities are data-oriented. The overload of data can be managed efficiently through technology like artificial intelligence (AI). Marketing campaigns are a direct technique to approach customers for product visibility (Davis, J. 2012a). Understanding the customer base is essential for a successful marketing campaign and integration of different marketing networks (Davis, J. 2012b). Customized and personalized marketing campaigns increase profits and sales (Reutterer, T. et al. 2006). Campaigns are influenced by several factors: the launch time, objective, and previous campaigns (Cacciarelli, D & Boresta, M. 2022). Campaigns focus more on customer participation (Ratnakaran S.T. & Edward, 2019). AI, a disruptive technology, is changing the marketing landscape and bringing efficiency to business (Noble, S.M & Mende. M, 2023). AI-enabled marketing campaigns increase profits, enhance high returns, and ignite organizational success (Jose Ramon Saura et al. 2024). Numerous benefits are gained by marketers by including AI in their marketing strategies (V. Kumar et al., 2024). AI-based marketing is more advantageous in determining the customer's need in real time. AI-enabled target marketing enables easy reach of customers suggesting the best channel to reach them (Abid Haleem, et al., 2022). The efficiency

DOI: 10.1201/9781003625452-7

of AI motivates many marketers to adopt AI-enabled marketing campaigns (Jochen Hartmann, et al., 2024). AI-enabled marketing campaigns provide personalization with predictive analytics enabling brand loyalty (Sujata Joshi., et al 2025). AI enables marketers to generate and distribute high volumes of individual marketing campaigns in seconds (Jana T. Winterstein et al., 2025). AI-generated campaigns are used by marketers to entice customers (Kirk & Givi., 2025). Generating AI-enabled personalized campaigns is possible to suit the needs of local and global customers (Suraksha Gupta et al., 2025). Successful campaigns have been personalized to attract territorial customers (Ernawati, E et al., 2021). Efficiency with enhanced user experience is the major benefit derived from AI-enabled marketing campaigns (Elhajjar, S. 2024). Segmenting the consumers for marketing campaigns with AI provides profound insights into consumer needs and wants (Alijoyo et al., 2025). The effectiveness of the marketing campaigns can be analyzed through AI (Campbell et al., 2020). Measuring the performance of AI-enabled marketing campaigns increases their implications (V. Kumar et al., 2024). AI-enabled marketing campaigns facilitate the measurement of return on investment (ROI) (Mer, A. & Virdi, A.S, 2022). Customer engagement through AI-generated content aids in refining the content for targeted campaigns (Oc, Y., et al, 2023). Insights gathered from data analytics are used for improved strategic marketing campaigns with enhanced user involvement (Mohapatra, A.G et al., 2025). Companies adopting AI-enabled strategic marketing attain more growth (Wu, C.-W. & Monfort, A. 2023). Enhanced sales are possible with AI campaigns (Muruganantham, G. & Aswanth, G. 2024). Marketing campaigns aimed to attract customers toward the products and services can be increased with AI. Proper implementation of AI coupled with targeted marketing can help companies reach their goals. Marketing through hybrid channels is possible with AI implementation.

7.2 REVIEW OF LITERATURE

With rapid business changes, companies are competing with each other to grow and sustain. Advancements in technology coupled with globalization have changed the business landscape. New-age technology has significantly impacted the way businesses operate. Consumers are more informed, and attracting and maintaining them are profound tasks of business. AI has emerged as a grip for companies to sustain in the market. AI-enabled marketing campaigns address the needs of the consumers (Ankitha, K. et al. 2025). AI-enabled marketing campaigns are experiencing a growing trend (Florido-Benítez 2024). Customer engagement is the new mantra for businesses to address (Emrich, T. 2024). Content marketing campaigns, a modern marketing strategy, are enhanced through AI (Sarstedt, M. et al, 2024).

Consumer behavior and perception can change considerably with a carefully designed campaign. Creating content, creating mains, reducing costs, and enhancing user experience are the major benefits of AI-enabled campaigns (Van Esch, P. & Black, S, 2021). Operational efficiency is increased by real-time data analytics with AI (Egorenkov, D. 2022). A substantial increase in customer satisfaction is achieved with AI-enabled campaigns. Social media has given many opportunities for the effective promotion of green campaigns (Kim, S., et al 2023). The strategy of approaching customers is different in each social media is different (Lee, J. 2018). Campaigns should focus on customers based on their preferences (Sun, Y. 2021). Campaigns can be designed to create awareness and pass information (Graham, J. & Ferguson, Y.M, 2020). Favorable behavior can be influenced when marketers target the emotional state of individuals (Manohar, S. et al. 2023). Advancements in digital channels provide a better opportunity for more visibility of a product. Targeted emotional campaigns trigger favorable responses from customers (Pirraglia, E. et al, 2023). To understand the evolving dynamics of digitalization, this study integrates insights from scholarly literature on business-to-business AI adoption with the concept of authenticity. Marketing campaigns focusing on a particular group of customers are successful. Despite all the benefits derived from AI-enabled marketing campaigns in customer engagement, operational efficiency, and enhanced customer satisfaction, research on the long-term impact of AI-driven campaigns is limited. This research is an exploration of the future of AI-enabled marketing campaigns.

7.3 RESEARCH QUESTIONS

- How do AI-powered customer profiling and predictive analysis contribute to more targeted and personalized marketing messages, and what is the impact on customer engagement and conversion rates? (Benefits of marketing campaigns)
- How do real-time data analysis and predictive modelling enable more effective campaign scheduling and adjustments, and how does this impact campaign performance? (Real-time and prediction in marketing campaigns)

- How can organizations effectively overcome the challenges of implementing AI-driven automation in their marketing campaigns?
  (Challenges in AI marketing campaigns)

7.4 CUSTOMER PROFILING AND PREDICTIVE ANALYSIS IN TARGETED MARKETING

In today's changing landscape of the dynamic and data-enabled marketplace, understanding and connecting with customers are significant for business success. Traditional marketing focused on general messages and audience is futile with less effectiveness and waste of resources. However, the invention of AI has changed marketing enabling marketers to engage in targeted marketing. Customers are not similar in their views and opinions (Calvo-Porral, C. & Lévy-Mangin, J.-P., 2020). Customer profiling involves segmenting them based on demographics to engage in deeper prediction. Target marketing involves segmenting the customer and reaching out to them continuously (Salazar-Santander, et al., 2025). Marketing based on individual preference empowers businesses to succeed in this competitive world (Mishra, K.K. et al., 2024). Marketing strategies based on individual consumer behavior increase favorable decision-making (Srivastava, G. & Bag, S. 2024). Predictive analytics aids in accurately predicting customer behavior (Naz, H. & Kashif, M., 2025). Previously customer analysis was ineffective as data was analyzed manually, currently, predictive analysis is a breakthrough providing more valuable insights (Shah, M.A. & Kumar, P. 2024). Leveraging customer profiling using AI with a target market enhances marketing success (Braca, A. & Dondio P.,, 2023). Customer retention is a major challenge addressed by AI (Singh, C et al., 2024). Profiling customers based on commitment will give lifetime value (Fullerton, G. 2020). Demographics is not the only market segment; there are other customer segments based on shopping attitude (Belwal, R et al., 2025). Understanding customers' needs enables marketers to segment customers and customize products and services as per their requirements (Koziel., A.M. & Shen, C.W. 2025). Customers are segmented as customers are heterogenous (Haverila, M et al 2020) AI-enabled personalization must lead to customer retention (Gao, Y. & Liu 2023). AR applied to marketing strategy leads to customer engagement and easy decision-making (Cuomo, M.T et al, 2020). Leveraging AI to segment customers and enable customer satisfaction is the need of the hour (Tewari, S.K. 2025). Customer profiling helps in customer retention (Sinha et al., 2025). Fluctuating needs of the customers can be addressed through AI-driven marketing strategies (Tan, S.Z. et al 2023). Precise target with the usage of AI drives businesses to success (Rana, A et al., 2022). Predicting customer behavior is essential for business growth and success (KabirMamdouh & Kök, A. G. 2025). Various paybacks are derived from predicting customer behavior loyalty, satisfaction, and business growth; this also aids in retaining existing customers by understanding their needs (Akhavan & Hassannayebi, E. 2024). Predictive analysis reduces the time and cost of future prediction, precautionary measures can be taken to reduce the future impact of sales (Virkar, G.R. & Shinde, S.S. 2020). Engaging the customers helps in predicting future behavior like value, positive recommendations, understanding purchase intention, and satisfaction (Abbasi et al., 2024). Continuous engagement coupled with emotional attachment provides greater satisfaction (Anwar. et al., 2025). Effectively implementing target marketing increases customer adoption (Tanveer et al., 2025). Modern marketing with AI requires a deeper understanding of customer behavior to engage the target audience. The old technique of broad-brush marketing is ineffective due to technological advancements. AI-enabled customer profiling goes beyond demographic segmentation to gain a better insight into individual preferences, behavior, and needs. Leveraging predictive analysis helps to accurately predict customer behavior for the future needs of the customers. Merging profiling and prediction of better target campaigns can be created to engage customers, improve satisfaction, and enhance loyalty, ultimately leading to business growth.

7.5 REAL-TIME DATA ANALYSIS AND PREDICTIVE MODELLING IN EFFECTIVE CAMPAIGN PERFORMANCE

Real-time data analysis and predictive modelling are the significant enablers of successful marketing campaigns. Data-driven decision-making is important to understand customer behavior, anticipate the needs, and deliver a positive campaign outcome. Real-time data analysis enables marketers to track key metrics, identify lesser-performing elements to make necessary adjustments, making agile decisions in the AI-enabled digital environment, where customer behaviors are rapidly changing. Businesses create real-time campaign models for automatic decision-making instead of relying on managers to decide on campaigns (Ayvaz.,et al., 2021). Real-time data analysis is crucial for user experience and positive purchase decisions by e-shop visitors (Gao, H. 2023). The unpredictable becomes predictable with the implementation of AI (Raneri, S. et al. 2023). Based on the historical data real-time insights can be analyzed (Shahidzadeh, M.H. & Shokouhyar, S 2024). Improved insights coupled with increased performance and growth can be achieved with real-time data (Contreras Pinochet et al., 2021). Forecasting demand using AI is possible for the effective management of logistics in real time (Walter,et al., 2025). Converting data into images to better understand its perceptions is probable (Sabri, R. & Amir, T.S 2024).

Future trends are predicted to gain optimized results (Mer, A et al., 2024). Real-time customer engagement in social media through events increases brand perspectives among customers (Harrison, E.N.B. & Kwon, W.-S 2023). Analyzing shopping preferences in real-time enhances service quality and increases customer satisfaction (Alfian, G et al., 2019). Marketers use programmatic advertisement to align with the organizational goals, by understanding the customer data and behavior (Kerr, G et al., 2023). Customer touch points to enhance customer experience and customer loyalty (Stein, & Ramaseshan, B 2020). Analyzing the observation of a consumer will help in the accurate prediction of consumer behavior (Rumpf et al., 2020). Businesses can use data mining tools to make accurate predictions of target marketing like customer segmentation and customer profiling (Olson, D.L & Chae, B 2012). The effectiveness of the segmentation is entirely based on the size of the organization, customer reach, and usage of distribution channels (Verhoef, P.C. et al, 2003). Compared to the traditional models the social media review is one of the most effective predictive tools for analyzing consumer behavior (Kim, W.G. & Park, S.A. 2017). Business needs to analyze customer data, segmenting them to make them actionable predictions (Hauser, W.J. 2007) Models developed through statistics a proven model for market prediction (Schoen, H et al., 2013) Predicting the outcomes of the campaign poses a challenge to business (Yao, X. & Wang, Y. 2024). Marketers to address these challenges to cope with the competition in the digital age. Real-time analysis and predictive modelling are significant contributors to effective marketing campaigns. Overthrowing the traditional, static approach the advanced technology enables the application of a dynamic, data-centric approach for customer engagement. Leveraging real-time data for immediate action in the campaign increases its effectiveness to maximize its returns. Being proactive and forecasting future trends for optimum utilization of resources is the major advantage derived from predictive modelling. Personalized experiences for better customer satisfaction and loyalty are the outcomes of AI-enabled marketing. By analyzing customer behavior and processing real-time data businesses can personalize their offers and create an engaging customer voyage.

7.6 CHALLENGES IN AI MARKETING CAMPAIGNS

AI-enabled marketing campaigns have many challenges, hindering their effectiveness. Technological, ethical, and operational issues are the major challenges. Businesses must effectively overcome these challenges for successful implementation. The major challenges faced in AI implantation in marketing are wrongly set objectives, no proper learning setup, AI biases, and AI control (De Bruyn,et al., 2020). Many businesses implement AI without having a proper plan. Marketing plans should be specific, measurable, reachable, relevant, and time-oriented, if not it's difficult to track the progress of the AI marketing success. One more pitfall is the business focuses more on technology rather than being strategic, leading to wasteful resources. The business has to have patience to reap the benefits of AI implementation, dramatic results cannot be expected. Leveraging AI tools is essential for marketing success, without proper training marketers may not succeed. The implementation and maintenance cost of AI is very high causing many marketers not to adopt the same. Most of the prediction and guidance of AI is based on historical data, thus biases cannot be avoided leading to unfair judgments and predictions. AI-enabled marketing lacks transparency, it is difficult to understand the algorithm (L. Ma & Sun, B 2020). Potential biases and errors cannot be avoided in AI marketing campaigns. Business needs to address ethical issues when opting for AI-enabled marketing campaigns. The successful implementation of AI-enabled marketing campaign is hindered by many challenges like technological, ethical, and operational. Businesses to address these issues for successful marketing campaigns to set realistic goals emphasizing strategy over technology. Tackling these challenges in a multifaceted approach like data governance, training, transparency, and a commitment to ethical practices. By addressing these issues, the full potential of AI-enabled marketing campaigns can be achieved.

7.7 CONCLUSION

Exploring the role of AI in transforming modern marketing campaigns, by analyzing key marketing areas such as segmentation, personalization, and target campaigning, this study is relevant in demonstrating the power of AI to marketers in reaching extraordinary levels of efficiency, personalization, and success. AI-enabled marketing includes predictive analysis in real time, leading to customer engagement, an increase in positive decision-making and more return on investment. Successful implementation of AI has significant challenges, including robust data infrastructure, skilled marketers, and a clear ethical consideration. Setting realistic goals, focusing on strategic implementation, and addressing bias issues are vital for enhancing the benefits of AI-enabled marketing campaigns. Leveraging the power of AI and overcoming the barriers, businesses can unlock new potentials, build strong relationships, and develop a competitive advantage for business success and growth.

REFERENCES

Abbasi, A. Z., Qummar, H., Bashir, S., Aziz, S., Ting, D. H. (2024). Customer engagement in Saudi food delivery apps through social media marketing: Examining the antecedents and consequences using PLS-SEM and NCA. *Journal of Retailing and Consumer Services*, 81, 104001, ISSN 0969-6989, https://doi.org/10.1016/j.jretconser.2024.104001

Abid Haleem, M. J., Qadri, M. A., Singh, R. P., Suman, R. (2022). Artificial intelligence (AI) applications for marketing: A literature-based study. *International Journal of Intelligent Networks*, 3, 119–132, ISSN 2666-6030, https://doi.org/10.1016/j.ijin.2022.08.005

Akhavan, F., Hassannayebi, E. (2024). A hybrid machine learning with process analytics for predicting customer experience in online insurance services industry. *Decision Analytics Journal*, 11, 100452, ISSN 2772-6622, https://doi.org/10.1016/j.dajour.2024.100452

Alfian, G., Ijaz, M. F., Syafrudin, M., Syaekhoni, M. A., Fitriyani, N. L., Rhee, J. (2019). Customer behavior analysis using real-time data processing: A case study of digital signage-based online stores. *Asia Pacific Journal of Marketing and Logistics*, 31(1), 265–290. https://doi.org/10.1108/APJML-03-2018-0088

Alijoyo, F. A., Aziz, T. S. A., Omer, N., Yusuf, N., Kumar, M. D., Ramesh, A. V. N., Ulmas, Z., El-Ebiary, Y. A. B. (2025). Personalized marketing: Leveraging AI for culturally aware segmentation and targeting. *Alexandria Engineering Journal*, 119, 8–21, ISSN 1110-0168, https://doi.org/10.1016/j.aej.2025.01.074

Ankitha, K., Kanchan, J., Kunder, H., Shetty, S.S., Ganaraj, K., Hegde, M. (2025). Fusing new age technologies with marketing management. In *Artificial Intelligence-Enabled Businesses*, S. Dixit, M. Maurya, V. Jain and G. Subramaniam (Eds.) https://doi.org/10.1002/9781394234028.ch6

Anwar, R. S., Ahmed, R. R., Streimikiene, D., Strielkowski, W., Streimikis, J. (2025). Customer engagement, innovation, and sustainable consumption: Analyzing personalized, innovative, sustainable phygital products. *Journal of Innovation & Knowledge*, 10(1), 100642, ISSN 2444-569X, https://doi.org/10.1016/j.jik.2024.100642

Ayvaz, D., Aydoğan, R., Akçura, M. T., Şensoy, M. (2021). Campaign participation prediction with deep learning. *Electronic Commerce Research and Applications*, 48, 101058, ISSN 1567-4223, https://doi.org/10.1016/j.elerap.2021.101058

Belwal, R., Belwal, S., Morgan, Z., Al Badi, L. H. (2025). Profiling consumers for their shopping motivations in modern retail formats in Oman. *International Journal of Retail & Distribution Management*, 53(1), 74–93. https://doi.org/10.1108/IJRDM-09-2023-0581

Braca, A., Dondio, P. (2023). Persuasive communication systems: A machine learning approach to predict the effect of linguistic styles and persuasion techniques. *Journal of Systems and Information Technology*, 25(2), 160–191. https://doi.org/10.1108/JSIT-07-2022-0166

Cacciarelli, D., Boresta, M. (2022). What drives a donor? A machine learning-based approach for predicting responses of nonprofit direct marketing campaigns. *Journal of Philanthropy and Marketing*, 27(2), e1724. https://doi.org/10.1002/nvsm.1724

Calvo-Porral, C., Lévy-Mangin, J.-P. (2020). An emotion-based segmentation of bank service customers. *International Journal of Bank Marketing*, 38(7), 1441–1463. https://doi.org/10.1108/IJBM-05-2020-0285

Campbell, C., Sands, S., Ferraro, C., Tsao, H.-Y., Mavrommatis, A. (2020). From data to action: How marketers can leverage AI. *Business Horizons*, 63(2), 227–243, ISSN 0007-6813, https://doi.org/10.1016/j.bushor.2019.12.002

Contreras Pinochet, L.H., Amorim, G.D.C.B., Lucas Júnior, D. and Souza, C.A.D. (2021). Consequential factors of big data's analytics capability: How firms use data in the competitive scenario. *Journal of Enterprise Information Management*, 34(5), 1406–1428. https://doi.org/10.1108/JEIM-11-2020-0445

Cuomo, M. T., Tortora, D., Festa, G., Ceruti, F., Metallo, G. (2020). Managing omni-customer brand experience via augmented reality: A qualitative investigation in the Italian fashion retailing system. *Qualitative Market Research*, 23(3), 427–445. https://doi.org/10.1108/QMR-11-2017-0142

Davis, J. (2012a). *Direct Marketing Gross Profit Magic Numbers for Consumer Marketing*, John Wiley & Sons (Asia) Pte. Ltd., 2005: 274–276. https://doi.org/10.1002/9781119199205.ch59

Davis, J. (2012b). *Direct Marketing ROI. Magic Numbers for Consumer Marketing*, John Wiley & Sons (Asia) Pte. Ltd., 2005: 278–280. In Measuring Marketing, https://doi.org/10.1002/9781119199205.ch61

De Bruyn, A., Viswanathan, V., Beh, Y., Brock, J., Von Wangenheim, F. (2020). Artificial intelligence and marketing: Pitfalls and opportunities. *Journal of Interactive Marketing*, 51, 91–105. https://doi.org/10.1016/j.intmar.2020.04.007

Egorenkov, D. (2022). AI-powered marketing automation: Revolutionizing campaign management. *International Journal for Multidisciplinary Research*. https://doi.org/10.36948/ijfmr.2022.v04i02.23358

Elhajjar, S. (2024). Unveiling the marketer's lens: exploring experiences and perspectives on AI integration in marketing strategies. *Asia Pacific Journal of Marketing and Logistics*, Vol. ahead-of-print No. ahead-of-print. https://doi.org/10.1108/APJML-04-2024-0485

Emrich, T. (2024). Marketing in an Augmented World. In *The Next Dimension*, T. Emrich (Ed.). https://doi.org/10.1002/9781394310487.ch4

Ernawati, E., Baharin, S. S. K., Kasmin, F. (2021, April). A review of data mining methods in RFM-based customer segmentation. *Journal of Physics: Conference Series*, 1869(1), 012085. IOP Publishing.

Florido-Benítez, L. (2024). Digital Channels Improve Promotion and Communication Campaigns. *Airport Marketing Strategies*, Emerald Publishing Limited, Leeds, pp. 109–154. https://doi.org/10.1108/978-1-83608-082-420241007

Fullerton, G. (2020). "Using latent commitment profile analysis to segment bank customers." *International Journal of Bank Marketing*, 38(3), 627–641. https://doi.org/10.1108/IJBM-04-2019-0135

Gao, H., Liu, H., Lin, W., Chen, C. (2023). Graph-theoretic approach to detecting real-time intents within purchase conversion funnel using clickstream data. *Kybernetes*, 52(11), 5139–5163. https://doi.org/10.1108/K-06-2021-0473

Gao, Y., Liu, H. (2023). Artificial intelligence-enabled personalization in interactive marketing: A customer journey perspective. *Journal of Research in Interactive Marketing*, 17(5), 663–680. https://doi.org/10.1108/JRIM-01-2022-0023

Graham, J., Ferguson, Y. M. (2020). The case of the "This Is Not A Game" campaign in Zambia: An analysis of the messaging strategies used to deter illegal bushmeat consumption. *Psychology & Marketing*, 37, 1696–1702. https://doi.org/10.1002/mar.21417

Gupta, S., Wang, Y. C., Patel, P., Czinkota, M. (2025). Navigating the future of AI in marketing: AI integration across borders, ethical considerations, and policy implications. *International Journal of Information Management*, 82, 102871, ISSN 0268-4012, https://doi.org/10.1016/j.ijinfomgt.2025.102871

Harrison, E. N. B., Kwon, W.-S. (2023). Brands talking on events? Brand personification in real-time marketing tweets to drive consumer engagement. *Journal of Product & Brand Management*, 32(8), 1319–1337. https://doi.org/10.1108/JPBM-10-2022-4180

Hartmann, J., Exner, Y., Domdey, S. (2024). The power of generative marketing: Can generative AI create superhuman visual marketing content? *International Journal of Research in Marketing*. ISSN 0167-8116, https://doi.org/10.1016/j.ijresmar.2024.09.002

Hauser, W. J. (2007). Marketing analytics: The evolution of marketing research in the twenty-first century. *Direct Marketing: An International Journal*, 1(1), 38–54. https://doi.org/10.1108/17505930710734125

Haverila, M., McLaughlin, C., Haverila, K. C., Arora, M. (2020). Beyond lurking and posting: Segmenting the members of a brand community on the basis of engagement, attitudes and identification. *Journal of Product & Brand Management*, 30(3), 449–466. https://doi.org/10.1108/JPBM-08-2019-2543

Joshi, S., Bhattacharya, S., Pankaj Pathak, N.A. Natraj, J. S., Goswami, S. (2025). Harnessing the potential of generative AI in digital marketing using the Behavioral Reasoning Theory approach. *International Journal of Information Management Data Insights*, 5(1), 100317, ISSN 2667-0968, https://doi.org/10.1016/j.jjimei.2024.100317

KabirMamdouh, A., Kök, A. G. (2025). A personalized content-based method to predict customers' preferences in an online apparel retailer. *International Journal of Production Economics*, 280, 109487, ISSN 0925-5273, https://doi.org/10.1016/j.ijpe.2024.109487

Kerr, G., Valos, M., Luxton, S., Allen, R. (2023). Understanding the link between an IMC technology capability and organisational integration and performance. *European Journal of Marketing*, 57(8), 2048–2075. https://doi.org/10.1108/EJM-05-2022-0373

Kim, S., Childs, M. L., Baek, T. H. (2023). Awe and guilt: Desirability and feasibility appeals in social media green campaigns. *Journal of Consumer Behaviour*, 22(2), 314–328. https://doi.org/10.1002/cb.2127

Kim, W. G., Park, S.A. (2017). Social media review rating versus traditional customer satisfaction: Which one has more incremental predictive power in explaining hotel performance?. *International Journal of Contemporary Hospitality Management*, 29(2), 784–802. https://doi.org/10.1108/IJCHM-11-2015-0627

Kirk, C. P., Givi, J. (2025). The AI-authorship effect: Understanding authenticity, moral disgust, and consumer responses to AI-generated marketing communications. *Journal of Business Research*, 186, 114984, ISSN 0148-2963, https://doi.org/10.1016/j.jbusres.2024.114984

Koziel, A. M., Shen, C.-W. (2025). Psychographic and demographic segmentation and customer profiling in mobile fintech services. *Kybernetes*, 54(2), 1262–1288. https://doi.org/10.1108/K-07-2023-1251

Kumar, V., Ashraf, A. R., Nadeem, W (2024). AI-powered marketing: What, where, and how?, *International Journal of Information Management*, 77, 102783, ISSN 0268-4012, https://doi.org/10.1016/j.ijinfomgt.2024.102783

Lee, J. (2018). A guide to building successful social media campaigns. In *Business Hack*, J. Lee (Ed.). https://doi.org/10.1002/9781119542322.ch8

Ma, L., Sun, B. (2020). Machine learning and AI in marketing: Connecting computing power to human insights. *International Journal of Research in Marketing*. https://doi.org/10.1016/j.ijresmar.2020.04.005

Manohar, S., Kumar, R., Saha, R., Mittal, A. (2023). Examining the effect of emotional branding in building brand equity of social marketing campaigns: a case on Swachh Bharat, India. *Society and Business Review*, 18(2), 197–218. https://doi.org/10.1108/SBR-09-2021-0159

Mer, A., Singhal, K., Virdi, A. S. (2024). A review of the role of artificial intelligence in banking and stock market trading. In *Finance Analytics in Business* (*Emerald Studies in Finance, Insurance, and Risk Management*), Taneja, S., Kumar, P., Sood, K., Özen, E. and Grima, S. (Eds.) Emerald Publishing Limited, Leeds, pp. 175–198. https://doi.org/10.1108/978-1-83753-572-920241009

Mer, A., Virdi, A. S. (2022). Artificial intelligence disruption on the brink of revolutionizing HR and marketing functions. In *Impact of Artificial Intelligence on Organizational Transformation* S. Balamurugan, S. Pathak, A. Jain, S. Gupta,S.SharmaandS.Duggal(Eds).https://doi.org/10.1002/9781119710301.ch1

Mishra, K. K., Pant, P., Singh, H., Mishra, S. K. (2024). The Philosopher's stone: Applications of data alchemy—customer personalization, profiling, and retention. In *Data Alchemy in the Insurance Industry*, S. Taneja, P. K. Kumar,

M. Reepu, and E. Özen (Eds.), Emerald Publishing Limited, Leeds, pp. 77–95. https://doi.org/10.1108/978-1-83608-582-920241015

Mohapatra, A. G., Mohanty, A., Mohanty, S. K., Mahalik, N. P., Nayak, S. (2025). Personalization and customer experience in the era of data-driven marketing. In *Artificial Intelligence-Enabled Businesses*, S. Dixit, M. Maurya, V. Jain and G. Subramaniam (Eds.). https://doi.org/10.1002/9781394234028.ch26

Muruganantham, G., Aswanth, R. S. (2024). Role of artificial intelligence in marketing. In *Computational Intelligence*, T.A. Kumar, E.G. Julie, V.R. Burugadda, A. Kumar and P. Kumar (Eds.) https://doi.org/10.1002/9781394214259.ch16

Naz, H., Kashif, M. (2025). Artificial intelligence and predictive marketing: An ethical framework from managers' perspective. *Spanish Journal of Marketing - ESIC*, 29(1), 22–45. https://doi.org/10.1108/SJME-06-2023-0154

Noble, S. M., Mende, M. (2023). The future of artificial intelligence and robotics in the retail and service sector: Sketching the field of consumer-robot-experiences. *The Journal of the Academy of Marketing Science* 51, 747–756. https://doi.org/10.1007/s11747-023-00948-0

Oc, Y., Plangger, K., Sands, S., Campbell, C. L., Pitt, L. (2023). Luxury is what you say: Analyzing electronic word-of-mouth marketing of luxury products using artificial intelligence and machine learning. *Psychology & Marketing*, 40, 1704–1719. https://doi.org/10.1002/mar.21831

Olson, D. L., Chae, B.(Kevin) (2012). Direct marketing decision support through predictive customer response modeling. *Decision Support Systems*, 54(1), 443–451, ISSN 0167-9236, https://doi.org/10.1016/j.dss.2012.06.005

Pirraglia, E., Giuliani, F., De Cicco, R., Di Berardino, C., Palumbo, R. (2023). The role of emotions in B2B product advertising on social media: A family business case study. *Journal of Family Business Management*, 13(1), 146–165. https://doi.org/10.1108/JFBM-12-2021-0157

Rana, A., Bansal, R., Gupta, M. (2022). Big data: A disruptive innovation in the insurance sector. In *Big Data Analytics in the Insurance Market* (*Emerald Studies in Finance, Insurance, and Risk Management*), K. Sood, B. Balusamy, S. Grima and P. Marano (Eds.), Emerald Publishing Limited, Leeds, pp. 165–183. https://doi.org/10.1108/978-1-80262-637-720221009

Raneri, S., Lecron, F., Hermans, J., Fouss, F. (2023). Predictions through Lean startup? Harnessing AI-based predictions under uncertainty. *International Journal of Entrepreneurial Behavior & Research*, 29(4), 886–912. https://doi.org/10.1108/IJEBR-07-2021-0566

Ratnakaran, S. T., Edward, M. (2019). Evaluating cause-marketing campaigns in the Indian corporate landscape: The role of consumer skepticism and consumer attributions of firm's motive. *International Journal of Nonprofit and Voluntary Sector Marketing*, 24, e1638. https://doi.org/10.1002/nvsm.1638

Reutterer, T., Mild, A., Natter, M., Taudes, A. (2006). A dynamic segmentation approach for targeting and customizing direct marketing campaigns. *The Journal of Interactive Marketing*, 20, 43–57. https://doi.org/10.1002/dir.20066

Rumpf, C., Boronczyk, F., Breuer, C. (2020). Predicting consumer gaze hits: A simulation model of visual attention to dynamic marketing stimuli. *Journal of Business Research*, 111, 208–217, ISSN 0148-2963, https://doi.org/10.1016/j.jbusres.2019.03.034

Sabri, R., Amir, T. S. (2024). Data management and analytics in finance. In *Strategic Financial Management*, M. Ali, L. Choi-Meng, C.-H. Puah, S.A. Raza and P. Sivanandan (Eds.), Emerald Publishing Limited, Leeds, pp. 93–118. https://doi.org/10.1108/978-1-83608-106-720241007

Salazar-Santander, C., Mac Cawley, A. F., Martinez-Troncoso, C. (2025). An optimal effectiveness-driven target segment selection modelling approach for marketing campaign management. *Computers & Industrial Engineering*, 2025, 110945, ISSN 0360-8352, https://doi.org/10.1016/j.cie.2025.110945

Sarstedt, M., Adler, S. J., Rau, L., Schmitt, B. (2024). Using large language models to generate silicon samples in consumer and marketing research: Challenges, opportunities, and guidelines. *Psychology & Marketing*, 41, 1254–1270. https://doi.org/10.1002/mar.21982

Saura, J. R., Škare, V., Dosen, D. O. (2024). Is AI-based digital marketing ethical? Assessing a new data privacy paradox. *Journal of Innovation & Knowledge*, 9(4), 100597, ISSN 2444-569X, https://doi.org/10.1016/j.jik.2024.100597

Schoen, H., Gayo-Avello, D., Takis Metaxas, P., Mustafaraj, E., Strohmaier, M., Gloor, P. (2013). The power of prediction with social media. *Internet Research*, 23(5), 528–543. https://doi.org/10.1108/IntR-06-2013-0115

Shah, M. A., Kumar, P. (2024). Leveraging machine learning techniques to project customer behaviour through predictive analysis and ethical marketing. In *Market Grooming*, S.S. Dadwal, H. Jahankhani and K. Revett (Eds.), Emerald Publishing Limited, Leeds, pp. 121–138. https://doi.org/10.1108/978-1-83549-001-320241006

Shahidzadeh, M. H., Shokouhyar, S. (2024). Unveiling just-in-time decision support system using social media analytics: A case study on reverse logistics resource recycling. *Industrial Management & Data Systems*, 124(6), 2251–2283. https://doi.org/10.1108/IMDS-12-2023-0921

Singh, C., Dash, M. K., Sahu, R., Kumar, A. (2024). Artificial intelligence in customer retention: A bibliometric analysis and future research framework. *Kybernetes*, 53(11), 4863–4888. https://doi.org/10.1108/K-02-2023-0245

Sinha, S., Malik, S., Mahajan, V., ter Hofstede, F. (2025). Retain, reactivate or acquire: Can nonprofits reliably use community profiles as an alternative to past donation data? *Journal of Business Research*, 186, 114997, ISSN 0148-2963, https://doi.org/10.1016/j.jbusres.2024.114997

Srivastava, G., Bag, S. (2024). Modern-day marketing concepts based on face recognition and neuro-marketing: A review and future research directions. *Benchmarking: An International Journal*, 31(2), 410–438. https://doi.org/10.1108/BIJ-09-2022-0588

Stein, A., Ramaseshan, B. (2020). The customer experience – loyalty link: Moderating role of motivation orientation. *Journal of Service Management*, 31(1), 51–78. https://doi.org/10.1108/JOSM-04-2019-0113

Sun, Y., Luo, B., Wang, S., Fang, W. (2021). What you see is meaningful: Does green advertising change the intentions of consumers to purchase eco-labeled products? *Business Strategy and the Environment (BSE)*, 30, 694–704. https://doi.org/10.1002/bse.2648

Tan, S. Z., Chan, K., Tan, P. L. (2023). Segmenting the Malaysian female young adolescent market based on gender roles and identities. *Young Consumers*, 24(6), 704–720. https://doi.org/10.1108/YC-01-2023-1675

Tanveer, U., Sahara, S. N. A., Kremantzis, M., Ishaq, S. (2025). Integrating circular economy principles into a modified theory of Planned Behaviour: Exploring customer intentions and experiences with collaborative consumption on Airbnb. *Socio-Economic Planning Sciences*, 98, 102136, ISSN 0038-0121, https://doi.org/10.1016/j.seps.2024.102136

Tewari, S. K. (2025). Data-driven marketing in emerging markets: Navigating challenges for sustainable development. In *Digital Transformation for Business Sustainability and Growth in Emerging Markets*, P. Kumar, S. Dadwal, R. Verma and S. Kumar (Eds.), Emerald Publishing Limited, Leeds, pp. 171–196. https://doi.org/10.1108/978-1-83549-109-620251007

Van Esch, P., Black, S. (2021). Artificial Intelligence (AI): Revolutionizing digital marketing. *Australasian Marketing Journal*, 29, 199–203. https://doi.org/10.1177/18393349211037684

Verhoef, P. C., Spring, P. N., Hoekstra, J. C., Leeflang, P. S. H. (2003). The commercial use of segmentation and predictive modeling techniques for database marketing in the Netherlands. *Decision Support Systems*, 34(4), 471–481, ISSN 0167-9236, https://doi.org/10.1016/S0167-9236(02)00069-6

Virkar, G. R., Shinde, S. S. (2020). Predictive analysis: Comprehensive study of popular open-source tools. In *Data Science and Analytics*, S. Kumari, K.K. Tripathy and V. Kumbhar (Eds.), Emerald Publishing Limited, Leeds, pp. 41–70. https://doi.org/10.1108/978-1-80043-876-720211004

Walter, A., Ahsan, K., Rahman, S. (2025). Application of artificial intelligence in demand planning for supply chains: A systematic literature review. *The International Journal of Logistics Management*, Vol. ahead-of-print No. ahead-of-print. https://doi.org/10.1108/IJLM-02-2024-0120

Winterstein, J. T., Abels, J., Kuehn, A., Carl, N., Wies, C., Brinker, T. J. (2025). AI-generated cancer prevention influencers can target risk groups on social media at low cost. *European Journal of Cancer*, 217, 115251, ISSN 0959-8049, https://doi.org/10.1016/j.ejca.2025.115251

Wu, C.-W., Monfort, A. (2023). Role of artificial intelligence in marketing strategies and performance. *Psychology & Marketing*, 40, 484–496. https://doi.org/10.1002/mar.21737

Yao, X., Wang, Y. (2024). Using neural data to forecast aggregate consumer behavior in neuromarketing: Theory, metrics, progress, and outlook. *Journal of Consumer Behaviour*, 23(4), 2142–2159. https://doi.org/10.1002/cb.2324

CHAPTER 8

Enhancing Customer Loyalty with AI Solutions

Mitra Madanchian and Alireza Rafiee

8.1 INTRODUCTION

Customer loyalty is widely recognized as a critical element of corporate success due to its direct impact on profitability and sustainability. Loyal consumers contribute to the development of long-term revenue streams and the promotion of favorable word-of-mouth advertising by consistently purchasing products or services and referring brands to others. Loyalty is a critical determinant of long-term success, as it is significantly less costly to retain existing clients than to attract new ones [1]. In congested marketplaces, loyalty is essential for maintaining a competitive advantage, as it reduces customer attrition rates [2].

There is a robust correlation between corporate performance and customer loyalty. Loyal consumers are less susceptible to price fluctuations and are more likely to remain loyal to a brand, even when competitors offer comparable products [1]. This resilience guarantees enhanced brand equity and stable market positioning. Brand loyalty is the likelihood that consumers will not switch to another brand, particularly in the event of price or feature changes. Consumers who are satisfied are more inclined to establish strong emotional connections with brands and make additional purchases [2]. Satisfaction levels are significantly increased by personalized benefits and tailored offers, which in turn increase loyalty. For example, loyalty program rewards that are customized to individual preferences result in a higher level of perceived value and affective engagement [3].

DOI: 10.1201/9781003625452-8

Customer satisfaction is enhanced by loyalty rewards, in addition to relevance and service quality [4]. These systems employ discounts, special offers, tailored suggestions, and points accumulation to promote recurring business [2].

Behavioral and attitudinal dimensions are frequently prioritized in conventional consumer loyalty strategies. Attitudinal loyalty is defined by emotional attachment and commitment to a brand, while behavioral loyalty is defined by repeated purchases. It is demonstrated the progression from cognitive loyalty (based on information) to affective loyalty (emotional connection), conative loyalty (intention to repurchase), and ultimately action loyalty (habitual repurchase). These models emphasize the significance of satisfaction as a precursor to loyalty; however, they frequently concentrate on linear relationships between satisfaction and loyalty, neglecting the intricacies introduced by contemporary technological advancements [5, 6]. Loyalty was classified into three categories: behavioral, intentional, and emotional. They underscored the importance of emotional resonance in the development of more profound consumer relationships. Traditional strategies frequently prioritized product quality, price, and service attributes as loyalty drivers, with minimal emphasis on dynamic customer engagement or personalization [6, 7].

Digital tools and platforms are integrated into contemporary methodologies to increase consumer engagement and cultivate loyalty. Social networks have become essential platforms for fostering consumer loyalty and establishing connections. Companies are now able to create interactive experiences that are in accordance with the preferences of their consumers by utilizing platforms such as Facebook and Instagram. This enables real-time communication and personalized marketing strategies [5]. Social networks have been recognized as spaces for connection, which can function as supplementary channels for cultivating customer-brand relationships [5].

Loyalty programs have undergone substantial transformations. Modern programs emphasize the establishment of emotional connections by means of exclusive offers, personalized experiences, and community development [8]. Meta-analytic studies indicate that contemporary loyalty strategies are influenced by the interconnectedness of perceived service quality, satisfaction, and value. These factors either directly or indirectly contribute to loyalty through mediated models, such as the "Dual Partial Mediation Model," which underscores the interaction between quality, satisfaction, and value [7]. In contrast to conventional strategies, which emphasize product-centric factors such as price and quality, contemporary approaches emphasize customer-centric strategies that utilize technology to enhance engagement and personalization. Traditional models frequently regard loyalty as a static consequence of satisfaction; however, contemporary frameworks perceive it as a dynamic process that is influenced by experiential factors, including brand identification and delight [9]. The transition from conventional loyalty programs to artificial intelligence (AI)-driven personalization strategies is illustrated in Figure 8.1.

The digital-first environment presents distinctive obstacles to sustaining customer loyalty, primarily as a result of the abundance of options and the reduced cost of transitioning for consumers. Organizations may encounter challenges in consistently providing customers with seamless, personalized, and omnichannel experiences. Trust is also a critical factor, as digital interactions frequently lack the personal contact of face-to-face engagements. Research has demonstrated that trust is a mediator of consumer engagement and loyalty; however, it can be compromised by perceived risks or inconsistencies in digital platforms [10]. The global nature of digital enterprises complicates efforts to establish and maintain loyalty due to cultural differences [11, 12].

By facilitating hyper-personalization, predictive analytics, and automation, AI has emerged as a transformative instrument for addressing these challenges. AI-powered systems analyze extensive behavioral data to anticipate consumer preferences and requirements, thereby enabling businesses to provide customized experiences that improve loyalty and satisfaction [13]. For instance, loyalty programs that are AI-driven employ machine learning algorithms to personalize rewards and communications in real time, thereby nurturing stronger relationships with customers [14, 15].

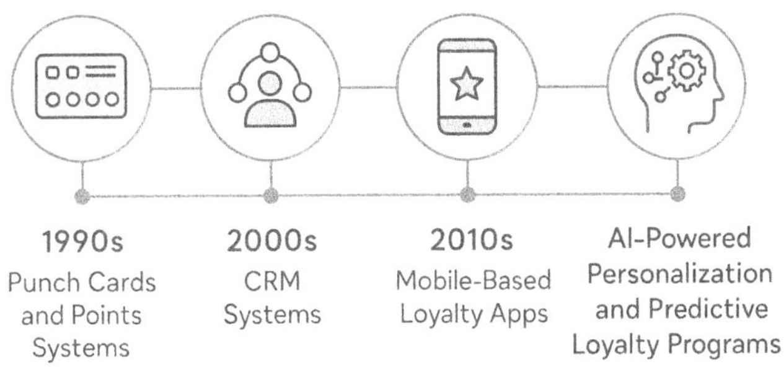

FIGURE 8.1 Evolution of customer loyalty strategies in the digital age.

AI also plays a substantial role in customer retention by utilizing predictive analytics to identify at-risk customers. Businesses can proactively mitigate potential attrition by implementing targeted interventions during the analysis of patterns such as purchase history and engagement metrics [16]. AI chatbots offer personalized interactions and 24/7 support, which are particularly effective in establishing trust across cultural contexts [17]. The integration of AI is not without its challenges, however. Research suggests that AI has the potential to improve engagement through personalization, but it may also negatively moderate the relationship between trust and loyalty if consumers perceive it as intrusive or impersonal [10]. This underscores the necessity of meticulous implementation strategies that strike a balance between automation and human-like empathy.

This chapter examines the transformative role of AI in contemporary customer loyalty strategies, examining the ways in which technologies such as machine learning, predictive analytics, and natural language processing are transforming brand-consumer relationships. Our objective is to offer a comprehensive comprehension of the ways in which AI can improve engagement, drive retention, and cultivate deeper emotional connections by analyzing real-world applications, frameworks, and future trends. Additionally, we will address the ethical considerations and strategic implications that are essential for sustainable success in a data-driven marketplace.

8.2 AI TECHNOLOGIES POWERING CUSTOMER LOYALTY

AI is being used more and more in a variety of sectors, such as banking, hospitality, and retail, to provide individualized experiences that increase client happiness and engagement. AI technologies are changing the traditional value chain in the retail industry by making it possible for merchants to be more adaptable and customer-focused. AI has been recognized as a disruptive force in retail, enabling companies to improve consumer engagement, streamline operations, and optimize inventory management [18]. Knowledge management, inventory optimization, and customer engagement are just a few of the steps in the authors' proposed AI-enabled retail value chain that incorporates many AI technologies. In addition to increasing operational effectiveness, this strategy improves the general customer experience, which boosts loyalty.

AI has also been adopted by the hospitality sector to enhance client satisfaction and service. The function of AI-powered chatbots in the tourism industry, which act as a bridge between AI technologies and client loyalty, is highlighted by research by Khana et al. [19]. In the end, these chatbots increase customer loyalty by offering individualized service, answering consumer questions, and improving the user experience. As Narayan et al. [20] highlight, the incorporation of AI into feedback systems enables hospitality companies to collect real-time data on consumer satisfaction and preferences, allowing them to customize their offerings accordingly.

AI-powered tailored offerings are transforming consumer interaction in the finance industry. For example, Personetics Technologies analyzes consumer transaction data using AI to provide customized financial management insights. By successfully meeting each customer's unique needs, this degree of customization not only increases consumer satisfaction but also cultivates loyalty. The application of AI in communication management highlights how crucial it is to inform communication professionals about AI's capacity to enhance client engagement and interactions [21].

AI is being used by e-commerce sites like Shopee to improve consumer experiences and foster loyalty. AI technologies, such as chatbots and tailored recommendations, significantly increase customer happiness and service responsiveness [22]. AI helps e-commerce companies to develop customized shopping experiences that appeal to customers by examining their behavior and preferences. This boosts client retention and loyalty. Core AI technologies (ML, NLP, Predictive Analytics, and Recommendation Engines) linked to loyalty functions are depicted in Figure 8.2.

The way businesses interact with their consumers is changing as a result of the incorporation of AI into CRM platforms and loyalty programs. AI improves CRM systems by making predictive modeling, tailored customer interactions, and advanced data analytics possible. AI-powered CRM systems, for instance, are able to analyze vast amounts of client data and spot patterns and trends, which enables companies to efficiently customize their offers and communications. By providing pertinent incentives and rewards based on each customer's preferences and actions, this personalization increases customer loyalty [23–25].

AI is important for loyalty program optimization as well. It makes possible fraud detection, real-time customer segmentation, and predictive analytics for incentive recommendations, all of which are essential for preserving program effectiveness and consumer confidence. Chatbots and virtual assistants driven by AI further improve loyalty programs by providing real-time engagement and feedback analysis, which raises customer satisfaction and retention. However, issues including interoperability with

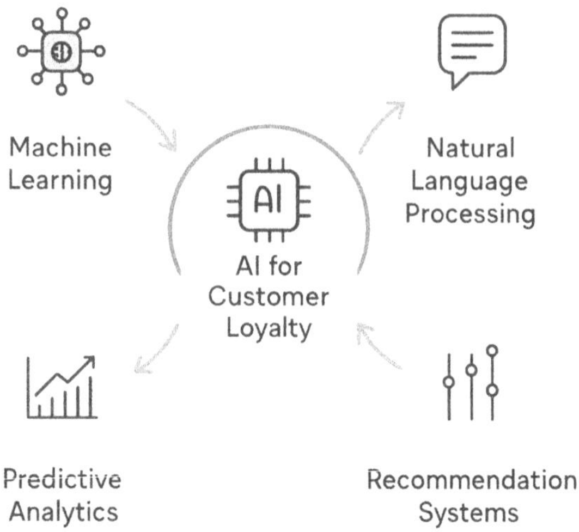

FIGURE 8.2 Key AI technologies driving customer loyalty.

existing systems, ethical considerations, and data privacy concerns continue to be major obstacles to broad adoption [24, 25].

Automation and real-time data processing are essential elements of contemporary AI-powered CRM systems. These features enable companies to react quickly to consumer actions and offer individualized experiences on a large scale. CRM solutions can now monitor real-time consumer interactions and forecast future behaviors thanks to AI technologies like machine learning, which promotes dynamic decision-making. Predictive analytics, for example, can drive engagement and conversions by suggesting the best course of action or customized promotional offers for each unique consumer [26].

AI-powered automation also reduces manual intervention, which streamlines CRM procedures. By automating processes like data input, customer segmentation, and campaign management, resources may be allocated to more strategic endeavors. By guaranteeing that client interactions are smoothly connected across many touchpoints, such as call centers or e-commerce platforms, real-time automation improves operational efficiency [24]. Notwithstanding these developments, effective deployment necessitates strong data governance frameworks to guarantee moral AI application and adherence to privacy laws.

8.3 PERSONALIZATION AND CUSTOMER ENGAGEMENT

E-commerce has undergone a revolution thanks to AI-driven personalized recommendations that improve customer satisfaction and increase sales. In order to provide personalized product recommendations, contemporary AI systems use machine learning algorithms to examine enormous datasets, such as browser history, purchase trends, and demographic data. These systems increase customer satisfaction by making recommendations that are pertinent to each user's interests. A systematic analysis, for example, emphasizes how AI-based recommendation engines use dynamic data points to improve user interaction and refine predictions [27, 28]. By producing immersive shopping experiences that speak to customer demands, the combination of AI and augmented reality (AR) has been demonstrated to increase customer usage intention [29].

Because AI allows firms to offer highly tailored messages at scale, it has revolutionized targeted marketing strategies. Based on behavioral insights, marketers can produce dynamic content for particular customer segments using predictive analytics and natural language processing (NLP). AI solutions, for instance, examine real-time data from CRM systems, e-commerce sites, and social media to pinpoint touchpoints and maximize campaign timing [30]. By attending to each customer's unique demands at every stage of the purchasing process, these tactics increase engagement and conversion rates. Beyond tailored suggestions, AI is also used in marketing automation. Email campaigns driven by AI use consumer data to create personalized content that dramatically raises open and click-through rates. AI-powered targeted advertising makes it possible to precisely segment audiences according to their demographics, interests, and past purchases. Launching hyper-targeted campaigns that connect with customers on a personal level has been successful with this strategy [31].

It is becoming more widely acknowledged that flexible loyalty programs are an essential instrument for improving client retention and engagement. These initiatives increase the perceived value of involvement by using data-driven insights to customize incentives and rewards to the preferences of specific customers. Loyalty programs are organized instruments for customer relationship management that have a lot to offer businesses and customers alike. They must be strategically designed and implemented, nevertheless, to avoid problems like overcomplication or a failure to meet client expectations, in order to be effective [32]. Qualitative research in the Chinese hotel sector shows that cultural quirks have a big impact on the success and design of loyalty programs, which emphasizes the necessity of localized adaptation [33].

Thanks to developments in AI and machine learning, dynamic pricing and content personalization have become essential tactics in contemporary marketing. Businesses can modify prices using dynamic pricing in response to current market conditions, customer behavior, and demand. The idea of "open pricing" in hotel revenue management is presented by Talón-Ballestero et al. [34], going beyond static models to one-to-one pricing methods catered to specific clients. Tomczyk et al. [35] investigate individualized dynamic pricing in the hospitality industry, emphasizing how it might maximize revenue potential while improving consumer perceptions of fairness. Content customization complements dynamic pricing by delivering individualized experiences that resonate with consumer preferences. Integrating technology-enabled customization in retail stores can overcome hurdles to adoption and drive customer satisfaction [35]. AI applications in dynamic pricing have been carefully assessed for their capacity to maximize pricing strategies while retaining transparency and confidence among consumers [36]. Figure 8.3 depicts how customer data is processed by AI to provide tailored loyalty experiences.

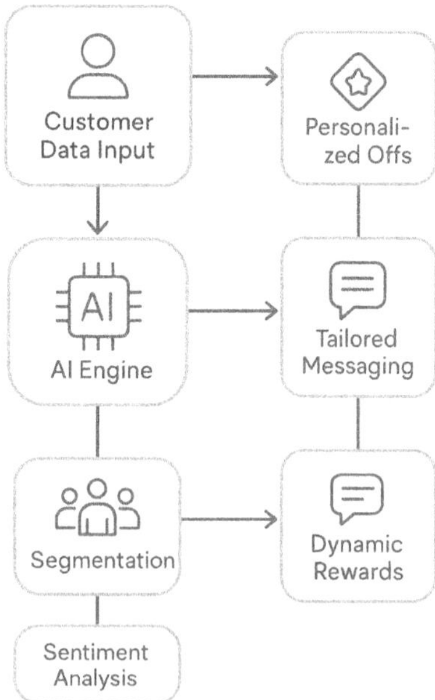

FIGURE 8.3 AI-Powered personalization flow in loyalty programs.

8.4 PREDICTIVE ANALYTICS FOR CUSTOMER RETENTION

Businesses looking to improve customer retention and maximize marketing efforts are finding that integrating AI into customer churn and customer lifetime value (CLV) prediction is a crucial tactic. A company's revenue and growth potential are greatly impacted by customer churn, which is defined as the loss of clients or customers. Organizations can take proactive steps to keep important clients by understanding the variables that contribute to churn. Keeping an existing client is far less expensive than finding a new one. For this reason, churn prediction is a crucial area of study for many businesses, including retail banking and telecoms [37]. To forecast churn and calculate CLV, AI-driven models use a variety of data sources, such as transaction history, customer interactions, and sentiment on social media. For example, machine learning methods like decision trees and logistic regression have been successfully used to identify customers who are at risk and predict their potential lifetime value [38, 39]. Businesses can target high-value consumers with customized marketing tactics by examining trends in customer behavior. This increases retention rates and maximizes profitability [40].

Sentiment analysis has become a potent instrument for comprehending consumer sentiments and opinions as they are communicated through social media interactions and online reviews. Businesses can examine enormous volumes of unstructured data to learn more about how customers feel about their goods and services by utilizing natural language processing (NLP) tools. In addition to aiding in the evaluation of customer satisfaction, this analysis is essential for forecasting churn [41]. For instance, sentiment scores and overall customer satisfaction ratings were found to be strongly correlated in a study that examined online hotel evaluations. This suggests that sentiment analysis is a useful tool for determining client sentiment and pinpointing areas that require improvement [41]. Social media platforms are also excellent sources of real-time feedback, which enables businesses to keep an eye on consumer opinions and quickly resolve issues [42]. Businesses can improve their comprehension of consumer needs and preferences and, eventually, increase retention rates by incorporating sentiment analysis into their customer relationship management (CRM) strategy.

Implementing proactive solutions that can reduce churn requires the identification of high-risk consumers. AI algorithms can examine consumer data to find trends that could point to churn, like declining engagement or unfavorable sentiment [43]. Businesses can focus their retention efforts on clients that display these risk characteristics by using predictive analytics, which enables focused marketing campaigns and individualized outreach [39, 44]. For example, a telecom operator developed a churn prediction model with an astonishing 93.3% accuracy rate using machine learning algorithms. In order to improve its predictive skills, this model integrated social network analysis elements, which allowed the business to pinpoint the customers who were most likely to leave and put retention plans in place in a timely manner [38]. In addition to aiding in client retention, these proactive steps also promote enduring loyalty and raise the average customer lifetime value.

Numerous real-world case studies demonstrate how AI may be effectively applied to improve customer engagement and forecast churn. A case study in the retail banking industry showed how well logistic regression approaches predict client attrition, enabling the bank to target particular customer segments with its marketing initiatives [37]. Similar to this, a study on online gaming companies emphasized the significance of predicting the individual customer lifetime value, demonstrating how AI may enhance income creation and optimize marketing choices [40].

Businesses in the telecom sector have been using sentiment analysis powered by AI to track user reviews on social media. These businesses can lower churn rates and improve customer happiness by proactively addressing any problems by examining sentiment patterns [6, 11]. These case studies highlight how AI has the ability to revolutionize customer relationship management and how companies must implement data-driven strategies to stay competitive in the ever-changing market environment of today.

8.5 CONVERSATIONAL AI AND CUSTOMER SUPPORT

The capacity of chatbots to respond instantly to consumer questions is one of its main benefits, greatly increasing responsiveness. Businesses have used round-the-clock chatbots as a result of consumers' expectations for rapid access to information [26]. In addition to satisfying customer requests for prompt assistance, this round-the-clock availability lowers operating expenses related to conventional customer support techniques. Mehrolia et al.'s study [45] highlights how customer happiness and their propensity to stick with the service are directly impacted by the quality of chatbot interactions, which are defined by responsiveness, interactivity, and dependability.

For customer support systems to be optimized, human agents and AI-powered chatbots must work together. Routine questions can be handled by chatbots, freeing up human agents to work on more difficult problems that call for emotional intelligence and subtle comprehension. Customer happiness and overall service efficiency are improved by this division of labor. Al-Mekhlal et al. [46] claim that by delivering timely and pertinent information, the use of AI technologies in customer service not only improves operational efficiency but also creates a more engaging customer experience. This partnership is further strengthened by chatbots' capacity to learn from interactions and becoming better over time, when discussing the significance of machine learning in boosting chatbot skills.

Customer happiness and chatbot interactions have a well-established relationship. According to Balasubramanian et al. [47], trust has a significant impact on how satisfied customers are in virtual settings. Chatbots' perceived reliability has a big impact on user loyalty and engagement. This is further explained by Khan et al. [48], who show that trust mediates brand engagement and experience, which in turn increases customer loyalty to online services. This implies that in order to improve customer happiness, businesses should place a high priority on establishing trust through efficient chatbot interactions.

Building trust requires that chatbot interactions be personalized. More customer pleasure and loyalty can result from tailored experiences [49]. The customer experience is enhanced and the brand's reputation as being aware of and responsive to individual requirements is strengthened by chatbots' capacity to deliver personalized responses based on user data.

8.6 ETHICAL CONSIDERATIONS AND DATA PRIVACY

Data privacy and ethical issues have become crucial to strategic planning and execution as companies use AI technologies more and more to increase client loyalty. In order to produce insights and provide individualized experiences, AI systems mostly rely on client data, which includes behavioral patterns and purchase histories. This data-driven strategy can greatly increase engagement and retention, but it also brings up important issues about the collection, storage, and use of data. Consumers are growing increasingly conscious of their digital footprints, and any abuse or perceived invasion may swiftly damage trust and destroy the very loyalty that companies seek to cultivate.

Informed consent is one of the main ethical issues with AI-powered loyalty programs. Users frequently don't realize how much of their data is being collected or how algorithms are using it to evaluate it. Although terms and conditions may legally satisfy legal requirements, they are often too complicated or unclear. Transparency is essential for the ethical application of AI; businesses must explain what information is being gathered, why, and how it will improve the customer experience. Opt-in procedures and straightforward, uncomplicated privacy policies promote confidence and provide consumers the power to make educated decisions. Algorithmic bias is another significant problem that may unintentionally impact the distribution of customer loyalty. AI systems may prioritize some client segments over others if they are trained on biased or insufficient data, giving high-spending customers better incentives or engagement while ignoring those with differing spending patterns or demographics. Regular audits and fairness checks should be a part of ethical AI to make sure that loyalty programs don't inadvertently discriminate or perpetuate current injustices. The foundation of AI decision-making must be inclusiveness and fair opportunity.

Protecting client loyalty requires data security just as much. Businesses become more appealing targets for hackers the more data they collect. In addition to adhering to data protection laws such as the CCPA or GDPR, ethical responsibility entails proactively implementing strong security infrastructures, such as encryption, access control, and breach response procedures. Years of devotion can be ruined and a brand's reputation permanently harmed by a single data leak. As a result, making an ethical commitment to clients through data security is more than just a technological choice. Human control is necessary for the ethical use of AI in loyalty programs. Even while automation increases productivity, human judgment must always be used when handling delicate client decisions, complaints, or award distribution. AI should not take the place of human engagement in decision-making, especially in complex or emotionally charged loyalty cases. This collaboration between humans and AI guarantees that the consumer experience will continue to incorporate empathy, justice, and contextual awareness. Figure 8.4 illustrates the trade-offs between privacy and personalization.

8.7 FUTURE TRENDS AND STRATEGIC IMPLICATIONS

It is anticipated that as AI develops further, it will become more deeply integrated into customer loyalty plans, changing the way that companies engage with their target audience. The transition from reactive to proactive loyalty initiatives is one of the most important themes of the future.

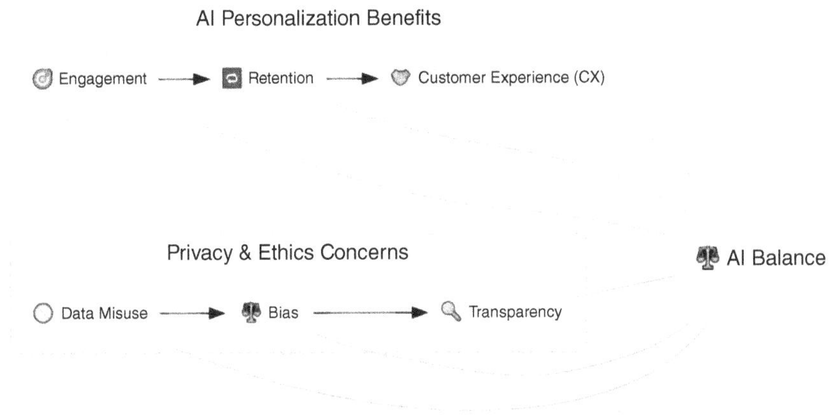

FIGURE 8.4 Ethical considerations in AI-driven loyalty systems.

AI systems are progressing toward anticipating client demands and intents before they materialize, rather than merely rewarding previous behavior. Businesses will be able to provide rewards and solutions before a client expresses a demand directly because to sophisticated data modeling and real-time behavioral tracking, changing the loyalty paradigm from transactional to anticipatory.

The combination of AI and immersive technologies like virtual reality (VR), augmented reality (AR), and the internet of things (IoT) is another new trend. AI will be essential in evaluating contextual data, such as location, mood, or even biological feedback, to provide hyper-personalized experiences as smart devices and linked settings proliferate. AI may be used, for instance, by a smart retail store to recognize when a regular customer walks in and turn on personalized welcomes, ambient music, or product recommendations via digital screens.

Conversational AI and voice-activated interfaces are also anticipated to play a bigger role in determining loyalty experiences. Businesses can employ digital assistants as continuous relationship channels as they grow more human-like and integrated into everyday life. By serving as both a brand ambassador and a loyalty strategist, these AI companions can offer personalized promos, remind users of their loyalty points, and provide real-time customer support. The end effect is a smooth, dialogue-based engagement loop that gradually deepens emotional ties with clients.

From a strategic standpoint, businesses need to start seeing AI as a partner in customer relationship management rather than just a tool. This suggests that internal operations need to be reorganized, teams need to invest in AI literacy, and data architecture needs to be in line with long-term loyalty objectives. Additionally, companies must give top priority to AI solutions that are adaptable, comprehensible, and able to change to meet the needs of their clients. Given the speed at which technology is developing and the way that consumer values are changing, strategic agility will be essential because static loyalty models could soon become outdated.

The development of AI in loyalty programs will continue to be influenced by ethical and legal factors. The need to protect privacy and maintain algorithmic fairness grows as personalization increases. Future approaches must provide people control over the use of their data and incorporate inherent transparency elements, including explainable AI (XAI). Long-term customer trust is crucial for sustaining loyalty, and businesses that approach data ethics as a core value rather than a compliance duty are more likely to gain and keep it.

8.8 CONCLUSION

In the present day, consumers anticipate interactions that are personalized, seamless, and meaningful to their individual interests and behaviors. Businesses can now transition from one-size-fits-all loyalty programs to dynamic, data-driven strategies as a result of the powerful arsenal of AI. Businesses may cultivate more robust relationships with their clients that are based on trust, expectation, and relevance, in addition to rewards, through the use of AI.

This chapter investigated the ways in which the loyalty market is being transformed by AI tools, such as machine learning, natural language processing, predictive analytics, and recommendation systems. Companies can engage with clients at the appropriate time, in the appropriate medium, and with the appropriate message with the assistance of these tools. The integration of AI has shifted the focus from transactional loyalty to experiential loyalty, fostering a sense of appreciation, understanding, and engagement among all customers. Examples of this include real-time attrition prediction, conversational assistance, and AI-powered personalization engines.

However, the immense technological power that it possesses also entails a significant amount of responsibility. The application of AI in consumer loyalty necessitates a steadfast dedication to ethical principles and data privacy. As algorithms influence the identification, reward, and retention of consumers, transparency and fairness become indispensable. Organizations must maintain a vigilant approach to the collection, processing, and utilization of consumer data in order to establish trust and ensure regulatory compliance through open communication and consent-based procedures.

The future of consumer loyalty will belong to businesses that employ AI for automation and analytics, as well as to establish genuine, enduring relationships. In the AI era, loyalty encompasses more than merely retaining clients; it also involves consistently learning from them, meeting their needs, and providing value during each interaction. Companies that combine AI innovation with customer-centric principles will not only retain their current clientele but also foster a community of devoted supporters who support long-term expansion and brand equity.

REFERENCES

1. Moisescu, O.-I., *Assessing customer loyalty: A literature review*. 2014.
2. Myftaraj, E. and B. Trebicka, Analyzing the impact of loyalty card programs on customer behavior: insights from the Albanian market. *F1000Research*, 2023. **12**: p. 1028.
3. Meyer-Waarden, L., The impact of reward personalisation on frequent flyer programmes' perceived value and loyalty. *Journal of Services Marketing*, 2013. **27**(3): p. 183–194.
4. Singh, V., et al., Service quality, customer satisfaction and customer loyalty: A comprehensive literature review. *Journal of Survey in Fisheries Sciences*, 2023. **10**(4S): pp. 3457–3464.
5. Dávila Espuela, N., M.D. Reina Paz, and C. Sevilla Sevilla, Social networks and customer loyalty: review of loyalty keys and main social networks publications' characteristics. *Frontiers in Psychology*, 2023. **14**: p. 1286445.
6. Khadka, K. and S. Maharjan, *Customer satisfaction and customer loyalty: Case trivsel städtjänster (trivsel siivouspalvelut)*. 2017. Pietarsaari, Finland: Centria University of Applied Sciences.
7. So, K.K.F., Y. Yang, and X. Li, Fifteen years of research on customer loyalty formation: a meta-analytic structural equation model. *Cornell Hospitality Quarterly*, 2025. **66**(2): pp. 253–272.
8. Chen, Y., T. Mandler, and L. Meyer-Waarden, Three decades of research on loyalty programs: A literature review and future research agenda. *Journal of Business Research*, 2021. **124**: pp. 179–197.
9. Desveaud, K. *A Customer Loyalty Conceptual Framework: A Grounded Theory Review Approach*. in *Proceedings of the European Marketing Academy*. 2019.
10. Chen, Y., et al., The influence of customer trust and artificial intelligence on customer engagement and loyalty–The case of the home-sharing industry. *Frontiers in Psychology*, 2022. **13**: p. 912339.
11. Nam, H. and P. Kannan, Digital environment in global markets: Cross-cultural implications for evolving customer journeys. *Journal of International Marketing*, 2020. **28**(1): pp. 28–47.

12. Zhang, L., Y. Yi, and G. Zhou, Cultivate customer loyalty in national culture: a meta-analysis of electronic banking customer loyalty. *Cross Cultural & Strategic Management*, 2022. **29**(3): pp. 698–728.
13. Rane, N., *Enhancing customer loyalty through Artificial Intelligence (AI), Internet of Things (IoT), and Big Data technologies: improving customer satisfaction, engagement, relationship, and experience.* Internet of Things (IoT), and Big Data Technologies: Improving Customer Satisfaction, Engagement, Relationship, and Experience (October 13, 2023), 2023.
14. Rane, N., et al., Artificial intelligence in sales and marketing: Enhancing customer satisfaction, experience and loyalty. *Experience and Loyalty* (May 17, 2024), 2024.
15. Sharma, A., N. Patel, and R. Gupta, Enhancing Personalized Loyalty Programs through Reinforcement Learning and Collaborative Filtering Algorithms. *European Advanced AI Journal*, 2022. **11**(10).
16. Adekunle, B.I., et al., Improving customer retention through machine learning: A predictive approach to churn prevention and engagement strategies. 2023; 9(4): 507–523.
17. Vashishth, T.K., et al., Artificial intelligence (AI)–powered chatbots: Providing instant support and personalized recommendations to guests 24/7, in *Technology and Luxury Hospitality*. 2024, Routledge. pp. 211–236.
18. Oosthuizen, K., et al., Artificial intelligence in retail: The AI-enabled value chain. *Australasian Marketing Journal*, 2021. **29**(3): pp. 264–273.
19. Khan, A., et al., Effectiveness of artificial intelligence in building customer loyalty: Investigating the mediating role of chatbot in the tourism sector of Pakistan. *International Journal of Academic Research in Business and Social Sciences*, 2023. **13**(9): pp. 657–671.
20. Narayan, R., et al., Hospitality feedback system 4.0: Digitalization of feedback system with integration of industry 4.0 enabling technologies. *Sustainability*, 2022. **14**(19): p. 12158.
21. Zerfass, A., J. Hagelstein, and R. Tench, Artificial intelligence in communication management: a cross-national study on adoption and knowledge, impact, challenges and risks. *Journal of Communication Management*, 2020. **24**(4): pp. 377–389.
22. Khansa, A. and T. Sutabri, *Pengembangan Customer Experience Berbasis Artificial Intelligence pada Startup Marketplace Shopee. Router: Jurnal Teknik Informatika dan Terapan*, 2024. **2**(4): pp. 28–39.
23. Kushnarevych, A. *Researching the Topic of Al Data Analysis in Loyalty Programs. in Proceedings of the 23rd European Conference on Research Methodology for Business and Management Studies*. 2024. Academic Conferences and publishing limited.
24. Ledro, C., A. Nosella, and A. Vinelli, Artificial intelligence in customer relationship management: literature review and future research directions. *Journal of Business & Industrial Marketing*, 2022. **37**(13): pp. 48–63.
25. Iqbal, T. and M.N. Khan, *The Impact of Artificial Intelligence (AI) on CRM and Role of Marketing Managers*. 2021. Gävle, Sweden: University of Gävle.

26. Jenneboer, L., C. Herrando, and E. Constantinides, The impact of chatbots on customer loyalty: A systematic literature review. *Journal of theoretical and applied electronic commerce research*, 2022. **17**(1): pp. 212–229.
27. Necula, S.-C. and V.-D. Păvăloaia, AI-driven recommendations: A systematic review of the state of the art in E-commerce. *Applied Sciences*, 2023. **13**(9): p. 5531.
28. Al-Hasan, T.M., et al., From traditional recommender systems to gpt-based chatbots: A survey of recent developments and future directions. *Big Data and Cognitive Computing*, 2024. **8**(4): p. 36.
29. Adawiyah, S.R., et al., The influence of AI and AR technology in personalized recommendations on customer usage intention: A case study of cosmetic products on shopee. *Applied Sciences*, 2024. **14**(13): p. 5786.
30. Patil, D., Artificial intelligence for personalized marketing and consumer behaviour analysis: Enhancing engagement and conversion rates. Available at SSRN 5057436, 2024.
31. Ziakis, C. and M. Vlachopoulou, Artificial intelligence in digital marketing: Insights from a comprehensive review. *Information*, 2023. **14**(12): p. 664.
32. Ahmed, G. and H. Alzoubi, Loyalty program effectiveness: Theoretical reviews and practical proofs. *Uncertain Supply Chain Management*, 2020. **8**(3): pp. 599–612.
33. Gubíniová, K., et al., Loyalty programmes and their specifics in the Chinese hospitality industry: Qualitative study. *Administrative Sciences*, 2023. **13**(6): p. 152.
34. Talón-Ballestero, P., M. Nieto-García, and L. González-Serrano, The wheel of dynamic pricing: Towards open pricing and one to one pricing in hotel revenue management. *International Journal of Hospitality Management*, 2022. **102**: p. 103184.
35. Tomczyk, A.T., et al., Price-personalization: Customer typology based on hospitality business. *Journal of Business Research*, 2022. **147**: pp. 462–476.
36. Chenavaz, R.Y. and S. Dimitrov, Artificial intelligence and dynamic pricing: A systematic literature review. *Journal of Applied Economics*, 2025. **28**(1): p. 2466140.
37. Mutanen, T., S. Nousiainen, and J. Ahola, Customer churn prediction–a case study in retail banking, in *Data Mining for Business Applications*. 2010, IOS Press. pp. 77–83.
38. Ahmad, A.K., A. Jafar, and K. Aljoumaa, Customer churn prediction in telecom using machine learning in big data platform. *Journal of Big Data*, 2019. **6**(1): pp. 1–24.
39. Ike, C.C., et al., Advancing machine learning frameworks for customer retention and propensity modeling in ecommerce platforms. *GSC Advanced Research and Reviews*, 2023. **14**(2): p. 17.
40. Zhao, S., et al., perCLTV: A general system for personalized customer lifetime value prediction in online games. ACM Transactions on Information Systems, 2023. **41**(1): pp. 1–29.

41. He, W., et al., Application of social media analytics: A case of analyzing online hotel reviews. *Online Information Review*, 2017. **41**(7): pp. 921–935.
42. Ogudo, K.A. and D.M.J. Nestor. *Sentiment analysis application and natural language processing for mobile network operators' support on social media.* in *2019 International Conference on Advances in Big Data, Computing and Data Communication Systems (icABCD).* 2019. IEEE.
43. Ogbu, D., Leveraging AI models to measure customer upsell. 2024.
44. Olaiya, O.P., et al., The impact of big data analytics on financial risk management. *International Journal of Science and Research Archive*, 2024. **12**(2): pp. 821–827.
45. Mehrolia, S., et al., Will users continue using banking chatbots? The moderating role of perceived risk. *FIIB Business Review*, 2023: p. 23197145231169900.
46. Al-Mekhlal, M., M. Al-Buraik, and M. Al-Lubli. *Digital transformation: AI-powered bot solutions and automation for customer services.* in *2023 International Conference on Digital Applications, Transformation & Economy (ICDATE).* 2023. IEEE.
47. Balasubramanian, S., P. Konana, and N.M. Menon, Customer satisfaction in virtual environments: A study of online investing. *Management Science*, 2003. **49**(7): pp. 871–889.
48. Khan, I., et al., Brand engagement and experience in online services. *Journal of Services Marketing*, 2020. **34**(2): pp. 163–175.
49. Winata, H., et al., From experience to loyalty: understanding the dynamics of customer trust in Indonesia's mobile banking industry. *Journal of Lifestyle and SDGs Review*, 2025. **5**(1): pp. e02597.

CHAPTER 9

Strategic Selection and Integration of AI Tools in Data-Driven Marketing

Mitra Madanchian and Hamed Taherdoost

9.1 INTRODUCTION

Data-driven decision-making in marketing refers to the systematic process of using factual data, metrics, and analytics to guide strategic choices rather than relying on intuition or gut feeling. This approach involves collecting relevant data from various sources such as customer interactions, market trends, and campaign performance, and then analyzing this information to extract actionable insights. By grounding decisions in verified data, marketers can better understand customer needs, optimize resource allocation, and align their efforts with overarching business objectives. This method reduces uncertainty and increases confidence in marketing strategies, ultimately leading to more predictable and measurable outcomes [1].

In the context of modern marketing, artificial intelligence (AI) tools have become indispensable due to their ability to process and analyze vast amounts of data quickly and accurately. AI enhances the data-driven approach by automating routine tasks, identifying patterns, and generating predictive insights that humans alone would struggle to uncover. These capabilities enable marketers to personalize customer experiences at scale, optimize campaign targeting, and improve the efficiency of

DOI: 10.1201/9781003625452-9

marketing workflows. The integration of AI into marketing strategies thus transforms raw data into refined, actionable intelligence, allowing businesses to engage their audiences more effectively and maximize return on investment [2].

The intersection of data and AI creates a powerful synergy that significantly enhances marketing effectiveness. Data provides the foundational insights into consumer behavior and market dynamics, while AI amplifies the ability to interpret and act on these insights in real time. For example, AI-driven algorithms can analyze historical customer data to predict future buying behaviors, segment audiences more precisely, and tailor messaging to individual preferences. This dynamic interplay enables marketers to move beyond broad, generic campaigns to highly targeted and adaptive marketing efforts that respond to evolving customer needs and market conditions [3].

Moreover, AI tools facilitate continuous learning and optimization by monitoring campaign performance and adjusting tactics based on near real-time data. This agility is crucial in today's fast-paced digital environment, where consumer preferences and competitive landscapes shift rapidly. By leveraging AI-powered analytics and automation, marketers can make informed decisions quickly, test different strategies efficiently, and scale successful initiatives with confidence. This iterative process driven by data and AI leads to improved customer engagement, higher conversion rates, and ultimately, stronger business growth [4].

The importance of AI in modern marketing strategies also lies in its ability to handle the complexity and volume of data generated by digital campaigns. Traditional marketing methods often struggle to keep pace with the exponential growth of data from multiple channels such as social media, email, websites, and mobile apps. AI systems can integrate and analyze these diverse data streams, uncovering hidden insights and correlations that inform smarter marketing decisions. This comprehensive understanding helps marketers allocate budgets more effectively, select optimal channels, and personalize content to resonate with specific audience segments [5].

In summary, data-driven decision-making supported by AI tools represents a fundamental shift in marketing from intuition-based to evidence-based strategies. This approach empowers marketers to harness the full potential of their data assets, enabling more precise targeting, enhanced personalization, and continuous optimization. As AI technologies continue to evolve, their role in transforming marketing decision-making will only grow, driving innovation and competitive advantage in an increasingly data-centric business landscape [6].

9.2 UNDERSTANDING DATA-DRIVEN MARKETING

Data-driven marketing is a strategic approach that relies on collecting and analyzing customer data to guide marketing decisions and actions (Figure 9.1). Unlike traditional marketing, which often depends on intuition or broad assumptions about audiences, data-driven marketing uses concrete information about customer behaviors, preferences, and interactions to create more personalized and effective campaigns. This method enables marketers to understand their customers on a deeper level, tailoring messages and offers to meet specific needs and improve engagement. The ultimate goal is to optimize marketing efforts by using data as the foundation for decision-making, thereby enhancing the relevance and impact of marketing activities [7].

Traditional marketing typically involves broad audience targeting through channels like print ads, television, and radio, where marketers rely on experience, creativity, and general market knowledge to reach potential customers. This approach often lacks precise measurement and personalization, leading to less efficient use of resources and sometimes lower return on investment. In contrast, data-driven marketing leverages detailed customer data and advanced analytics to segment audiences more

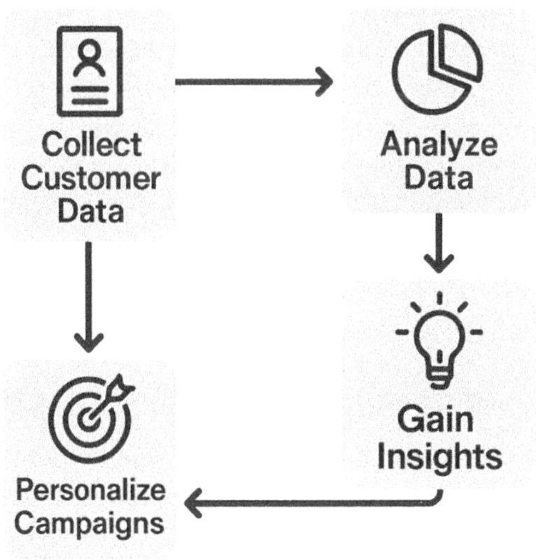

FIGURE 9.1 Understanding data-driven marketing.

accurately and deliver highly targeted messages. This shift from a one-size-fits-all strategy to a more focused, personalized approach allows marketers to allocate budgets more effectively and achieve better results by addressing the specific needs and behaviors of distinct customer groups [8].

One of the key differentiators of data-driven marketing is the use of real-time data and advanced analytics to inform decisions. While traditional marketing campaigns may be planned and executed based on historical data or fixed schedules, data-driven marketing continuously collects and analyzes fresh data from multiple sources such as website interactions, social media activity, and purchase history. This enables marketers to respond quickly to changing customer preferences, market trends, and campaign performance. Real-time insights allow for dynamic adjustments in targeting, messaging, and channel selection, which increases the agility and effectiveness of marketing efforts [9].

Advanced analytics play a crucial role in transforming raw data into actionable insights. Techniques such as predictive modeling, machine learning, and customer segmentation help marketers identify patterns and trends that would otherwise remain hidden. These insights enable the creation of personalized customer journeys, optimized content, and more efficient allocation of marketing resources. By understanding not just what customers have done but also what they are likely to do, marketers can anticipate needs and tailor their strategies accordingly, resulting in higher engagement and conversion rates [10].

The ability to monitor and adjust campaigns in real time also reduces waste and enhances return on investment. Data-driven marketing minimizes the risk of spending on ineffective channels or messaging by providing continuous feedback on campaign performance. This ongoing measurement allows marketers to test different approaches, learn from results, and refine their strategies to maximize impact. The data-centric approach thus fosters a culture of experimentation and learning, where decisions are validated by evidence rather than guesswork [11].

9.3 THE ROLE OF AI IN DATA-DRIVEN MARKETING

AI plays a transformative role in data-driven marketing by enabling the processing and analysis of vast and complex data sets that would be impossible for humans to handle manually. AI systems use advanced algorithms, including machine learning and natural language processing, to sift through large volumes of customer data collected from multiple channels such as social media, websites, email interactions, and purchase histories. This capability allows marketers to extract meaningful patterns and insights quickly and with high accuracy. By automating data analysis, AI frees marketers from time-consuming manual tasks and accelerates the decision-making process, making marketing strategies more responsive and precise [12].

One of the core capabilities of AI in marketing is predictive analytics, which uses historical data to forecast future customer behaviors and trends. AI-powered predictive models can identify which products a customer is likely to purchase next, predict the best time to engage with a prospect, or estimate customer lifetime value. This foresight enables marketers to proactively tailor campaigns, optimize pricing, and allocate resources efficiently. For example, Amazon's recommendation engine leverages predictive analytics to suggest products based on a customer's browsing and purchase history, significantly boosting sales. Predictive analytics thus shifts marketing from reactive to anticipatory, allowing businesses to stay ahead of customer needs [13].

Personalization is another key strength of AI in data-driven marketing. AI analyzes individual customer data points such as past purchases, browsing behavior, and engagement patterns to deliver highly customized marketing messages and offers. Unlike traditional segmentation based on broad demographics, AI-driven personalization creates dynamic, evolving customer profiles that adapt in real time. This enables marketers to serve content, product recommendations, and promotions that resonate on a personal level, increasing engagement and conversion rates. For instance, Netflix uses AI to personalize viewing recommendations for each subscriber, enhancing user satisfaction and retention [14].

Automation powered by AI further enhances marketing efficiency by enabling real-time adjustments and execution of campaigns. AI-driven marketing platforms can automatically trigger personalized email sequences, adjust ad bids, and modify website content based on user behavior without human intervention. This real-time marketing automation ensures that customers receive relevant messages at the right moment, improving the customer journey and campaign performance. Spotify's "Discover Weekly" playlists, which are generated and updated using AI based on a user's listening habits, exemplify how automation can deliver continuous, personalized experiences that keep users engaged [15].

Sentiment analysis is another important AI capability that benefits marketers by monitoring and interpreting customer opinions across social media, reviews, and feedback channels. AI algorithms use natural language processing to detect positive, negative, or neutral sentiments in large volumes of text data. This insight helps brands manage their reputation by quickly addressing negative feedback and amplifying positive sentiment. Coca-Cola, for example, employs AI-driven sentiment analysis to track online conversations and adjust marketing strategies accordingly, ensuring their messaging aligns with consumer perceptions and trends [16].

AI's ability to optimize content is also revolutionizing marketing. By analyzing user engagement data, AI tools can identify which headlines, images, and topics perform best, then generate or suggest content optimized for higher click-through and conversion rates. Tools like Persado use AI to craft emotionally resonant marketing messages by analyzing language patterns that drive customer responses. This data-driven content optimization helps marketers create more compelling and relevant communications, ultimately improving campaign effectiveness and ROI [17].

Customer segmentation is another area where AI excels by moving beyond static demographic categories to dynamic, behavior-based groups. AI analyzes multiple data dimensions, such as purchase frequency, browsing paths, and interaction history, to create nuanced segments that evolve over time. This allows marketers to target audiences more precisely and tailor strategies to specific customer needs. Netflix's AI-driven segmentation, which groups users by viewing habits rather than just age or location, is a prime example of how AI enhances targeting accuracy and personalization [18].

Moreover, AI enables marketers to continuously monitor campaign performance and optimize strategies in real time. By integrating AI analytics into marketing platforms, businesses can receive instant feedback on which tactics are working and which are not, allowing for rapid adjustments. This iterative process improves marketing agility and ensures resources are focused on the most effective initiatives. Google Analytics 4 and HubSpot now incorporate AI features that track user behavior patterns and suggest improvements, helping marketers refine their content and user experience [19].

In addition to improving targeting and personalization, AI-driven marketing tools also help businesses scale their efforts efficiently. Small and large enterprises alike benefit from AI's ability to automate complex tasks such as data integration, audience analysis, and campaign management. This scalability allows marketers to execute sophisticated, multi-channel campaigns without proportionally increasing their workload or costs. AI thus democratizes access to advanced marketing capabilities, enabling organizations of all sizes to compete more effectively in the digital marketplace [20].

9.4 CRITERIA FOR SELECTING AI TOOLS FOR MARKETING

Selecting the right AI tools for marketing requires a comprehensive understanding of how these tools align with your specific objectives and brand needs (Figure 9.2). It is essential to start by clearly defining your marketing goals and identifying the challenges you aim to address. Whether your focus is on increasing customer engagement, improving lead generation, or streamlining operational processes, your objectives will influence the features and functionalities you prioritize. For example, if personalization is a key goal, you should look for AI tools that excel in customer segmentation and content customization. Conversely, if automation and efficiency

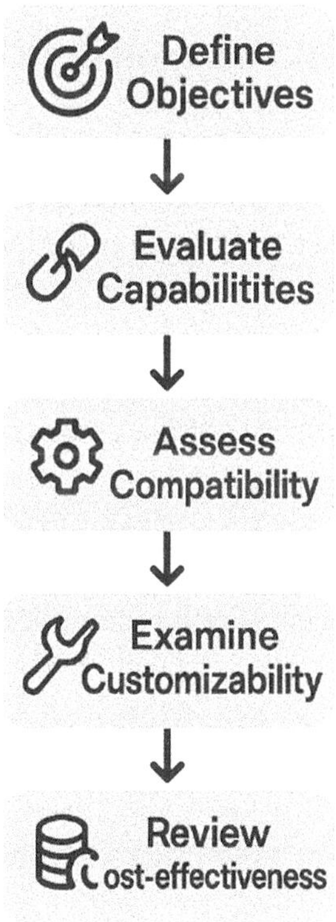

FIGURE 9.2 Criteria for selecting AI tools for marketing.

are priorities, tools with robust workflow automation capabilities will be more suitable. By aligning your objectives with the core functionalities of potential AI solutions, you can ensure that the tools you select will effectively support your strategic initiatives and contribute to long-term success [21].

Core capabilities are fundamental to evaluating AI tools for marketing. Predictive analytics is a critical feature that enables forecasting customer behaviors and market trends, allowing proactive decision-making. Real-time insights are equally vital, as they provide immediate feedback on campaign performance and customer interactions, facilitating agile adjustments. Automation features, such as automated email campaigns, social media scheduling, and chatbots, help reduce manual workload and improve operational efficiency. When assessing these capabilities, it's important to consider how accurately and reliably the AI system can deliver predictions, insights, and automated actions. The effectiveness of these features directly impacts the ROI and overall success of your marketing efforts, making them key criteria in your evaluation process [22].

Integration with your existing marketing technology stack is another crucial factor. An AI tool should seamlessly connect with your current systems, including customer relationship management (CRM) platforms, email marketing software, analytics tools, and content management systems. Compatibility through APIs and data sharing capabilities ensures that the AI solution enhances your existing workflows rather than complicating them. Proper integration allows for a unified data environment, enabling comprehensive analysis and more cohesive marketing strategies. Before committing to a particular tool, it's advisable to verify its compatibility with your current infrastructure and to consider whether it can be easily integrated without extensive customization or additional costs. This integration capability ensures that your investment in AI technology maximizes its potential and minimizes operational disruptions [23].

User-friendliness and accessibility are vital considerations, especially since marketing teams often include members with varying levels of technical expertise. An AI tool should feature an intuitive interface that allows non-technical users to navigate and leverage its functionalities effectively. Clear dashboards, straightforward reporting, and minimal setup complexity contribute to faster adoption and better utilization. Hands-on testing through demos or trial periods can provide valuable insights into the tool's usability. If the tool is overly complex or requires extensive training, it may hinder productivity and delay the realization of benefits.

Therefore, selecting an AI solution that balances advanced capabilities with ease of use is essential for ensuring widespread adoption and sustained value [24].

Customizability and flexibility are equally important, as each brand has unique needs and evolving requirements. An AI tool should offer configurable features, allowing you to tailor algorithms, data inputs, and reporting formats to fit your specific marketing strategies. For instance, customizable dashboards enable teams to focus on metrics most relevant to their goals, while adaptable algorithms can refine predictions based on your industry or customer base. The ability to modify and extend the AI's functionalities ensures that the tool remains relevant over time and can adapt to changing market conditions or new marketing channels. Tools that lack flexibility may become obsolete quickly or require costly modifications, limiting their long-term utility [25].

Data security, compliance, and ethical considerations are paramount when selecting AI tools, given the sensitive nature of customer data involved. It is essential to verify that the AI solution adheres to relevant data privacy regulations such as GDPR, CCPA, or other regional laws. The tool should incorporate features like data encryption, access controls, and automated redaction of personally identifiable information (PII) to safeguard user privacy. Regular audits and transparency in data handling practices foster trust with customers and protect your organization from legal liabilities. Ethical AI use also involves ensuring that algorithms do not perpetuate biases or unfair practices. Prioritizing security and compliance not only mitigates risks but also enhances your brand's reputation and customer trust [26].

Cost-effectiveness and the expected return on investment (ROI) are critical considerations, especially for organizations operating within budget constraints. While some AI tools come with high upfront costs, others offer subscription models or pay-as-you-go pricing, making them accessible to a wide range of businesses. When evaluating costs, it's important to consider the potential savings in time and resources, as well as the revenue growth enabled by improved targeting and personalization. An AI tool that automates routine tasks, enhances campaign performance, and provides actionable insights can generate substantial ROI over time. Additionally, be mindful of hidden costs such as training, ongoing support, and future upgrades, which can influence the overall value proposition. A cost-benefit analysis helps ensure that your investment aligns with your strategic priorities and delivers measurable results [27].

Selecting the appropriate AI tools for marketing involves a careful balancing of multiple criteria. Aligning the tools with your specific goals ensures relevance and effectiveness. Evaluating core capabilities like predictive analytics, real-time insights, and automation guarantees that the tools can deliver tangible benefits. Seamless integration with your existing technology stack maximizes efficiency and data coherence. Prioritizing user-friendliness encourages adoption across your team, while customization and flexibility ensure the tools remain adaptable to future needs. Security, compliance, and ethical considerations safeguard your brand and customer trust. Finally, assessing cost-effectiveness and ROI ensures that your investment delivers sustainable value. By systematically considering these factors, you can make informed decisions that enhance your marketing capabilities and drive long-term success [28].

9.5 DATA INFRASTRUCTURE AND PREPARATION

Clean, structured, and integrated data form the foundation of effective AI-driven marketing strategies. AI models rely heavily on the quality of the data they are trained on; if the data is inconsistent, incomplete, or siloed, the AI's outputs will be flawed, leading to misguided decisions and poor customer experiences. The principle of "garbage in, garbage out" is particularly relevant here: AI systems learn from historical data patterns, so any errors or gaps in the data are amplified in the AI's predictions and recommendations. Therefore, maintaining a comprehensive, well-organized data infrastructure that captures customer interactions across all touchpoints, from real-time browsing behavior to long-term transaction history, is essential for training AI models that can accurately predict customer behavior and personalize marketing efforts effectively [29].

To achieve this, marketers must implement robust tools and processes for data collection, normalization, and management. Data collection should encompass all relevant sources, including CRM systems, marketing automation platforms, social media channels, and website analytics, ensuring a holistic view of customer data. Normalization is a critical step that standardizes data from diverse sources into a consistent format, making it comparable and analyzable. This involves selecting appropriate normalization methods, such as min-max scaling or z-score standardization, and applying them carefully to avoid introducing bias or errors. Once normalized, data can be integrated into a unified system where it is accessible and usable for AI training and analysis. Employing data profiling tools helps identify patterns and relationships between datasets, facilitating more accurate normalization and integration [30].

Despite best efforts, data quality challenges are common and can significantly hinder AI effectiveness. Inaccurate data, often caused by manual entry errors or poor integration, leads to misdirected marketing efforts and wasted resources. For example, incorrect contact details reduce campaign reach, while duplicated or inconsistent customer records impair personalization and segmentation. To overcome these issues, automation and integration tools should be employed to minimize manual data entry, and regular audits and validation checks must be conducted to ensure data accuracy. Additionally, investing in premium data verification services can enhance the reliability of contact information, improving outreach success rates. Establishing organizational data quality standards and training staff on data management best practices further supports ongoing data integrity [31].

Structured data plays a pivotal role in optimizing AI performance. Unlike unstructured data such as emails or social media posts, structured data is organized in predefined formats like databases or spreadsheets, making it easier for AI algorithms to process and analyze. Structured data enables AI models to efficiently identify patterns and relationships, resulting in more accurate and reliable predictions. This is particularly important in marketing applications where precision in customer segmentation, behavior prediction, and campaign optimization is crucial. The clarity and consistency of structured data also facilitate traceability and auditability, which are vital for maintaining data quality over time and ensuring compliance with regulatory standards [32].

Integrating both structured and unstructured data can further enrich AI's capabilities. While structured data provides a solid foundation, unstructured data, such as customer reviews, social media comments, and multimedia content, adds depth and nuance to customer insights. Advanced AI techniques, including natural language processing and image recognition, can convert unstructured data into structured formats, enabling a more comprehensive analysis of customer sentiment and preferences. This integration allows marketers to develop richer, more personalized campaigns that resonate with their audiences on multiple levels, enhancing engagement and loyalty [33].

Addressing data quality challenges requires a proactive and multifaceted approach. Incomplete data sets, where critical information is missing, can distort AI models and lead to inaccurate conclusions. To mitigate this, marketers should employ diverse data collection methods, including surveys, interviews, and observational data, to fill gaps and ensure comprehensive coverage. Machine learning algorithms can also be used to predict and impute missing values based on existing data patterns, enhancing dataset completeness. Furthermore, implementing rigorous data quality control measures, such as validation during data entry, anomaly detection, and periodic audits, helps maintain high data standards. Organizations that prioritize data quality often see measurable improvements in marketing outcomes, including higher customer satisfaction and increased revenue [34].

9.6 DEVELOPING A DATA-DRIVEN AI MARKETING STRATEGY

Developing a data-driven AI marketing strategy begins with defining clear and specific marketing objectives that will guide the selection and implementation of AI tools. Without a well-articulated goal, AI initiatives risk becoming unfocused and ineffective. Whether the aim is to increase customer acquisition, improve retention, optimize ad spend, or enhance personalization, clarity in objectives allows marketers to choose AI solutions that are best suited to meet those targets. This focus ensures that the AI tools are not just adopted for their novelty but serve a strategic purpose aligned with broader business goals. Clear objectives also provide measurable benchmarks to evaluate the success of AI-driven campaigns [35].

Building a marketing plan using AI involves several critical steps, starting with comprehensive data collection. AI thrives on large volumes of diverse and high-quality data, which must be gathered from multiple sources such as CRM systems, social media platforms, website analytics, and customer feedback channels. Once collected, this data undergoes rigorous analysis using AI algorithms that identify patterns, segment audiences, and predict customer behaviors. These insights form the basis for personalization, enabling marketers to tailor messages, offers, and experiences to individual preferences and behaviors. Following personalization, channel optimization ensures that marketing efforts are deployed through the most effective channels at the right times, maximizing engagement and conversion rates. This end-to-end process leverages AI's ability to turn raw data into actionable marketing strategies [36].

Training and upskilling marketing teams to work effectively with AI-generated insights is a vital component of a successful AI marketing strategy. AI tools can produce complex data outputs and predictive models that require interpretation and contextual understanding. Marketers need foundational knowledge of AI concepts such as machine learning, natural language processing, and predictive analytics to fully harness the technology's potential. Equipping teams with these skills fosters confidence and encourages the creative application of AI insights. Moreover, ongoing training promotes collaboration between marketing, data science, and IT departments, ensuring that AI initiatives are integrated smoothly into existing workflows and that human expertise complements algorithmic outputs [37].

Continuous monitoring, iteration, and optimization are essential to sustain the effectiveness of AI-driven marketing campaigns. Unlike traditional campaigns that might run on fixed schedules, AI-enabled campaigns benefit from real-time data feedback and automated adjustments. Marketers must establish processes to regularly review performance metrics, such as conversion rates, engagement levels, and return on ad spend, to identify what is working and what needs refinement. AI platforms often include optimization engines that automatically tweak bids, reallocate budgets, or modify creative elements based on ongoing results. This iterative approach allows campaigns to adapt dynamically to changing customer behaviors and market conditions, maintaining relevance and maximizing impact over time [38].

The integration of AI into marketing strategies also demands a cultural shift within organizations, emphasizing agility and data-driven decision-making. Teams must embrace a mindset that values experimentation, learning from data, and rapid response to insights. This cultural adaptation is supported by AI's capacity to reduce manual workload through automation, freeing marketers to focus on strategic thinking and creative problem-solving. By fostering an environment where AI tools are seen as collaborators rather than replacements, organizations can unlock the full potential of data-driven marketing and drive innovation [39].

Finally, successful AI marketing strategies begin modestly and scale thoughtfully. Starting with a single dataset, a focused goal, and one or two AI tools allow teams to learn and demonstrate value without overwhelming resources. As confidence and expertise grow, marketers can expand AI applications across channels and campaigns, continuously refining their approach. This phased adoption reduces risk, encourages iterative improvement, and builds a foundation for sustained competitive advantage in an increasingly data-centric marketing landscape [36].

9.7 CHALLENGES AND CONSIDERATIONS

Relying on AI tools for marketing presents several significant challenges that organizations must navigate carefully. One of the most concerning pitfalls is algorithmic bias, which occurs when AI systems produce unfair or discriminatory outcomes. These biases often stem from the training data itself rather than from the algorithms being inherently prejudiced. For example, if historical marketing data reflects societal biases or underrepresents certain demographics, AI systems may perpetuate or even amplify these biases in their predictions and recommendations. Research has shown that over 38% of data in large AI databases contains biases, which can lead to skewed targeting that disproportionately favors certain groups while excluding others. This was demonstrated in a recent study where Facebook's ad targeting system showed delivery driver job advertisements differently based on gender stereotypes, with Pizza Hut ads shown primarily to men and Instacart ads to women, despite identical job qualifications. Such biases not only raise ethical concerns but also have legal implications under regulations like GDPR and CCPA, potentially resulting in fines and damaged brand reputation [40].

Over-automation represents another significant challenge in AI marketing implementation. While AI excels at automating repetitive tasks and streamlining processes, excessive automation can lead to marketing that feels impersonal and robotic. AI-generated content, though efficient to produce, often lacks the emotional nuance, creativity, and personal touch that human-created content providers. This can result in generic, predictable content that fails to engage audiences on a deeper level or establish meaningful connections. Additionally, AI tools sometimes prioritize technical optimization over user experience, such as when SEO tools overload content with keywords at the expense of readability and natural flow. This over-optimization can ultimately harm engagement metrics and lower organic search rankings, counteracting the intended benefits of using AI for marketing optimization [41].

Balancing human expertise with AI insights is crucial for effective marketing strategies. While AI is powerful at analyzing data, identifying patterns, and executing routine tasks, it has limitations when it comes to uniquely human qualities such as creativity, emotional understanding, and strategic decision-making. As computer scientist Mesan Ali noted, AI should be viewed as a tool to assist and enhance human decision-making, not as a replacement for human intuition and expertise. The most successful AI marketing implementations recognize that AI and human marketers have complementary strengths. Humans provide the strategic direction, creative vision, and ethical oversight, while AI delivers the data processing power, pattern recognition, and execution efficiency. This balanced approach prevents the "AI dependence trap" where organizations might over-rely on automation at the expense of human judgment [42].

Data privacy and security concerns present another significant challenge in AI marketing. AI systems collect and process vast amounts of personal data to deliver accurate targeting and personalization, but this extensive data collection raises serious privacy considerations. Violating data protection regulations like GDPR or CCPA can result in substantial financial penalties and, more importantly, a loss of customer trust that can be difficult to rebuild. To address these concerns, organizations must implement transparent data collection practices, clearly disclose how customer data is used, limit data collection to what is necessary, and prioritize obtaining explicit user consent. Selecting AI tools with built-in compliance features can help ensure that marketing activities remain within legal boundaries while still leveraging the benefits of data-driven personalization [43].

The rapid evolution of AI technology presents an ongoing challenge for marketing teams trying to keep pace with innovations. As new AI capabilities emerge and existing tools advance, organizations must continuously evaluate, adapt, and update their marketing technology stack. This requires not only financial investment but also a commitment to ongoing education and skills development. The knowledge gap around AI represents a significant barrier to effective implementation, with many marketers lacking comprehensive understanding of AI capabilities, limitations, and best practices. Overcoming this challenge requires dedicated learning through courses, research, and peer discussions, followed by knowledge sharing across marketing teams. Organizations that fail to keep up with AI advancements risk falling behind competitors who more effectively leverage these technologies for marketing advantage.

9.8 CONCLUSION

In conclusion, leveraging AI in marketing offers transformative opportunities to enhance personalization, efficiency, and strategic decision-making through data-driven insights. However, the successful adoption of AI tools requires careful consideration of multiple factors, including aligning technology with specific business goals, ensuring data quality, and fostering organizational agility. While AI has the potential to revolutionize marketing practices, organizations must remain vigilant about potential pitfalls such as biases, ethical concerns, and over-automation. Balancing human expertise with AI capabilities is essential to craft authentic, impactful campaigns that resonate with customers and uphold brand integrity. As AI technology continues to evolve at a rapid pace, ongoing learning, adaptation, and ethical oversight will be vital. By thoughtfully navigating these challenges and capitalizing on AI's strengths, marketers can unlock new levels of insight, engagement, and growth, positioning themselves for success in an increasingly data-centric digital landscape.

REFERENCES

1. Adepoju, A.H., et al., Developing strategic roadmaps for data-driven organizations: A model for aligning projects with business goals. *Int J Multidiscip Res Growth Eval*, 2023. **4**(6): pp. 1128–1140.
2. Emma, O., M. Maddog, and S. Templer, *Automated Personalized Marketing: Build A Platform That Uses Customer Data for Targeted Marketing Campaign Automation*. 2023. https://www.researchgate.net/profile/Emma-Oye/publication/389211521_Automated_Personalized_Marketing_Build_A_Platform_That_Uses_Customer_Data_for_Targeted_Marketing_Campaign_Automation/links/67b8f234461fb56424e4fe6a/Automated-Personalized-Marketing-Build-A-Platform-That-Uses-Customer-Data-for-Targeted-Marketing-Campaign-Automation.pdf?__cf_chl_tk=e_vLHnPFvFZjVwikdJCpy.Cglz_QvVVMnHFBgcC_vY-1750942802-1.0.1.1-os.zCEkJ34vzoUd3w1pzmemUSOXep5tZ1kAwrsC6jMU
3. Raju, V., et al., AI in data-driven marketing: Decoding consumer choices and behaviours, in *Data Engineering for Data-driven Marketing*. 2025, Emerald Publishing Limited. pp. 33–45.
4. Okuyelu, O. and O. Adaji, AI-driven real-time quality monitoring and process optimization for enhanced manufacturing performance. *Journal of Advances in Mathematics and Computer Science*, 2024. **39**(4): pp. 81–89.
5. Anastasios, P. and G. Maria, Predictive AI in business intelligence enhancing market insights and strategic decision-making. *American Journal of Technology Advancement*, 2024. **1**(8): pp. 72–90.
6. Mahabub, S., M.R. Hossain, and E.Z. Snigdha, Data-driven decision-making and strategic leadership: AI-powered business operations for competitive advantage and sustainable growth. *Journal of Computer Science and Technology Studies*, 2025. **7**(1): pp. 326–336.
7. Potter, K., F. Olaoye, and L. Doris, Analyzing the effectiveness of personalized marketing strategies in improving customer engagement and loyalty. *Marketing*, 2024.
8. Sinha, R., A comparative analysis of traditional marketing vs digital marketing. *Journal of Management Research and Analysis*, 2018. **5**(4): pp. 234–243.
9. Tarabasz, A., The impact of digital on marketing strategy, in Paulo Botelho Pires, José Duarte Santos, and Inês Veiga Pereira *Digital Marketing*. 2024, CRC Press. pp. 21–37.

10. Druen, P., *Leveraging Advanced Machine Learning and Predictive Analytics for Deeper Market Insights*. 2024. https://www.researchgate.net/publication/387307094_Leveraging_Advanced_Machine_Learning_and_Predictive_Analytics_for_Deeper_Market_Insights
11. Powell, G., S. Groves, and J. Dimos, *ROI of Social Media: How to Improve the Return on Your Social Marketing Investment*. 2011: John Wiley & Sons.
12. Zong, Z. and Y. Guan, AI-driven intelligent data analytics and predictive analysis in Industry 4.0: Transforming knowledge, innovation, and efficiency. *Journal of the Knowledge Economy*, 2024: 30, pp. 1–40.
13. Okeleke, P.A., et al., Predictive analytics for market trends using AI: A study in consumer behavior. *International Journal of Engineering Research Updates*, 2024. **7**(1): pp. 36–49.
14. Bhardwaj, S., et al., *Marketing Through AI-Driven Personalization Strategies*. https://www.researchgate.net/profile/Nirmesh-Sharma/publication/380121620_Enhancing_Customer_Targeting_in_E-Commerce_and_Digital_Marketing_through_AI-Driven_Personalization_Strategies/links/678fb5e482501639f500f8fe/Enhancing-Customer-Targeting-in-E-Commerce-and-Digital-Marketing-through-AI-Driven-Personalization-Strategies.pdf#
15. Janice, N. and N. Kusumawati, Harmonizing algorithms and user satisfaction: Evaluating the impact of spotify's discover weekly on customer loyalty. *Journal Integration of Management Studies*, 2024. **2**(2): pp. 174–188.
16. Inampudi, M.S., et al., *Sentiment Analysis and Social Media Marketing*, in *Predictive Analytics and Generative AI for Data-Driven Marketing Strategies*. Chapman and Hall/CRC. pp. 149–158.
17. Senyapar, H.N.D., Artificial intelligence in marketing communication: A comprehensive exploration of the integration and impact of AI. *Technium Social Sciences Journal*, 2024. **55**: p. 64.
18. Sarin, A.B., The evolution of consumer behavior and the role of artificial intelligence in shaping it: AI in marketing, in *Decoding Consumer Behavior Using the Insight Equation and AI Marketing*. 2025, IGI Global Scientific Publishing. pp. 21–40.
19. Najafov, E., AI-Driven User Experience (UX) and Dynamic Landing Page Design, in *ChatGPT for Marketing: Learn Practical Applications of ChatGPT for Marketing*. 2024, Springer. pp. 133–151.
20. Kumar, V., A.R. Ashraf, and W. Nadeem, AI-powered marketing: What, where, and how? *International Journal of Information Management*, 2024. **77**: p. 102783.
21. Sabitha, J., AI-Driven customer segmentation and personalization. *Zibaldone Estudios Italianos*, 2024. **11**(2): pp. 1–20.
22. Mortaji, S.T.H. and M.E. Sadeghi, Assessing the reliability of artificial intelligence systems: Challenges, metrics, and future directions. *International Journal of Innovation in Management, Economics and Social Sciences*, 2024. **4**(2): pp. 1–13.
23. Chung, S.H., et al., An empirical study of the relationships between IT infrastructure flexibility, mass customization, and business performance. *ACM*

Sigmis Database: The Database for Advances in Information Systems, 2005. **36**(3): pp. 26–44.
24. Heijsters, F.A., et al., A usability evaluation of the perceived user friendliness, accessibility, and inclusiveness of a personalized digital care pathway tool. *International Journal of Medical Informatics*, 2023. **175**: p. 105070.
25. Kumar, A., From mass customization to mass personalization: A strategic transformation. *International Journal of Flexible Manufacturing Systems*, 2007. **19**: pp. 533–547.
26. Aldboush, H.H. and M. Ferdous, Building trust in fintech: An analysis of ethical and privacy considerations in the intersection of big data, AI, and customer trust. *International Journal of Financial Studies*, 2023. **11**(3): p. 90.
27. Munoz, M.D. and M.A. Munoz, *Evaluating Training: Return on Investment and Cost-Benefit Analysis*. 2000.
28. Stone, M., et al., Artificial intelligence (AI) in strategic marketing decision-making: A research agenda. *The Bottom Line*, 2020. **33**(2): pp. 183–200.
29. Machireddy, J., S.K. Rachakatla, and P. Ravichandran, Leveraging AI and machine learning for data-driven business strategy: A comprehensive framework for analytics integration. *African Journal of Artificial Intelligence and Sustainable Development*, 2021. **1**(2): pp. 12–150.
30. Misra, B.B., Data normalization strategies in metabolomics: Current challenges, approaches, and tools. *European Journal of Mass Spectrometry*, 2020. **26**(3): pp. 165–174.
31. Liang, W., et al., Advances, challenges and opportunities in creating data for trustworthy AI. *Nature Machine Intelligence*, 2022. **4**(8): pp. 669–677.
32. Velkova, I., Unstructured social media data processing with artificial intelligence. *Industry 4.0*, 2023. **8**(2): pp. 65–67.
33. Johnson, M., et al., Integrating human knowledge into artificial intelligence for complex and ill-structured problems: Informed artificial intelligence. *International Journal of Information Management*, 2022. **64**: p. 102479.
34. Bhaskaran, S.V., Integrating data quality services (dqs) in big data ecosystems: Challenges, best practices, and opportunities for decision-making. *Journal of Applied Big Data Analytics, Decision-Making, and Predictive Modelling Systems*, 2020. **4**(11): pp. 1–12.
35. Gabelaia, I., The applicability of artificial intelligence marketing for creating data-driven marketing strategies. *Journal of Marketing Research and Case Studies*, 2022. **466404**: p. 2022.
36. Huang, M.-H. and R.T. Rust, A strategic framework for artificial intelligence in marketing. *Journal of the Academy of Marketing Science*, 2021. **49**: pp. 30–50.
37. Lachmann, H., T. Schneider, and L. Wagner, AI revolution: Evolving skills in marketing agency jobs. *Special Issue Innovative Brand Management IV*, 2024, p. 53.
38. James, C., *AI-Driven Strategies for Marketing Campaign Optimization*. 2024. https://www.researchgate.net/publication/387947152_AI-Driven_Strategies_for_Marketing_Campaign_Optimization?utm_source=chatgpt.com

39. Gade, K.R., Data-driven decision making in a complex world. *Journal of Computational Innovation*, 2021. **1**(1), pp. 1–18.
40. Scatiggio, V., *Tackling the issue of bias in artificial intelligence to design ai-driven fair and inclusive service systems. How human biases are breaching into ai algorithms, with severe impacts on individuals and societies, and what designers can do to face this phenomenon and change for the better.* 2020.
41. Govindaraj, M., et al., Humanizing the digital touch: Strategies for balancing automation in modern marketing, in *Balancing Automation and Human Interaction in Modern Marketing*. 2024, IGI Global. pp. 175–202.
42. Boulos, M., *The Intersection of Artificial Intelligence and Digital Marketing: Balancing Automation with the Human Touch. Assessing the effects on Productivity, Cost, Quality, and their Implications for Employment in the Industry*. Assessing the effects on Productivity, Cost, Quality, and their Implications for Employment in the Industry (January 04, 2024), 2024.
43. Kumar, D. and N. Suthar, Ethical and legal challenges of AI in marketing: An exploration of solutions. *Journal of Information, Communication and Ethics in Society*, 2024. **22**(1): pp. 124–144.

CHAPTER 10

AI-Driven Marketing Strategies in the Digital Era

Jash Khatri and Hamed Taherdoost

10.1 INTRODUCTION

With the advent of artificial intelligence (AI), many industries have seen new ways of implementing AI in their day-to-day operations; from healthcare to education, AI has led to increased efficiency, profitability, and better end results (Franke, 2019; Garcia & Herrero, 2025; Huang & Rust, 2021). The use of AI has allowed businesses to save on resources, i.e., time and money, allowing for increased efficiency and a greater Return on Investment. One of these industries where AI has begun to garner movement is the marketing industry, with marketers directly using AI Models to create content and indirectly to analyze data and make decisions (Wilendra et al., 2023).

10.1.1 Background

Global advertising and marketing spending has steadily increased year over year, with US$1.8 trillion being spent on marketing activities in 2024 alone (Statista, 2025). With the ever-evolving marketing industry's playing field, marketers have begun to move from traditional marketing strategies to more modern solutions – for instance, the integration of AI models like ChatGPT (Wilendra et al., 2023). In 2023 alone, 73% of marketers in the United States reported that they used generative AI tools in their work (MarTech, 2023). This number is expected to grow as further developments occur within the industry requiring the use of AI tools in

DOI: 10.1201/9781003625452-10

order to keep up with competitors. Some businesses have already had great success in implementing generative AI into their marketing efforts, such as Heinz's award-winning "A.I. Ketchup" campaign (The One Club, 2023, as cited in Hartmann et al., 2025, p. 13).

However, while generative AI tools like ChatGPT serve as a method of copywriting, other tools have emerged for across-the-board use in marketing activities, such as image creation, data analysis and reasoning, and automations for customer targeting. These tools aid in maintaining brand identity, while also easing the strain on resources, such as time and money (Wilendra et al., 2023). This can be seen in companies like Lexus, which have used AI technologies [IBM Watson] to write their commercial scripts (Huang & Rust, 2021). There are also marketing tools, like HubSpot, Hootsuite, and Salesforce which integrate AI into their applications to offer better services and allow for advanced data analysis and automation (Gunduzyeli, 2024; Mostefaoui & Benkirat, 2024).

Another key example would be Meta Platforms, previously known as the Facebook Group, where they integrate AI into several parts of their platform, collecting data through user interactions and using this to train their AI to understand and predict their behavior (Mostefaoui & Benkirat, 2024). In turn, their AI is better able to target ads and personalize their social products to the user. This is considered to be Analytical AI, which Sarker (2022) explains makes use of large data sets by analyzing them and extracting trends and patterns, which are then used to make decisions.

In itself, AI being implemented in the marketing processes of businesses have significantly impacted customer engagement by enabling personalized interactions across varying platforms, such as social media, email, and chatbots. This, in turn, has allowed businesses to benefit from enhanced brand loyalty and customer retention (Huang & Rust, 2021).

10.1.2 Problem Statement

With the rapid integration of AI in marketing operations, businesses have been able to transform the way they engage their customers through data analysis to create on-brand and personalized campaigns. However, even though AI garners benefits in the areas of efficiency and increased return on investment, there remain the ever-present challenges it brings: for instance, the ethical issues of data privacy and hyper-personalization, such as in the case of Target's AI system, which once inadvertently revealed a teenager's pregnancy to her father before she could.

10.1.3 Research Questions

This study was based on and aims to answer the following research questions.

> **Question 1:** "How do businesses utilize Artificial Intelligence to enhance customer segmentation, personalization, and automation in Business-to-Consumer (B2C) marketing operations?"
> **Question 2:** "What are the ethical challenges and operational limitations which arise from the adoption of AI-Driven Marketing Strategies?"

Question 1 explores the varying ways AI is currently being implemented in day-to-day marketing operations, like data analysis and predictive analytics in segmentation, personalization, and automation. Question 2 aims to examine the implications of AI Marketing strategies by focusing on ethical concerns like data privacy and hyper-personalization while also looking at its operational challenges, such as its inability to understand emotions.

10.1.4 Objectives

This study aims to examine the current state of AI in business marketing strategies, focusing on the various methods being employed by marketers to increase engagement, while also identifying the potential challenges these AI Marketing strategies may face. It also aims to establish what future research may be required to improve or innovate upon the current implementations in order to solve existing challenges.

10.1.5 Scope

While the application of AI has been seen across varying marketing operations, this study will define its scope to only include B2C strategies, excluding AI implementation in Business-to-Business (B2B) marketing operations. Even though there are certain overlaps in how AI is implemented, the exclusion of B2B was done due to the fundamental differences in audience engagement strategies and decision-making processes. For instance, B2C marketing targets individual consumers, allowing for advanced personalization. However, B2B marketing focuses on organizational buying behaviors, which require varied approaches. The study considers its application on a global front, examining resources from varying backgrounds and perspectives. It will only include the use of secondary data, collected via academic database searches.

10.2 DEFINING KEY TERMS

10.2.1 Artificial Intelligence

While AI has had a major impact on our lives in more ways than one, finding agreement on a singular definition has proven difficult. Minsky (1968) wrote, "Artificial Intelligence ... is the science of making machines do things that would require intelligence if done by [hu]men" (Bolter, 1984, p. 1). This definition so far has kept its value; however, now, with AI models being fed large data sets in order to create predictions, it is questionable whether AI is necessarily doing what a human would be able to do.

Over time, with modern advancements in system computational power, increased storage capabilities, and access to a wider array of datasets, AI models have benefitted from faster response times and more accurate end results (Colther & Doussoulin, 2024). They continue that this innovation, coupled with the development of the global communication network, has allowed these models to access data sets which do not need to be stored locally.

With these improvements, offering new capabilities, the definition of AI has significantly changed, with it now being considered "[computer] programs, algorithms, systems and machines that demonstrate intelligence" (Shankar, 2018, as cited in Davenport et al., 2020, p. 25). We can no longer associate AI with being akin to the capabilities of humans, as they have been developed to the point where they carry out thorough processes which humans are incapable of doing without the aid of machines. This definition is further supported by Bruyn et al. (2020), who purports that the now "widely accepted definition of AI is intelligence demonstrated by machines" (p. 1).

This evolving definition, from mimicking human intelligence to actually demonstrating machine intelligence, has led to the implementation and development of more advanced marketing tools capable of analyzing large datasets and automating tasks, enhancing efficiency, and offering increased return on investment.

10.2.2 Marketing

Since the beginning of commerce, the need for marketing has existed; however, over time, the methods through which businesses appeal to customers have shifted. In itself, marketing is the process of adding value to a good or service by means of communication in order to convince customers (Skalen et al., 2022). Over time, the idea of marketing became more mainstream, leading to further study and development of the subject, with modern-day marketing featuring channels both traditional and digital.

Traditional being those of coupons, ad spaces in public areas, ads on TV and Radio Channels, and in-store promotional sampling. However, with the invention of mobile phones and faster network speeds, we are able to access the internet anywhere and anytime, given there is a connection. This has led to the evolution of marketing toward a more digital front, with varying marketing initiatives like ads on social media platforms, digital coupons, sponsored content, and much more.

10.3 AI-DRIVEN MARKETING STRATEGIES

As previously mentioned, many companies around the world have actively begun to implement AI tools in their marketing operations, with an aim to increase audience engagement and resource allocation efficiency in their operations. AI implementation has taken on several forms, respective toward using data to do the following:

- Segment the market and aid in targeting customers.
- Predict consumer behavior through analytics to offer a more personal experience.
- Implement automations for efficient customer outreach and lead generation.

10.3.1 Customer Segmentation and Targeting

One key aspect of traditional marketing which has lapsed over to modern marketing is market segmentation. A method first theorized by Wendell Smith (1956), "Market segmentation involves viewing a heterogenous aggregate market as decomposable into a number of smaller homogeneous markets in response to the heterogeneous preferences attributable to the desires of consumers for more precise satisfaction of their varying wants and needs" (p. 6). Similarly, Huang and Rust (2021) define segmentation as the act of "slice[ing] the market into pieces, with customers in each piece having unique needs and wants" (p. 37). In other words, market segmentation is the process of dividing the entire market for a particular product into smaller versions based on specified niches in order to optimize the final product toward the end consumer. According to Ding et al. (2020), while the initial segmentation model has endured, several changes have occurred as businesses began to realize that on an individual scale, customers are unique when referencing their demographic data. Thus, the addition of psychographic data, otherwise considered likes and dislikes, attitudes, and behaviors.

This process of market segmentation is supported through a vital foundation of market research which is necessary if segments are to be correctly drawn. Preda and Dumitru (2024) share that AI has enhanced the segmentation process by allowing for audiences to be segmented more efficiently in order to maximize the effectiveness of campaigns and reduce resource usage.

Many businesses have successfully integrated AI-driven segmentation tools into their marketing operations. A key example of this is Amazon and its utilization of AI systems to further improve its recommendation engine. Amazon uses a combination of demographic and psychographic data to segment its customers, often offering further analysis using customer data from their purchase history, browsing behaviors, and product feedback (Seth, 2023). This implementation has allowed them to generate 35% more of its yearly revenue. However, even though companies like Amazon have seen great returns, it is necessary to highlight the potential risk that lies in the over-reliance of data-driven segmentation, which may overlook nuanced consumer preferences, especially when data sets are generalized.

Huang and Rust (2021) proposed a three-step framework which would make use of AI to not only conduct research but also to form a marketing strategy based on the compiled data and execute the strategy. Most importantly, however, they classified the AI processes as "Mechanical AI … Thinking AI … [&] Feeling AI" (p. 2).

To clarify, Mechanical AI was meant to act in routine, such as continuously collecting data, organizing it, and segmenting it. Thinking AI sided more, as the name suggests, on taking in the data initially collected by mechanical AI and processing it to find insights or end conclusions. Finally, Feeling AI acted more on the part, in tandem with human input [in terms of the end-user or the consumer], giving responses based on the prior processed data.

Huang and Rust's (2021) three-part model divides the use of AI into the sections of marketing research, marketing strategy, and marketing action. In the marketing research stage, AI collects and analyses consumer data.

Then, in the marketing strategy phase, the data is processed to identify trends and patterns, which are used to optimize resource allocation for a campaign. And in the final stage, AI automates the process of interacting with customers through executing personalized campaigns.

However, in highlighting consumer segmentation, the main area of focus will remain on Mechanical AI. Huang and Rust (2021) indicate that the implementation of such a structure enables a constant standard across the methods by which consumer data is collected and organized, resulting in a more effective overall strategy. This standard allows for there to be no gaps in the data collected as it keeps constant monitoring and will not neglect any constraints based on biases, allowing for the correct segment to be targeted.

10.3.2 Personalization, Automation, and Customer Experience

Customer experience can make a difference in gaining a sale, and marketing plays a crucial role in attaining the customer through the use of data. These days, when it comes to consumer data, there is a blatant abundance available on the web indirectly through third-party sites and applications, like social media platforms, search engines, mobile games, and other websites (Davis et al., 2021). The current model stands based on the collected data; advertised content is then shown to the potential consumer running off of an algorithm created by the host company, such as Google, Meta, or even TikTok.

This is considered personalization, as the content is tailored to the individuals' own needs and wants based on their previous aggregated data. Thinking back to Huang and Rust (2021), this falls under the second part of the structure, known as Thinking AI, as the algorithm works to establish conclusions on whether the end user would be more likely to act on the presented content.

Taking a step back, the role of AI in marketing can also be integrated as part of the customer journey, guiding the consumer from touchpoint to touchpoint until finally a decision is made (Chen & Prentice, 2024). One example by which this integration has taken form is through AI Chatbots and Robo-advisors (Wang & Song, 2025; Hao & Li, 2025). These can begin either through contact by the customer or through a business to the customer.

For instance, in the case of "to the customer," a business can send a message via email, SMS, or Social Platform, marketing an item or service. Instead of a message, they may also initiate a phone call. For either to work, however, they rely on the recipient [prospective customer] to respond. Looking at a "by the customer" interaction, it would require the individual to reach out via one of the aforementioned methods and would then be connected to an AI Chatbot or a Robo-advisor.

Both means of interaction are enabled by an AI assistant which aims to replicate human interaction (Hao & Li, 2025). This version is more preferred by businesses as it alleviates costs while also decreasing response times effectively bridging touchpoints along the customer journey more efficiently.

While we have already established specific automation in relation to AI Chatbots and Robo-advisors, it is important to know that there is a multitude of automations which integrate the use of AI. Automations are also applicable to marketing campaign positioning and repositioning – as the AI monitors the campaign data, such as how many likes, shares, and comments, it can better determine what direction is best, thus recommending human intervention. Preda and Dumitru (2024) purport that the use of AI in creating automated tasks improves efficiency and can reduce costs by around 10%–20%. Referring back to Huang and Rust (2021) and their three-part framework, automation is considered under the established structure of Mechanical AI.

While AI-driven personalization and automation have allowed businesses to deliver a better customer experience, building customer engagement, and increased return on investments, it has also led to increased consumer expectations for tailored and custom experiences. Businesses now face the issue where they have to balance the benefits and limitations of AI in maintaining personal connections, often working with human interaction to mitigate this issue (Figure 10.1).

Ethical Challenges in AI-Driven MarketingWhile studies like Huang and Rust (2021), Hao and Li (2025), and Wang and Song (2025) indicate that the use of AI in marketing enables efficiency and leads to better end results, it is pertinent that we also identify the particular challenges AI-Driven marketing strategies face.

Muhlhoff (2023) argues that the main challenge arises in the protection of data, which is used by AI to form predictive analytics, by claiming that by using mass data, predictions may fall victim to bias, leading to social inequality, discrimination, and exclusion within marketing operations. He establishes the term "Predictive Privacy," furthering that even if the sample size was relevantly large, AI models could possibly make a prediction which harms one individual or a group of individuals who were not

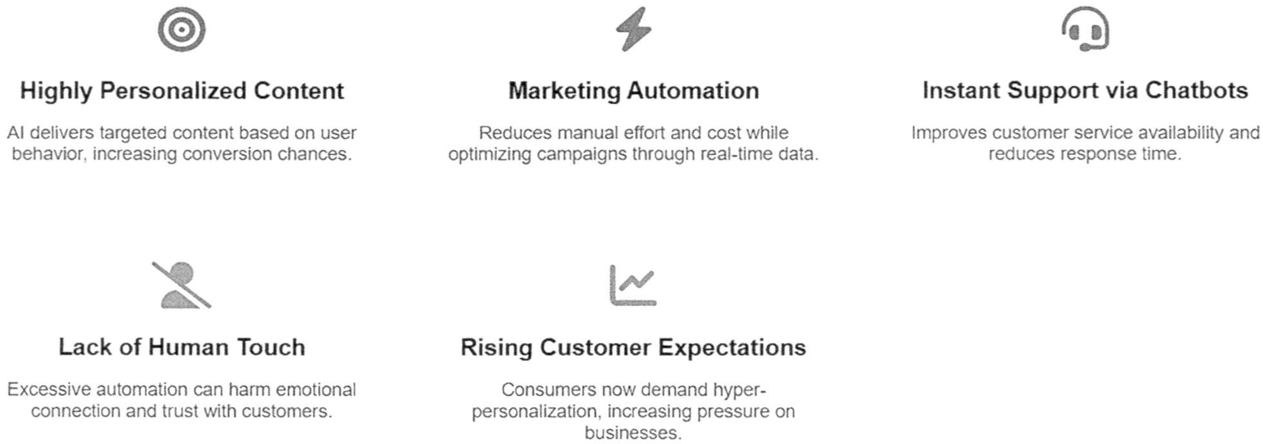

FIGURE 10.1 AI in customer experience: Key advantages and limitations.

reflected in the original training data set. Similarly, Simion and Popescu (2023) raise concerns that with the extensive collection of personal data that AI models collect to evaluate their future decisions, end consumers might find themselves at the end of a hyper-personalized marketing campaign, which feels invasive or unwanted. Muhlhoff (2023) also questions the existing privacy regulations, such as the EU's GDPR which only focuses on individual rights rather than aggregated data. On the other hand, Braun (2024) holds that AI in itself should not be regulated, given that it is a broad umbrella term encompassing varying kinds of models.

Hari et al. (2025) share agreement with the idea presented by Muhlhoff; however, highlights a more direct ethical issue of AI integration. First, they highlight the issue of privacy in the use of Conversational AI, or in other words, Chatbots and Robo-Advisors. The data being collected may be at risk of data breaches bringing to question the security of consumer information. Shanmugam et al. (2023) share a similar concern, highlighting that consumer data may be stored for a longer period of time given the decreased cost of storage and the increased capabilities of AI models. Hari et al. (2025) continue to highlight that these AI models can become biased since the algorithms are trained on data under little to no regulation, which in turn can lead to discrimination – further supporting the claims of Muhlhoff. They also mentioned the "Uncanny Valley Paradox," which Kim et al. (2022) explain that, "[an] increased human-likeness of artificial entities, ironically, could elicit a surge of negative reactions from people" (p. 1). In other words, when AI begins to feel too human, we will tend to develop a sense of fear or creepiness toward it.

Chander et al. (2025), while highlighting potential solutions, also raise concern over these issues. Additionally, they indicate that even in the case where data sets are generalized to maintain individual privacy, it hinders the representation of other diverse groups as they may be considered outliers, further supporting the ideas presented by Muhlhoff.

While studies mention that AI's development of the likeness of humans, others such as Bruyn et al. (2020) highlight the lack of common sense these AI models may suffer from (p. 96). They further that even though AI possesses the capability of recognizing emotions, it lacks the ability to understand them and may lead to issues in communication between the AI and the end consumer. For example, think of a customer leaving a Google Review for a retail store stating that their experience at the business was bad. The AI can most likely identify that the reviewers experience was bad, however, it cannot relate to it and thus leads to an improper understanding of how to truly respond.

10.3.3 Real-World Case: Target

AI models are keen on picking up on patterns and trends from data which would be impossible for humans given the complexities of data sets. However, sometimes these patterns can lead to issues in understanding and impact customer privacy. One example of this is a case in 2012 where Target, an American retail corporation, implemented an AI system to analyze customer data and automatically market customers with products they would most likely need (Hill, 2012). The model was built to understand when an individual was pregnant, using predictive analytics to analyze customer purchase data linked to their accounts. It aimed at targeting soon-to-be mothers to get them to shop at target – and it did exactly as it was meant to do. It had sent maternity coupons to a girl who was still in high school, offering discounts on cribs and baby clothes. However, the first person to see the coupons was her father, and it turned out that the girl was indeed pregnant. Target's AI was able to predict a pregnancy based on consumer purchase data, however, it failed to show an appropriate response.

This supports the concerns of researchers like Muhlhoff (2023) and Simion and Popescu (2023), who bring to light the potential flaws of predictive analytics in AI models. Models may fall victim to "Predictive Privacy" issues and lead to a hyper-personalized marketing initiative.

10.4 METHODOLOGY

This study has focused on evaluating how AI has been implemented by businesses in marketing strategies while also looking to see what challenges these implementations may face. It has specifically been done using secondary data from peer-reviewed academic journals, which later were employed in structuring a literature review. Most of the data is considered qualitative. Figure 10.2 gives a visual overview of the steps taken to conduct this study.

First, in order to identify what research studies would be used in this project, several keywords were identified based on the research questions. These included, but were not limited to, "Marketing," "Digital Marketing," "AI," "Artificial Intelligence," "Segmentation," "Automation," "AI Marketing Strategies," and "AI Marketing Ethics." After keywords were identified, several searches were conducted in academic databases, such as JSTOR, ScienceDirect, MDPI, and the UCW Library.

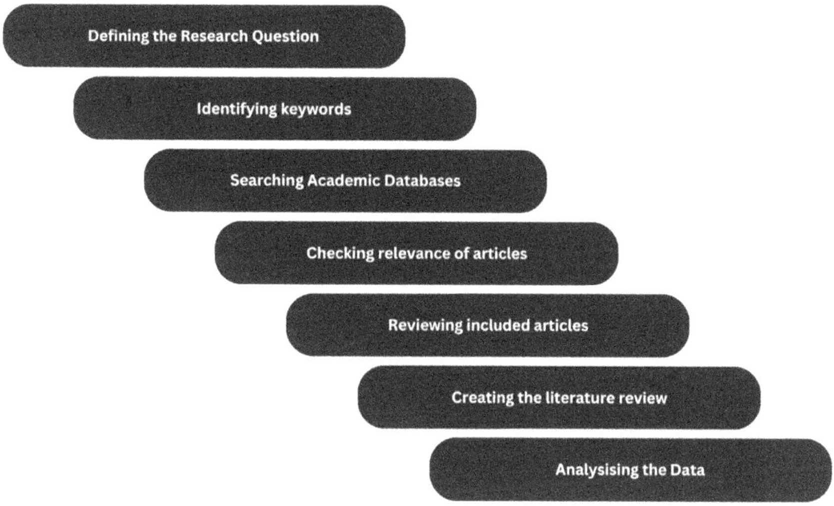

FIGURE 10.2 Research methodology.

The retrieved articles, based on the above keyword searches, were evaluated to check if they were relevant to answering the research questions. Articles which directly addressed the implementation of AI in marketing were included in this study, while those which did not meet the specific requirements were excluded. Articles were also checked for their currency, excluding those which were over five years old. This made sure that the information being used was both current and relevant to the study.

Then, the included articles were reviewed to grasp an understanding of existing knowledge in AI marketing strategies. It was then compiled into a comprehensive literature review to identify how businesses are currently implementing AI in their marketing operations, what challenges they may face, and what future research should examine.

10.5 ANALYSIS

With the data collected, and aiming to answer the research questions, the following is an in-depth analysis of the theories and models which were found through this study, as well as the challenges and ethical considerations which researchers in the field have raised awareness of.

10.5.1 AI-Driven Marketing Strategies

When it comes to the AI marketing strategies which businesses are currently working into their operations, several key findings were identified.

First, Huang and Rust's (2021) framework is a key basis for understanding how AI is implemented in the operation. While other researchers have not directly used these names or cited their work, it is apparent upon inspection that the concepts and processes being defined in their studies do, in fact, fit under the three-part model.

Researchers identified and agreed that in the area of customer segmentation and targeting, the use of AI has many advantageous results. With the ability to analyze large sets of data and identify patterns and trends within them, AI is able to segment consumer markets more efficiently and with greater precision.

When it comes to garnering a better customer experience, researchers found that AI can aid in developing more personalized experiences given its ability to better understand what each and every individual's preferences are. It was found that AI can even offer a more personalized option of communication between customers and businesses through the use of AI Chatbots and Robo-Advisors, which are becoming overly popular among businesses.

Lastly, in line with the use of AI to create automations, such as email campaigns, it was found that marketing operations experienced an increase in efficiency and return on investment, while also maintaining around 10%–12% reduction in costs.

Overall, on the side of the AI Marketing Strategies which were covered by this study, it can be said that they were aligned with many positive outcomes. However, while AI implementation may have its positive impacts, there are many negatives which must be covered.

10.5.2 Challenges and Ethical Considerations

Without a doubt, it can be said that AI will bring great benefits to any industry they are incorporated into, however, there are also negatives which we must look toward to better understand where the technology stands and how it can be improved upon.

First, it was found that while many researchers approve of using AI in marketing operations, they have particular concerns over consumer data privacy and security. With AI models benefiting from advancements in computational power, coupled with the increased affordability of storage and wider access to data sets, businesses are able to hold on to data for longer periods of time. This opens the data up to risks, given that at any point an individual or group with malintent may act toward conducting a data breach. Concerns were also seen in the area of predictive analytics, particularly by Muhlhoff. Given that AI technologies are still developing and changing, regulations have been slow to come into effect. This is a key area where further inquiry and development must be made.

Another key area of issue is that of potential bias and discrimination. Researchers claimed that data sets which were used to train AI models could possibly become biased, since models look for patterns and trends. This can lead to smaller groups or minorities being seen as outliers, and the resulting action of AI could be tainted. Groups cannot be singled out, nor can they be generalized.

While biases occur when data is not specific to a particular individual or group, there is another concern over when data becomes too specified. Researchers coined this to be hyper-personalization. The main concern across the board being that since Models do not have a sense of boundaries, it can sometimes cause interactions to feel invasive or unwanted.

Lastly, it was found that while AI possesses the "intelligence" to analyze data, it lacks the ability to act with common sense. As humans, we have developed a perception of emotions and, with it, an ability how to appropriately respond; however, when it comes to AI, responding to emotions can be difficult. That is to say, it will respond, but it can sometimes feel off or inaccurate.

It should be noted that while the existing literature highlights the benefits of AI in marketing, a deeper look finds that in order for it to be successfully implemented, there needs to be careful consideration of the ethical and practical challenges which it may pose, such as data privacy and algorithmic biases (Figure 10.3).

10.6 DISCUSSION

With the growing adoption of AI in business operations, especially marketing, this study aimed to investigate the methods of AI usage in marketing strategies in a B2C model and what potential challenges they may face. While other studies have explored the usage of AI in varying industries, only a few have examined those in Marketing, while those which do have done so in a broader aspect.

After a careful review and analysis of the existing literature, it was found that the usage of AI in marketing brought many benefits to businesses, such as increased efficiency and greater return on investment. It was also found that mainly businesses used AI to (1) analyze customer data and segment the market to target required audiences, (2) offer personalized experiences to their customers, and (3) create smart automations to improve efficiency.

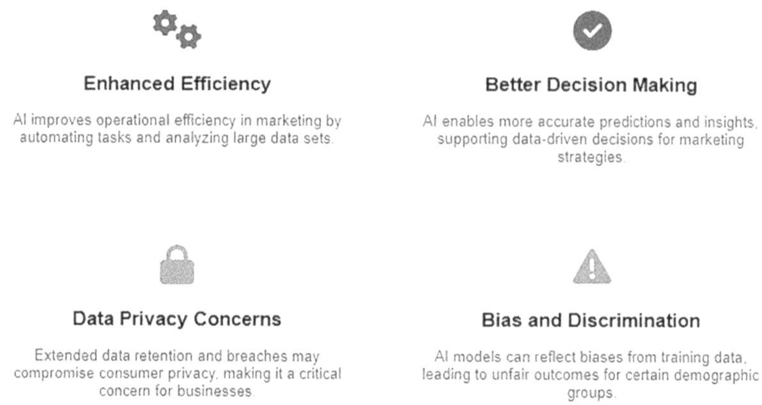

FIGURE 10.3 AI in marketing: Key benefits and ethical challenges.

In searching for what potential ethical concerns and challenges businesses may have to face in implementing AI into their marketing strategy, it was found that the main issues were related to (1) privacy and security of consumer data, (2) potential for bias and discrimination in predictive analytics, (3) hyper-personalization making marketing efforts feel unwanted, and (4) the limitation of AI models to comprehend and respond to human emotions.

Although Braun (2024) claims that AI should not be regulated, this study stands to disprove this given the many challenges its integration is and will possibly still face in the future. Regulations will allow for an ease in ethical concerns and possibly lay the groundwork for a stable framework to be adopted.

While this study looked to see how businesses are employing AI-driven marketing strategies in their operations, it should be noted that not all methods of implementation were covered. This study focused more on the side of analytical tools, with a slight look at generative methods as well.

10.7 FUTURE RESEARCH

With the findings of the study, it can be concluded that this field yet requires more research to be done in order to improve upon the existing AI models. During the study, it became evident that a standard framework, like Huang and Rust's (2021) three-part cycle, needed to be developed for AI models to use. Further research into how their framework can be improved upon is strongly encouraged.

It is also necessary for additional research in the area of addressing privacy and security concerns. As new AI models begin to pop up the importance of making sure the data used to train them is safe and secure is paramount.

It is also suggested for researchers to inspect and find ways to improve AI's intractability when it comes to emotional responses. While AI no longer is meant to be human intelligence, it should still strive to align itself with understanding and responding to human common sense.

10.8 CONCLUSION

While the integration of AI models into the marketing operations of businesses provide many benefits, such as increased efficiency in resource allocations, better customer experiences, and smoother customer journeys, we must realize that since AI is still a relatively new concept for many industries, including marketing, that there are potential risks which may harm not only the consumer but also the business in itself. This being said, it would be advisable that future research goes into understanding how these AI frameworks can be built to effectively manage marketing efforts while also keeping in mind the risks of privacy and ethical implications.

REFERENCES

Braun, D. (2024). Why "Artificial Intelligence" Should Not Be Regulated. *Digital Government: Research and Practice*, "Accepted". https://doi.org/10.1145/3696010

Bruyn, A. D., Viswanathan, V., Beh, Y. S., Brock, K. B., & Wangenhim, F. V. (2020). Artificial Intelligence and Marketing: Pitfalls and Opportunities. *Journal of Interactive Marketing*, *51*(1), 91–105. https://doi.org/10.1016/j.intmar.2020.04.007

Bolter, D. J. (1984). Artificial Intelligence. *Daedalus*, *113*(3), 1–18. https://www.jstor.org/stable/20024925

Chander, B., John, C., Warrier, L., & Gopalakrishnan, K. (2025). Toward Trustworthy Artificial Intelligence (TAI) in the Context of Explainability and Robustness. *ACM Computing Surveys*, *57*(6), 1–49. https://doi.org/10.1145/3675392

Chen, Y., & Prentice, C. (2024). Integrating Artificial Intelligence and Customer Experience. *Australasian Marketing Journal*, *0*(0), 1–13. https://doi.org/10.1177/14413582241252904

Colther, C., & Doussoulin, J. P. (2024). Artificial Intelligence: Driving Force in the Evolution of Human Knowledge. *Journal of Innovation & Knowledge*, 9(4). https://doi.org/10.1016/j.jik.2024.100625

Davenport, T., Guha, A., Grewal, D., & Bressgott, T. (2020). How Artificial Intelligence will Change the Future of Marketing. *Journal of the Academy of Marketing Science*, *48*(1), 24–42. https://doi.org/10.1007/s11747-019-00696-0

Davis, B., Grewal, D., & Hamilton, S. (2021). The Future of Marketing Analytics and Public Policy. *Journal of Public Policy & Marketing*, *40*(4), 447–452. https://www.jstor.org/stable/27285955

Ding, Y., DeSarbo, W. S., Hanssens, D. M., Jedidi, K., Lynch, J. G., & Lehmann, D. R. (2020). The Past, Present, and Future of Measurement and Methods in Marketing Analysis. *Marketing Letters*, *31*(2/3), 175–186. https://www.jstor.org/stable/48739836

Franke, U. (2019). Harnessing Artificial Intelligence. *European Council of Foreign Relations*. https://www.jstor.org/stable/resrep21491

Garcia, A. G., & Herrero, A. P. (2025). Impact of Predictive Marketing Based on Artificial Intelligence: Transforming Communication and Sales Strategies in SMEs and Startups. *Visual Review*, *17*(1), 165–178. https://doi.org/10.62161/revvisual.v17.5394

Gunduzyeli, B. (2024). Artificial Intelligence in Digital Marketing Within the Framework of Sustainable Management. *Sustainability 16*(23), 10511. https://doi.org/10.3390/su162310511

Hao, R., & Li, C. (2025). How AI Chatbots Shape Satisfactory Experiences: A Combined Perspective of Competence Expansion and Emotional Extension. *Technological Forecasting and Social Change*, *212*(2025), 1–16. https://doi.org/10.1016/j.techfore.2025.123979

Hari, H., Sharma, A., Verma, S., & Chaturvedi, R. (2025). Exploring Ethical Frontiers of Artificial Intelligence in Marketing. *Journal of Responsible Technology*, *21*(2025), 1–13. https://doi.org/10.1016/j.jrt.2024.100103

Hartmann, J., Exner, Y., & Domdey, S. (2025). The Power of Generative Marketing: Can Generative AI Create Superhuman Visual Marketing Content? *International Journal of Research in Marketing*, *42*(1), 13–31. https://doi.org/10.1016/j.ijresmar.2024.09.002

Hill, K. (2012). How Target Figured Out A Teen Girl Was Pregnant Before Her Father Did. *Forbes*. https://www.forbes.com/sites/kashmirhill/2012/02/16/how-target-figured-out-a-teen-girl-was-pregnant-before-her-father-did/

Huang, M. H., & Rust, R. T. (2021). A Strategic Framework for Artificial Intelligence in Marketing. *Journal of the Academy of Marketing Science*, *49*(1), 30–50. https://doi.org/10.1007/s11747-020-00749-9

Kim, B., Visser, E., & Phillips, E. (2022). Two Uncanny Valleys: Re-evaluating the Uncanny Valley Across the Full Spectrum of Real-World Human-Like Robots. *Computers in Human Behaviour*, *135*(2022), 1–14. https://doi.org/10.1016/j.chb.2022.107340

MarTech. (2023). Share of Marketers Using Generative Artificial Intelligence (AI) in their Companies in the United States as of March 2023 [Graph]. *Statista*. https://www.statista.com/statistics/1388390/generative-ai-usage-marketing/

Minsky, M. (1968). Semantic Information Processing. The MIT Press.

Mostefaoui, I., & Benkirat, W. (2024). The Uses of Artificial Intelligence in the Economic Operations of the Enterprise Marketing in Meta Company as a model. *Journal of Economic & Financial Studies*, *17*(1), 39–58. https://research.ebsco.com/linkprocessor/plink?id=77a0dd68-ae39-37bf-b1a3-426f690da85e

Muhlhoff, R. (2023). Predictive Privacy: Collective Data Protection in the Context of Artificial Intelligence and Big Data. *Big Data & Society*, *10*(1), 1–14. https://doi.org/10.1177/20539517231166886

Preda, O., & Dumitru, N. R. (2024). The Role of Marketing Strategy in the Context of Artificial Intelligence. *Journal of Information Systems & Operations Management*, *18*(2), 172–184. https://research.ebsco.com/linkprocessor/plink?id=56a12047-df2e-38db-90f8-feaa3c9db1a4

Seth, S. (2023). Personalization at Scale: Data-Driven Approaches for Hyper-targeted Digital Marketing: A Case Study of Amazon. *International Journal of Creative Research Thoughts*, *11*(1), 492–499. https://ijcrt.org/papers/IJCRT2307768.pdf

Shankar, V. (2018). How Artificial Intelligence (AI) is Reshaping Retailing. *Journal of Retailing*, *94*(4), 6–11. https://doi.org/10.1016/S0022-4359(18)30076-9

Sarker, I. H. (2022). AI-Based Modeling: Techniques, Applications and Research Issues Towards Automation, Intelligent and Smart Systems. *SN Computer Science*, *3*(2), 158. https://doi.org/10.1007/s42979-022-01043-x

Shanmugam, G., Rajendran, D., Thanarajan, T., Murugaraj, S. S., & Rajendran, S. (2023). Artificial Intelligence as a Catalyst in Digital Marketing: Enhancing Profitability and Market Potential. *International Information and Engineering Technology Association*, *28*(6), 1627–1636. https://doi.org/10.18280/isi.280620

Simion, P. C., & Popescu, M. A. M. (2023). Assessing the Use of Artificial Intelligence in Digital Marketing. Evidence from Romanian Companies. *Proceedings of the International Conference on Business Excellence*, *17*(1), 1128–1138. https://doi.org/10.2478/picbe-2023-0101

Skalen, P., Cova, B., Gummerus, J., & Sihvonen, A. (2022). Marketing-as-Practice: A Framework and Research Agenda for Value-Creating Marketing Activity. *Marketing Theory*, *23*(2), 185–206. https://doi.org/10.1177/14413582221110450

Statista. (2025). Advertising and Marketing Spending Worldwide from 2021 to 2025 (in billion U.S. dollars) [Graph]. *Statista*. https://www.statista.com/statistics/1446002/advertising-marketing-spending-worldwide/

The One Club. (2023). A.I. Ketchup. https://www.oneclub.org/awards/theoneshow/-award/48285/ai-ketchup/

Wang, Q., & Song, J. (2025). The Application of Artificial Intelligence in Marketing: A Comprehensive Review and Future Research Directions. *International Conference on Computer Science and Management Technology (ICCSMT)*, *5*(1), 706–712. https://doi.org/10.1145/3708036.3708155

Wendell, R. S. (1956). Product Differentiation and Market Segmentation as Alternative Marketing Strategies. *Journal of Marketing*, *21*(1), 3–8. https://doi.org/10.2307/1247695

Wilendra, W., Nadlifatin, R., & Kusumawilan, C.K. (2023). ChatGPT: The AI Game-Changing Revolution in Marketing Strategy for the Indonesian Cosmetic Industry. *Procedia Computer Science*, *234*(2024), 1012–1019. https://doi.org/10.1016/j.procs.2024.03.091

Index

www.ingramcontent.com/pod-product-compliance
Ingram Content Group UK Ltd.
Pitfield, Milton Keynes, MK11 3LW, UK
UKHW021720240926
475702UK00029BA/1670
* 9 7 8 1 0 4 1 0 3 8 0 4 7 *